THE OTHER ENLIGHTENMENT

CARLA HESSE

THE *Other* ENLIGHTENMENT
How French Women Became Modern

PRINCETON UNIVERSITY PRESS
PRINCETON AND OXFORD

Published by Princeton University Press, 41 William Street, Princeton, New Jersey 08540
In the United Kingdom: Princeton University Press, 3 Market Place,
Woodstock, Oxfordshire OX20 1SY

Third printing, and first paperback printing, 2003
Paperback ISBN 0-691-11480-3

The Library of Congress has cataloged the cloth edition of this book as follows

Hesse, Carla Alison.
    The other Enlightenment : how French women became modern / Carla Hesse.
        p.   cm.
    Includes bibliographical references and index.
    ISBN 0-691-07472-0 (CL : acid-free paper)
    1. France—Intellectual life—19th century.   2. France—Intellectual life—
20th century.   3. Women—France—History—19th century.   4. Women—France—
History—20th century.   I. Shepley, John.   II. Title.

    DC33.6 .H46   2001
    944.06'082—dc21

                                                            2001021987

British Library Cataloging-in-Publication Data is available

This book has been composed in Palatino

Printed on acid-free paper. ∞

www.pupress.princeton.edu

Printed in the United States of America

10   9   8   7   6   5   4   3

Where would we be . . . if all women were

guided by what they call their own lights?

—Germaine de Staël, *Delphine* (1802)

CONTENTS

ILLUSTRATIONS AND TABLES

TABLES

This book is a history of how French women came into consciousness of themselves as modern individuals at the end of the eighteenth century. The notion of an "other Enlightenment" may seem at the outset to be a contradiction in terms, and indeed it would be if by "Enlightenment" we meant the belief in an apprehensible set of universal laws of human nature. A universal concept admits no "otherness." Therefore, many Enlightenment philosophers have been compelled to dehumanize, to one degree or another, those groups—women, servants, children, and non-Europeans—whom they could not admit as equally governable by universal laws. Of all these, woman is paradigmatic. Woman, as Simone de Beauvoir observed some fifty years ago, has been the most universal and most immutable category of "other" because her difference from, and her subordination to, man has been conceived from time immemorial as a biological fact rather than a historical or a cultural contingency. And beginning with *The Second Sex* (1949), feminist history has sought to document the terms and the processes by which this dehumanization of women has taken place—the story of women's exclusion from humanity has by now become well known.

But this book departs from another strain of Enlightenment thought, that of Immanuel Kant, in his famous 1784 essay "What is Enlightenment?" Though Kant was no friend to feminists, he makes the important observation, with reference to the duties and obligations of subjects to the sovereign, that it is possible to be subordinate and at the same time capable of independent reason. Political and civil equality, then, are not necessary preconditions for moral self-determination or participation in the advancement of public reason. If, like Kant, we take

critical reason, rather than universal laws of nature, as the defining feature of the Enlightenment, it becomes possible to see that "otherness"
can, in principle, have its own modern and public voice.

This book is the story of how one such "other"—woman—became
enlightened. It is a history of how French women came to participate in
the modern project of self-determination and public reason since the
eighteenth century. In a sense, it is an inversion of the project that Simone de Beauvoir set for herself. Instead of seeking to document the
terms of woman's subordination as "other," I have reconstructed how it
became possible for women, as "other," to acquire the capacity for self-
constitution and for participation in public reasoning. Finally, I have
sought to recover the particular forms that their participation in philosophical inquiry have taken since the French Revolution. Thus I hope
that this book will also be a contribution to the history of modern female
thought.

Modernity, most fundamentally, is the consciousness of oneself as
self-creating. It requires very specific intellectual skills and highly developed systems of communication. None is more critical than writing,
which enables us to separate ourselves from our ideas, to take possession of them, and to exchange them with others across space and time.
It creates a durable space of self-reflexivity unattainable in transitory
oral forms of expression. The spread of literacy in the late eighteenth
century was thus crucial in bringing the cultural ideal of the modern self
into being. Commercial print culture made it increasingly possible for
private selves to transform themselves into public ones, to evade the
censorship of traditional authorities, and to make their thoughts independently available to an anonymous and putatively universal public-
at-large.

Women's relationship to literacy, publishing, and authorship are
crucial to their becoming modern selves and these relationships are thus
the central themes of the first half of this book. Here I examine the specific terms in which they came to participate in the modern public
sphere. Chapter one charts the demise of the traditional roles women
had played in literary culture under the monarchy as virtuosi of the spoken word, most notably as *salonnières* and fishwives. A second chapter
documents the shift of women's cultural energies into written as opposed to oral forms of expression and the dramatic expansion of their
presence in print culture after 1789. And chapter three tells the story of
how women writers worked with (and around) the legal constraints
upon their freedom to publish under the new, postrevolutionary

regimes of the nineteenth and twentieth centuries. The fact of being a woman and, hence, juridically unequal to men until the French civil code was revised in 1965, gave a distinctive shape to both the circumstances and the strategies of modern French women authors. Nonetheless, by the end of the eighteenth century, women of letters, like their male counterparts, found a new commercial world of print more open to them than ever before, and they threw themselves enthusiastically into the revolutionary project of remaking themselves and the public world in new terms.

During the decade of the French Revolution, women in unprecedented numbers grappled publicly with the contingencies and possibilities that the loss of lineage-based identity and the new hope of self-determination presented. The book turns, in its second half, to how women took up their newfound cultural authority and intervened in the revolutionary philosophical debates concerning the nature of modern political sovereignty, the problem of moral autonomy, and the aesthetics of self-representation. In 1789 they, like men, faced the question of what new form of political sovereignty should replace the monarchy. Chapter four tells the story of how the greatest historian of women of the era—Louise de Kéralio-Robert—reworked the public ideal of female sovereignty, documenting the evils of the institution of queenship and inventing in its place a new, egalitarian, and sisterly ideal for women as republicans.

The rebuilding of the moral foundation of a Republic that had severed all formal, public ties with religious authorities became the central preoccupation of French intellectual elites after the fall of Robespierre. And within these discussions the problem of female moral autonomy especially vexed male philosophers and legislators. If women were to continue to be juridically and politically subordinated, as all but the most radical among them thought should be the case, their exclusion would have to be based on their alleged incapacity for moral self-government and their inability to maintain universal ethical rules. Divine precept would no longer do. Chapter five recounts the story of how these debates prompted the gifted novelist, Isabelle de Charrière, to write a powerful feminist critique of the possibility of universalist ethical systems, and to propose instead a skeptical and pragmatic response to modern ethical dilemmas.

By investigating the intellectual lives of French women of the revolutionary era as a group, I do not intend to imply that they shared some essential "feminine" identity. To the contrary, I hope that this book will reveal the extent to which women have struggled—and struggled successfully—over the course of the modern period against the reduction of their personhood to their bodies. But of course French women did share a distinctive set of sociopolitical circumstances from the French Revolution through the 1960s that subordinated them on the basis of sex. So in the last chapter of the book I explore how these shared historical circumstances produced what I would call a dissident style of self-constitution that is recognizable in the writings of women working in a surprisingly wide range of political and social situations, and often with disparate esthetic and ethical aims. By the end of the revolutionary era, both despite and because of their political and social subordination to men, modern French women writers had invented a distinctive poetics of self-making that I have chosen to call the "other Enlightenment."

It needs to be said, finally, that this is a work of avowedly liberal, as opposed to radical, feminism. Radical feminists have argued that modern republicanism, because it was rooted in an exclusively male social contract, supposedly produced a modern conception of citizenship that, while claiming to be universal, was, in fact, inherently masculine.[1] Whether in the imagined originary bargain that Rousseau thought brought civil society into being or the real-life compact enacted by the Third Estate and its allies meeting on a tennis court at Versailles in 1789, the core political arrangements upon which society was governed were made by men. "Fraternity" meant precisely that. The exclusion of women from active citizenship was thus an essential feature of the Republic's constitution. This exclusion, it is argued, put women who sought inclusion in the polity in the "paradoxical" position of either denying their difference from men, or affirming their womanhood and thus undermining their case.[2]

I disagree with the premise of this position. In my view, women were initially excluded from active citizenship not because citizenship was conceived as inherently masculine, but because women were not perceived to be either capable of self-governance or of reasoning about general rather than particular interests.[3] French Republicanism, because of its antipluralism, has been notoriously resistant to the political inclu-

---

[1] Carole Pateman, *The Sexual Contract* (Palo Alto CA: Stanford University Press, 1988).

[2] Joan Wallach Scott, *Only Paradoxes to Offer: French Feminists and the Rights of Man* (Cambridge, MA: Harvard University Press, 1996).

[3] Pierre Rosanvallon, *Le Sacré du citoyen: histoire du suffrage universel en France* (Paris: Gallimard, 1992).

sion of groups who play different roles in civil society. But the struggle for women to become the political equals of men has nonetheless had less to do with the undermining of a republican notion of citizenship than with achieving recognition of their capacity to make independent judgments (independent, especially, of their priests) and their capacity to represent something larger than their own sex. Rather than a structural "paradox," then, I view the origins of modern republicanism as having contained a historical contradiction—the promise of inclusion to all reasoning beings, and the contingent exclusion of women because of historical prejudices, often justified by untenable biological theories. Modern history has proved that these prejudices can, in fact, be overcome without a fundamental restructuring of the polity or a redefinition of the republican notion of citizenship on which it was based. It has been the cultural work of modern women to overthrow these prejudices, and to do so without renouncing their specific interests as women.

In a modern Republic, the real liberation for women comes not when their sex is represented (although this is an important and necessary part of the enterprise), but when they are perceived as capable, as well, of representing something larger than gender alone; when the political arena is for women, as for men, an arena of self-transcendence rather than mere self-affirmation. This is why, for Simone de Beauvoir, acquiring the vote and the ability to run for office were ultimately of little importance for the liberation of women if they were not coupled with the public recognition of women's capacity to create the world and themselves anew, be it in art or in politics. This book tells the story of how women, despite their political and civil subordination, used the cultural resources of modern commercial society to achieve that recognition and thus staked a successful claim for themselves as modern individuals in the public world.

Many institutions and people have helped to bring this book into being. The History Department and the Humanities Research Council at the University of California, Berkeley, funded the completion of the research embodied within it, and the Solomon R. Guggenheim Foundation gave me a precious year away from teaching in order to finish writing it. I am grateful to them both.

Portions of this book appeared in print in earlier guises. Sections of chapter two were published as "French Women in Print, 1750–1800: An Essay in Historical Bibliography," in *The Darnton Debate: Books and Revolution in the Eighteenth Century, Studies on Voltaire and the Eighteenth Cen-*

tury, vol. 358, (Oxford: Voltaire Foundation 1998). A preliminary version of chapter three appeared as "Reading Signatures: Female Authorship and Revolutionary Law in France, 1750–1850," *Eighteenth-Century Studies* vol. 22, no. 3 (Spring 1989). Parts of chapter four were published as "Revolutionary Histories: The Literary Politics of Louise de Kéralio, 1758–1822," in *Culture and Identity in Early Modern Europe, 1500–1800*, Barbara Diefendorf and Carla Hesse, eds. (Ann Arbor: University of Michigan Press, 1993). Finally, an earlier version of chapter five appeared as "Kant, Foucault and *Three Women*," in *Foucault and the Writing of History*, Jan Goldstein, ed. (London: Basil Blackwell, 1993).

This book really began in the 1980s at Princeton University, and I am very happy to have the chance to acknowledge the participants in the Graduate Research Colloquium in Women's Studies—especially Leyla Ezdinli, Mary Harper, Kirstie McClure, and Kari Weil—who convinced me to pursue this topic as a book. Since then, my colleagues in the History Department and on the editorial board of *Representations* at UC Berkeley have been an enormous source of encouragement and guidance. I have benefited, moreover, from the insights and criticisms of Susanna Barrows, David A. Bell, R. Howard Bloch, Roger Chartier, Robert Darnton, Natalie Z. Davis, Joan DeJean, Michel Feher, Geneviève Fraisse, Jan Goldstein, Stephen Greenblatt, Lynn Hunt, Colin Jones, Steven Kaplan, Sheryl Kroen, Jean-Yves Mollier, Aron Rodrigue, Harold Mah, Joan Wallach Scott, Lawrence Stone, and Rachel Weil. Elizabeth Dudrow, Marcia Norton, Chaela Pastore, and Paige Arthur provided excellent research assistance at various stages in the book. Brigitta Van Rheinberg, at Princeton University Press, had faith in the project and saw it into print. I thank her. Diana Drew did a superb job of copyediting the manuscript.

Catherine Gallagher and Martin Jay deserve special thanks for their careful readings and comments on the entire manuscript, as do Joan Landes and Margaret Waller. They have spared me many, but not all, errors. Carol J. Clover not only read and commented on the whole book, she has been a priceless friend over the years of its writing. My many conversations with Jane A. Dixon have also played an immeasurable role in shaping this book. I am very grateful to her. Finally, the generous love and historical brilliance of my husband, Thomas Walter Laqueur, has made the experience of writing this book richer and happier than I could have wished it to be. I dedicate it to him.

ABBREVIATIONS

ABF	*Archives Biographiques de France*
AD	*Archives Départementales de la Seine*
AL	*Année Littéraire*
AN	*Archives Nationales*
BGR	*Bibliographie du genre romanesque,* Martin, Mylne and Frautschi, eds. (Paris: Expansion, 1977)
BLC	*British Library Catalogue*
BN	*Bibliothèque Nationale de France*
CHF	*Catalogue de l'histoire de France, Bibliothèque Nationale*
FC	*Feuille de Correspondence du Libraire* (Paris: Aubry, 1791–1793)
JL	*Journal littéraire*
JT	*Journal Typographique*
Mag. Enc.	*Magasin encyclopédique*
Monglond	*La France révolutionnaire et impériale,* André Monglond, ed. (Grenoble: B. Arthaud, 1973–1978)
MW	*Catalogue des pamphlets, journaux et anonymes de la Révolution française à la Bibliothèque Nationale,* Martin et Walter, eds.
NL	*Nouvelliste Littéraire* (Paris: Marin & Lenoir, 1796–1806)
OF	*Opinion des Femmes. De la vielle au lendemain de la Révolution française* (Paris: des Femmes, 1989)
Sullerot	Evelyne Sullerot, *La Presse feminine* (Paris: Colin, 1963)

Note: All translations are my own unless otherwise indicated.

1789:
May 5, The Estates General meets in Versailles and the French Revolution begins
July 14, The Bastille is stormed by Parisian crowds
August 26, The Declaration of the Rights of Man is promulgated and freedom of the press is declared
October 5–6, Market women march to Versailles and bring the royal family back to Paris

1791:
October 1, Promulgation of the Constitution; women are excluded from active citizenship

1792:
August 10, The French monarchy is abolished and a Republic is declared
April 20, The French declare war on Austria

1793:
January 21, Louis XVI is executed
March 10, The Revolutionary tribunal is organized; the Terror begins
April 18, Mme Jeanne-Catherine Clere is executed by the revolutionary tribunal
November 8, Mme Maire-Jeanne Roland is tried and executed for treason

1794:
July 27 (9 Thermidor), Robespierre falls, the Terror ends, and the Thermidorian republic is installed

1795:
October, France creates a National Institute and Normal Schools that exclude women
from the professional study of philosophy

1799:
November 9–10, Coup d'Etat of Napoleon Bonaparte

1804:
May 18, Napoleon Bonaparte declares the French Empire

1790   1800   1810   1820   1830   1840   1850   1860   1870

1811:
*Mme Stéphanie de Genlis publishes De l'Influence des femmes sur la littérature française
(The Influence of Women on French Literature)*

1804:
*Fortunée Briquet publishes her Dictionnaire historique et biographique des françaises
(Historical and Biographical Dictionary of French Women)*

1800:
Mme Gemaine de Staël publishes On Literature

1795:
Isabelle de Charrière publishes her novel, Trois Femmes (Three Women)

1793:
Louise de Kéralio publishes The Crimes of the Queens of France, anonymously

1791:
*Olympe de Gouges publishes her
Declaration of the Rights of Women*

1789:
*August 10, Louise de Kéralio launches her newspaper,
Le Journal du Citoyen ou le Mercure National*

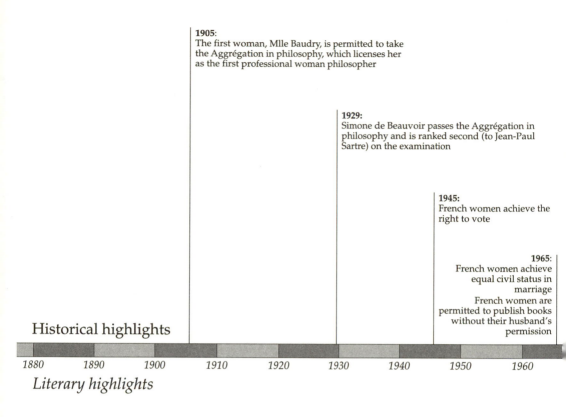

1905:
The first woman, Mlle Baudry, is permitted to take the Aggrégation in philosophy, which licenses her as the first professional woman philosopher

1929:
Simone de Beauvoir passes the Aggrégation in philosophy and is ranked second (to Jean-Paul Sartre) on the examination

1945:
French women achieve the right to vote

1965:
French women achieve equal civil status in marriage
French women are permitted to publish books without their husband's permission

Historical highlights

| 1880 | 1890 | 1900 | 1910 | 1920 | 1930 | 1940 | 1950 | 1960 |

Literary highlights

PART ONE

Women in the Modern Public Sphere

CHAPTER ONE

The Perils of Eloquence

Y'a d'la parole dans leux ventre p'us qu'dans l'Encirclopédie.
(There are more words in their lungs than in the *Encyclopedia*.)
—*Chanson poissarde* (1789)

Early in the spring of 1793, at the height of the revolutionary crisis in France, a middle-aged domestic cook named Jeanne-Catherine Clere frequented a Parisian café near her employer on the rue des Poules where she was in the habit of tippling a few and losing her senses.[1] Once she had had a few too many, she would take to singing at the top of her lungs. And recently she had begun saying that it was "wrong to kill the King and it would have been better to kill the Queen, who was far guiltier than he." The cafetier had had to throw her out of the establishment on several occasions.

Sometime in the first week of March she had also been heard by a local architect in another café, at the corner of the rue Mouffetard and the place de Contrescarpe, saying that "It won't be tolerated if they cut off the head of the son, as they did the father." Asked by another patron in the café who she meant by "the father," she responded, "The father who was in the Temple. Vive le roi!" A bartender warned her that if she said such things outside in the street, she would be arrested.

And that is precisely what happened. At eleven in the evening on March 7, Mme Clere was thrown out of the café Mouffetard after a few drinks. She began ranting loudly as she careened down the street. To be more exact, she was singing, verses ending in resounding choruses of *"Vive le roi."* A patriotic passerby, who turned out to be the President of her section, escorted her to the station of the local *Corps de Garde*. There,

---

[1]The case of Jeanne-Catherine Clere is found in the *Archives Nationales* (hereafter AN): W 268, no. 10 (28 *pièces*), April 8–18, 1793.

seeing the guard's muskets, she bragged of her father's service in the Army of the King and continued singing royalist war songs. She began denigrating soldiers who served the Republic. For several hours she held forth in the most unpatriotic terms: "The rabble that was sent to the army and was still being sent would be swept away by the 30,000 troops of our enemies"; "the rabble weren't the only ones to leave Paris," and that many honest men would die. And, she went on, according to the officers at the station: "The city of Lyon was under the white cocarde, and the province of Franche-Comté would defend Lyon, and would never betray that same cocarde"; "the Swiss Guards were of this faction"; "they too would stick up for the Franche-Comté and the city of Lyon"; "and the same was to be said for all the villages along the postal routes between France and her enemies." Finally, she opined that "the National Convention, as well as the Jacobins, should be lined up in two columns and pummeled. It was supposed to happen on the 25th of March." Asked if she wanted to have her head cut off, she said, "There will be a revolt soon, and this time it won't fail." Then, having said her peace, she fell asleep for several hours. When she woke up, Mme Clere found herself formally accused of treason and imprisoned.

On April 8, Mme Clere's case was sent to the newly constituted revolutionary tribunal. The interrogation that ensued helps to put some of Mme Clere's comments into perspective. She was married to a stagecoach driver from Lyon—hence her knowledge of affairs there. Moreover, she had sons in the Republican army, serving under General Adam Philippe Custine, who were, according to the official record, "known to be good citizens." Under interrogation, Clere first denied having made almost all of the statements attributed to her. She said that she remembered nothing except being escorted to the *Corps de Garde*. When the guards showed her their muskets, she told them that she was the daughter of a soldier who had served thirty-seven years for the King. To prove it, she began singing old war songs.

Pushed further, she admitted saying something about the white cocardes in Lyon, but claimed that she was only repeating what she had read in the old newspapers that she was asked to burn for her employer. She didn't think she was doing any harm in repeating what was already public news. Pushed again about her remarks, she admitted to having said something about plans for a revolt, but here, too, she claimed that she was only repeating things she had heard on the street. She had intended these remarks "without venom," she continued; she only wanted to say that there were "still a lot of crooks in Paris, and that until they were purged, honest men were not free to defend the Republic."

Witnesses from the neighborhood were called in to vouch for her character. Her employer, a "man of letters" named Noel-François de Wailly, testified that she had come to work for him five months ago with referrals and that she was a "good soul." He said, however, that "she was often drunk" and that he had castigated her and threatened to fire her if she didn't stop drinking. He added that when she is taken with drink (*prise de boisson*) she rambles until she sleeps it off. Another neighbor said she had never heard her say anything. The local bartender said she often got drunk and ranted. And the police, too, said that she showed all the "symptoms of drunkenness" when she was brought to the *Corps de Garde*.

The indictment against Mme Clere acknowledged her drinking, but insisted throughout the record of events that she was "better informed and more articulate (*mieux stylée*) than she makes out to be." It stated that, even though drunk, "her thoughts are clear and well-ordered," and that she was clearly "conscious of her criticisms of the volunteers sent to the army," that is, that some of them were "rabble." On April 18, 1793, just over a month after her arrest, Mme Clere was convicted by the revolutionary tribunal of Paris for having "uttered remarks intended to provoke murder, the dissolution of the representatives of the nation and the reestablishment of royalty."[2] She was put to death by guillotine the following day on the place de la Réunion.

Jeanne-Catherine Clere was one of the first people convicted by the revolutionary tribunal. I have dwelt upon her case at this length because it is not coincidental that this early convicted traitor to the new Republic was a woman, and that her crime was seditious speech. A whole group of market women were arrested for seditious speech as early as the October days of 1789.[3] Heated political speech by women on both sides of the political spectrum was treated as a particular threat to public order by revolutionary authorities. Just after the King's flight to Varennes in June of 1791, three notorious radical women, Constance

[2]*Jugement du tribunal-criminel révolutionnaire établi au Palais à Paris par la loi de 10 mars 1793, 2ème de la République françoise, qui condamne à la peine de mort Jeanne-Catherine Clere, pour avoir provoqué le rétablissement de la royauté en France [signé Fabricus, greffier]* (Paris: Imp. du Clément, [n.d]).

[3]Barry Shapiro, *Revolutionary Justice in Paris, 1789–90* (New York: Cambridge University Press, 1993), p. 215.

Evrad, Pauline Léon, and Léon's mother, were stopped by a troop of royal bodyguards in the Palais Royal and almost summarily executed for calling the King's actions treasonous.[4] Many examples of this sort could be cited, but the important point is that, from very early on in the Revolution, seditious speech was more heavily criminalized than any other form of political expression or activity.[5]

Still, from what we know about the social logic of the terror, Mme Clere's execution is surprising. Women, in general, were far less likely than men to be detained as suspects. They were less likely to be convicted by the revolutionary tribunal (they constituted less than 15 percent of those put to death). It is true that Parisian women represented almost half of all women convicted, but, in contrast to the social profile of male convicts, the great majority of these came from the upper classes.[6] What made Mme Clere such an exceptional figure?

This book begins with the revolutionary conjuncture of Parisian women and political speech because the unhappy fate of eloquent women in revolutionary politics marked a critical cultural turning point for French women more generally: The demise of the oral was the first chapter in the story of their entry into the modern world.

In retrospect, the conviction of Mme Clere may not seem difficult to explain. Her speeches *were* outrageously provocative. But on closer examination her case is more difficult to interpret. True, some of her remarks were flagrantly royalist, especially concerning the execution of the King. But she also suggested that the King was perhaps a mere victim of his wife's plotting and that the Queen should be killed for treason. And the impression that her record leaves is primarily that of a woman in distress—distress because her sons were at war and she was frightened for their safety, distress and anger because of the uncertainties of the Revolution. She blamed the new government, she longed for the security of the King. But her political views were not unambiguously royalist: Her remarks about all the "crooks in Paris" and her fears for the safety of Parisians if all the honest men went to war, were rem-

---

[4]See Darline Levy, Harriet Applewhite, and Mary Johnson, eds., *Women in Revolutionary Paris, 1789–1795* (Urbana: University of Illinois Press, 1979), pp. 158–160; Dominique Godineau, *Citoyennes tricoteuses* (Paris: Alinea, 1988), pp. 372, 375–376.

[5]Richard Mowery Andrews, "Boundaries of Citizenship: The Penal Regulation of Speech in Revolutionary France," in *French Politics and Society*, vol. 7, no. 3 (Summer 1989): 90–109.

[6]Women were 14.4 percent of the total number of defendants before the tribunal. See Stephanie Brown, *Women on Trial: The Revolutionary Tribunal and Gender*, Stanford Ph.D. dissertation 1996, pp. 53, 65–66, 89, 157, 387.

iniscent of the popular anxieties that resulted in the September massacres. And her invocation of a rumored popular revolt planned for March seems more likely to have referred to the plans for an ultrarevolutionary Hérbertist insurrection than to a counterrevolutionary uprising. What, finally, made the ranting of a drunken women seem like such a threat?

Before answering this question let us consider another case, taken from the other end of the sociocultural spectrum—the trial of the well-known Girondist *salonnière* and minister's wife, Marie-Jeanne Roland, eight months later, on November 8, 1793.[7] Mme Roland went to prison with high hopes that she would be able to use her well-known eloquence to recover her freedom. Indeed, in December of 1792 she had already successfully defended herself and her husband before the bar of the National Convention. On that occasion she had spoken with such eloquence that she had received a standing ovation from the deputies.[8]

Ten days after her arrest, Mme Roland was interrogated for the first time. She was asked if she had any special knowledge of the affairs troubling the Republic. She responded, like Mme Clere, that she had no knowledge of public affairs other than what she had read in the newspapers and heard about in public conversations. Moreover, everything that she had heard in conversation was always in a manner entirely in accordance with the principles of justice and liberty. The interrogator replied that "the words *liberty* and *justice* can become very equivocal ones when one doesn't add that equality is the basis of a Republic." Ever quick-witted, she responded that equality was "an inevitable consequence of liberty and justice." Language play was a game well suited to the talents of Roland.

Asked to name who composed her regular society, Mme Roland stressed that a great number of people passed through her house and that "she had never had what one would call a particular 'circle.'" The interrogators persistently tried to get Mme Roland to admit that she was the "director" of a secret "*bureau d'esprit*" that functioned as a propaganda center for the Federalist cause. She, in return, resisted characterization of herself as anything more than a helpmeet to her husband (his occasional secretary) and as having engaged only in casual conversation. Each time they suggested that she held private "meetings" at her

---

[7]For an excellent account of Mme Roland's arrest and trial, see Gita May, *Madame Roland and the Age of Revolution* (New York: Columbia University Press, 1970), pp. 262–288.

[8]May, *Madame Roland*, p. 250.

home, she corrected them, calling her gatherings public "conversations" as opposed to "conferences."

The interrogators became increasingly frustrated with her answers. As they put it:

> It was shocking that her responses were entirely generic and evasive of what the court wanted to hear, and we therefore required her to respond only by an affirmative or negative whether she had knowledge of an organized departmental force and whether she had agitated in favor of this in her conversations.

As she recalled this interrogation in her memoirs:

> The discussion was long and difficult. Before I could put my answers in writing they wanted to reduce them to a simple *yes* or *no*. They accused me of verbosity, and said that this wasn't the Ministry of the Interior; wit would get me nowhere. When the judge posed a question that the prosecutor didn't find to his taste, he would pose it in another manner, extending it, making it more complex or interrupting my responses, and then requiring me to abridge them. It was a real vexation."[9]

In the end, the prosecutor, Antione Quentin Fouquier-Tinville, indicted Mme Roland for counterrevolutionary conspiracy because of her correspondence and because of her private conversations, for having held "secret meetings in her home."[10]

Mme Roland's interrogation proceeded in precisely the opposite rhetorical direction from that of Mme Clere. In Mme Clere's case, the authorities worked to provoke her to greater eloquence in order to determine whether she should be judged to be the author of her own words; her culpability lay in the perception of her conscious ability to create political meanings. In Mme Roland's case, her ability to debate political meanings far exceeded that of her interrogators. They therefore pursued the opposite tactic—reducing her to two words alone.

Opposing strategies led, however, to the same end. In each case the police were determined to find these women guilty as the witting authors of their own speech, and to conclude that they deployed their speech with the intent of effecting political ends. In both cases—the

---

[9]Gérard Walter, ed., *Actes du tribunal révolutionnaire* (Paris: Mercure de France, 1986), pp. 266, 269.

[10]The *Act d'Accusation* can be found in AN: W 290, plaq. 227, p. 31.

one through her explicitness, the other through her evasiveness—the women were proved to be culpable.

While in prison, awaiting her trial, Roland still clung to hopes that once she was permitted to speak in the courtroom she would be able to sway the jurors with a rousing defense of her actions and motivations. But she was never to be given the opportunity. The moment she opened her mouth in the tribunal, she was interrupted by one of the judges and then silenced by deafening cries of "Long live the Republic, Down with the traitors," from the public galleries. Clearly, the only means to convict this eloquent woman was to silence her.[11]

Female eloquence became a central and a dangerous element in revolutionary politics. Spoken words, especially among Parisian women of the people, carried more weight—and a historically specific weight—in 1793 than they do today. Though urban France was becoming rapidly more literate, Mme Clere's world was essentially an oral one. Daniel Roche estimates that in the 1780s only about one in eight women in the Parisian popular classes could read, even if they could sign their names.[12] Illiteracy was a distinctly gendered phenomenon by the end of the Old Regime. Were we to draw a graph depicting the male and female paths to literacy beginning in roughly 1650, when all but a very small upper crust of society (say about 10 percent) could read, moving through the eighteenth century, we would see an increasing gap open up between the sexes, widening to the end of the eighteenth century and then slowly closing up toward 85 percent total literacy from the second half of the nineteenth century to the beginning of the twentieth. The Revolution thus occurred at a very particular moment in the history of literacy.

The last decade of the eighteenth century saw the greatest extent of the gender gap in literacy: Most French men were literate and most French women were not.[13] Illiteracy was a distinctly female phenomenon; women were perceived to be intimately connected with the oral.

Mme Clere claimed in her testimony to the police to be able to read newspapers. She would have been unusual in this regard and therefore especially powerful: Clere could act as a cultural bridge between her mostly illiterate milieu and the world of print. She had hoped that her claim to be merely repeating what she read in newspapers would di-

[11]May, *Madame Roland*, p. 284.

[12]Daniel Roche, *The People of Paris* (Berkeley: University of California Press, 1987), p. 213.

[13]François Furet and Jacques Ozouf, *Reading and Writing: Literacy in France from Calvin to Jules Ferry* (Cambridge, UK: Cambridge University Press, 1982), pp. 32–33, 46.

minish her culpability for the substance of her ranting. In fact, it may have had the opposite effect on the authorities: It made her appear that much more dangerous as a potential neighborhood agitator who combined the knowledge of print with the power of speech.

The sociology of women's speech in the period of the transition to literacy should also be situated in a precise cultural context. Under the Old Regime, it was not just women of the popular classes who were associated with verbal skill. Elite French women, too, enjoyed a reputation as particularly gifted when it came to spontaneous oral eloquence. As the French language came to be codified by written regulations, women's speech took on a particular set of cultural meanings. Beginning in the mid–seventeenth century, the French crown sponsored a series of cultural initiatives to define correct speech and regulate its public use. Louis XIII patronized the composition of French grammars and dictionaries of good usage, founded the French Academy in 1635 and set for it the task of writing the definitive dictionary of the language. Written rules thus introduced models of correct speaking intended to govern oral usage. The grace and the elegance of French rhetorical style came to be admired throughout Europe.[14]

By the 1660s, the Crown had created the first royal "police" force in Paris, precisely to ensure the "politeness" of public comportment, including public speech. Indeed, there is an intimate relationship between the idea of the "police," "*politesse*" and a "well-policed," or civilized, state. Public speaking, whether in the academy or on the street, thus came under the continuous surveillance of the royal ear. As these new institutions began for the first time to give shape to normative spoken French, nonnormative French—that is, slang and other forms of transgressive speech—also came to be defined. Two forms of speech, in particular, came to denote the transgression of good style: *poissarde* and *préciosité*, one plebian, one elite.

The history of the emergence of *préciosité* and the *précieuse* style has been well studied by literary historians of the seventeenth century. Its links to women, to salon culture, and its particular political associations with the anti-absolutist machinations of the *Fronde* are well documented. In the eyes of the Crown, and its most eminent cultural ex-

---

[14]See Marc Fumaroli, *L'Age de l'eloquence: rhétorique et "res literaria" de la Renaissance au seuil de l'époque classique* (Geneva: Droz, 1980), esp. pp. 647–672, "Le Parnasse de l'eloquence royale: L'Académie Française sous Richelieu." On the special relationship of French literature to oral conversation, see also Marc Fumaroli, *Le Genre des genres littéraires français: la conversation* (Oxford, UK: Clarendon Press, 1992).

ponents from Molière to Boileau, *préciosité* rapidly came to represent feminine rhetorical excess and hyper-refinement in literary expression.[15]

Précieuse cultural institutions and styles formed the infrastructure of enlightened anti-absolutist intellectual activity—the so-called "Republic of Letters"—over the course of the eighteenth century and right up to the revolutionary period.[16] Throughout the last century of the Old Regime, the salon functioned as a kind of shadow institution of the French Academy in cultural matters and the *Parlement* in politics. Jean-Jacques Rousseau thought that women's extraordinary verbal skills could only be explained physiologically. He suggested that their tongues must be more flexible than men's![17] Be that as it may, women's verbal virtuosity—their ability to stimulate witty and learned conversation—was critical to the salon's success. But excessive verbal skill could be politically dangerous, especially in the world of the royal court where the shaping of perceptions through word of mouth was critical in making and unmaking the credibility of courtiers.

At the other end of the social spectrum was *poissarde*, or fishwives' speech. The history of the word suggests that it first came into use at precisely the same moment as *préciosité*, roughly the 1640s, to refer to fishwives and their notoriously vulgar, yet captivating street cries. The term soon came to be used more generally to refer to the crude speech patterns of the popular classes. From the very beginning, the poetics of the popular slang of market women, and that of the aristocratic *précieuses* were linked in the minds of male literary critics as two related examples of excessively pretentious and hyperbolic speech forms.[18]

Initially a term of denigration, *poissarde* began to take on positive

---

[15]Some key signposts of this vast literature are Roger Lathuillère, *La Préciosité. Etude historique et linguistique* (Genève: Droz, 1966); Dorothy Backer, *Precious Women* (New York: Basic Books, 1974); Carolyn Lougee, *Le Paradis des Femmes: Women, Salons and Social Stratification in Seventeenth-century France* (Princeton: Princeton University Press, 1976); Renate Baader, *Dames de lettres: Autorinnen des preziosen, hocharistokratischen und "modernen" salons (1649–1698)* (Stuttgart: J. B. Metzlersche Verlagsbuch, 1986); Nicole Aronson, *Madame de Rambouillet, ou la magicienne de la chambre bleue* (Paris: Fayard, 1988); Erica Harth, *Cartesian Women: Versions and Subversions of Rationalist Discourse in the Old Regime* (Ithaca, NY: Cornell University Press, 1992).

[16]Dena Goodman, *The Republic of Letters: A Cultural History of the Enlightenment* (Ithaca, NY: Cornell University Press, 1994).

[17]Jean-Jacques Rousseau, *Emile: Or, On education*, Allan Bloom, trans. (New York: Basic Books, 1979), p. 376.

[18]A. P. Moore, *The Genre Poissard and the French Stage of the Eighteenth Century* (New York: Institute for French Studies, Columbia University, 1935), p. 31.

literary attributes by the eighteenth century—reflecting the raw eloquence of the people. *Poissarde* speech first began to become fashionable among elites through immoral farces known as *parades,* which were presented as *entr'actes* in popular theater.[19] Over the course of the century, aristocratic households, including the court at Versailles, produced *parades* as a form of light, evening entertainment in which the elite classes took on the roles of market women and longshoremen, imitating their slang, accents, and intonation. In 1777, it is reported, Marie Antoinette even went so far as to have actual market women brought to Versailles to serve as speech coaches for her ladies in waiting in the production of one of these *poissarde* plays.[20]

By the 1740s, *poissarde* had become a bona fide literary genre, distinguished by its ethnographic realism and vivid pastoralization of popular oral forms. It was written in a pseudophonetic form (most frequently identified by the use of the first-person singular pronoun with a plural verb form, for example, "*j'avons . . .*") with intentional phonetic misspellings of words. *Poissarde* produced social dissonance by combining popular expressions with higher poetic forms. Comic effects were produced by mispronunciation and misusage of words and figures of speech considered to be above the station of the speaker. *Poissarde* speech, like preciosity, was, above all, construed as hyperbolic—flattery too sweet or rage too strong.

It was a minor royal official, Jean-Joseph Vadé, who, in the 1740s, created the most lasting model of *poissarde* literature as a kind of fictionalized scripting of an ethnographic record of popular speech. He did this through the construction of a myth of the male author as a mere scribe of female speech, a man of letters who haunted marketplaces, taverns, and cafes of the popular neighborhoods of Paris, recording eloquent street disputes concerning jealous or ill-sorted loves, social pretensions, and just comeuppances (see Figure 1.1).

In the hands of a writer as gifted as Diderot, the fishwife became a figure of the sublime. Thus, he writes of Jean-Baptiste Greuze's portrait of his wife, shown at the 1765 *Salon:*

> This fine, fat fishwife, with her head twisted backwards, and whose pale coloring, and showy kerchief, all mussed, and expres-

---

[19]The most extensive study of this literature is Moore; *The Genre Poissard;* see also, Arthur Heulhard, *La Foire Saint-Laurent: son histoire et ses spectacles* (Paris: Alcan-Levy, 1877).

[20]Moore, *The Genre Poissard,* p. 291.

Figure 1.1 The Male Writer Transcribes Female Speech. "La vente de la seringue (The Sale of the Seringue)," from Jean Joseph Vadé, *Oeuvres poissardes, illustrées par Monsiau* (Paris: Defer de la Maisonneuve, an IV [1796]). Bancroft Library, University of California, Berkeley.

sion of pain mixed with pleasure depicts a paroxysm that is sweeter to experience than it is decorous to paint.[21]

Diderot's sublime figure of the *poissarde*, at once ecstatic and enraged, has come down to us today as the defining example of the word *poissarde* in the *Grand Robert* dictionary.[22] Greuze's painting betrays the elite literary origins of this image of the fishwife, and the power of the literary experience engendered by her speech: His wife's paroxysm is, it appears, a result of reading and writing (see Figure 1.2).

In cultural terms, women's speech in the period of the transition to literacy can be conceptualized as the two ends of a bell curve in which correct speech, linked with eloquent style, was figured as a masculine norm (the rhetoric of the academy, the pulpit, or the law courts). Female speech represented the two extremes of the curve: on the one hand the excessively vulgar, and on the other hand the excessively refined. Conversational rather than oratorical, these speech forms were recognized as powerful rhetorical elements, both eloquent and dangerous. Repartee, by nature an improvisational and open-ended game in which each party sought to exceed the other in wit, always carried the risk of going too far.

Each of these oral forms was associated with a particular sociocultural milieu—the salon and the marketplace. These were, then, two key feminine sites of interpretation and commentary in a social and political world that was still primarily an oral one. Not surprisingly, they were, by the end of the eighteenth century, heavily policed.[23] Courtiers discreetly listened in on the "gallant conversations" in aristocratic drawing rooms, while police spies circulated in the marketplaces of the capital.

Women's public speech, and especially the speech of market women, had, moreover, a recognized place in the political ritual of the Old Regime. The market women of Paris had had a special relationship

---

[21]Denis Diderot, *Salon de Greuze* (1765), in *Diderot on Art I: The Salon of 1765 and Notes on Painting*, John Goodman, trans. (New Haven, CT: Yale University Press, 1995), p. 102.

[22]See the definition of *poissarde*, in *Le Grand Robert de la langue française*, 2nd ed., vol. 7 (Paris: Le Robert, 1985).

[23]For regulation of popular public speaking, see Arlette Farge, *Le Dire et le mal dire* (Paris: Seuil, 1992); for the codification of *politesse* and the regulation of verbal expression in the salon, see Daniel Gordon, *Citizens Without Sovereignty* (Princeton, NJ: Princeton University Press 1994) and Goodman, *The Republic of Letters*. See also Lisa Jane Graham, *If the King Only Knew: Seditious Speech in the Reign of Louis XV* (Charlottesville: University of Virginia Press, 2000).

LA PHILOSOPHIE ENDORMIE.

Dediée à Madame Greuze

Figure 1.2 Diderot's Fishwife. "Madame Greuze or, 'La Philosophie Endormie' (Philosophy Sleeps)," engraving, Jacques Aliament, after Jean-Baptiste Greuze (1761). Metropolitan Museum of Art, New York.

to the King since the middle ages, when St. Louis granted destitute women the exclusive privilege to sell retail goods and, in particular, fish, at designated sites in the city markets. These retail locales came to be known as *places St. Louis.* The women who obtained the royal privilege to make use of these spaces were formed into a mutual aid society known as the "Confraternity of Saint-Louis."[24] Royal charity, thus, not only rescued desperate women from sinful forms of gain but also facilitated the observance of Lent by making fish more widely available.

Fish selling was no small matter. Fish, from biblical times, were considered a particularly pure species in both Aristotelian and biblical sources. Because fish shared neither of humankind's two environments (air and land), Aristotle saw them as living in another world. Biblical commentators found fish to have been exempted from God's curse in Genesis, never fallen, and therefore especially holy.[25] Before the Revolution, there were 138 fast days a year. On these days one abstained from all meat except fish. Supply was critical to observance. Fishwives thus played a central role in maintaining the ritual sanctity of the realm and they were regulated with special care by royal authorities in collaboration with the Church.[26]

Certain fish, notably the salmon and the whale, were considered "royal fish" and the King had special privileges in relation to their catch. Under Louis XV, salmon, in particular, took on special associations with the court when Mme de Pompadour chose it as an image for her china pattern. The market women of Paris, and especially the fishwives, thus owed a very special debt to the King for his protection, and they held a special place in his heart.

Over the course of the early modern period, this special relationship crystallized into the ritual reception of a delegation of market women by the King twice a year—on the Jour St. Louis (August 26) and at the New Year. They also visited the Queen on the day of the Assumption of the Virgin. And they appeared on special occasions such as royal mar-

---

[24]Little is known about this confraternity except that they dissolved themselves along with other royal corporations in 1791. See *Adresse des dames de la halle à l'assemblée nationale, séance du 27 août 1791.* (Paris: Imprimerie Nationale, 1791).

[25]For the best institutional history of the *Dames de la Halle* to date, see Rene S. Marion, *The Dames de la Halle: Community and Authority in Early Modern Paris*, Ph.D. dissertation, Johns Hopkins University, 1994; see also Nicolas Delamare, *Traité de la police* (Paris: J. P. Cot, 1705), entries on *poisson.*

[26]For the history of the administration of the principal market in Paris, *les Halles,* see Jean Martineau, *Les Halles de Paris des origines à 1789* (Paris: Editions Montchrestien, 1960).

riages and births or the recovery of health of a member of the King's family or the celebration of French military victories.

By the end of the eighteenth century, the ritual exchanges between the market women and the King had become rather elaborate. The women would make a procession from Paris to Versailles, or the King would take the occasion to visit the marketplace. The royal visit might include a feast, and on very special occasions a theater performance in which the King and Queen would sit next to a market woman and a longshoreman to ritually enact their communion with their people.[27]

The visits of the market women to Versailles and, reciprocally, their role in welcoming the King when he visited his capital, gave them a special privilege to offer the King their wares and, especially, a bouquet, along with a verbal toast to the health of the King and the royal family. Reciprocally, the visits gave the King an opportunity to inquire directly about the well-being of his people. These verbal exchanges between the King and the market women, could, however, in bad years—like 1750—become quite tense: Caught in the grips of a panic about the mysterious disappearance of street children, the market women of Paris threatened to go to Versailles and "tear the King's hair out" if he did not protect them from the police.[28] The market women of Paris thus acquired a kind of popular political legitimacy and a privilege to free political speech enjoyed by no other group in French society under the Old Regime.

But even without this intimate dialogue with the King, the public speech of fishwives was extremely powerful in shaping popular perceptions of the monarchy. Fishwives gathered daily in neighborhood wine bars, like the one frequented by Mme Clere on the rue Mouffetard, and held forth on the political issues of the day. Wine bars were thus key nodes in the oral networks of Parisian neighborhoods: It was here that political news was transmitted in an illiterate world.[29]

As with the salon, elites embraced *poissardes* not only for literary pleasure, but for political profit as well. Literary *poissardes* witnessed a

[27]See Marion, *The Dames de la Halle*. See also Louis Sébastien Mercier, *Le Tableau de Paris* (Amsterdam: n.p., 1782–1788).

[28]Farge, *Le Dire et le mal dire;* see also, Arlette Farge and Jacques Revel, *Logiques de la foule* (Paris: Hachette, 1988).

[29]David Garrioch, *Neighborhood and Community in Paris, 1740–1790* (Cambridge, UK: Cambridge University Press, 1986), pp. 182–183. See also W. Scott Haine, "A Voice of Their Own: Parisian Working Women and Café Politics, 1789–1800," in *Consortium on Revolutionary Europe, 1750–1850: Proceedings 1989* (Tallahassee, FL: Institute on Napoleon and the French Revolution, Florida State University, 1990), pp. 539–544.

slow but definitive politicization over the course of the eighteenth century. The fortuitous fact of Mme de Pompadour's maiden name—Mademoiselle Poisson—offered too fine an opportunity to her detractors not to make the unflattering linguistic link between the royal mistress and the haranguing fishwives. Thus a series of anonymous *poissonades* appeared in 1749, lampooning the marquise as a "*petite bourgeoise, elevée à la grivoise.*" ("A petty-bourgeois, of vulgar upbringing")[30] By the second half of the century, as the constitutional crisis between the Crown and the *Parlements* deepened, lawyers began to appropriate the voices of the market women and their privilege of political speech in order to compliment or correct the King.

Fishwives were mobilized from the 1750s onward to the cause of the Jansenist church leaders in Paris who sought to restore the Church to a more rigorous moral purity.[31] By the 1770s, following the crisis over the Crown's attempt to deregulate commerce, the market women of Paris had taken up the cause of the *Parlementaires* against royal attempts to impose "unconstitutional" economic reforms. On November 21, 1774, for example, a delegation of market women greeted the restored *Parlement* and offered its president, Etienne-François d'Aligre, a bouquet in homage.[32] By 1787, when the standoff between *Parlement* and Crown became a matter of life and death for the regime, the market women of the capital were fully politicized on behalf of the constitutional cause.[33] As an act of overt protest, they refused to come to Versailles on the Queen's Saint day to offer their compliments. By the eve of the Revolution in 1789, the *poissarde* alliance with the party of reform was made vividly clear by the arrangement for the appearance of several fishwives on the stage of a performance of the *Souper de Henri IV* at the *Théâtre de Monsieur,* to drink a toast to Henry IV, the most popular of all French Kings. The performance was an explicit political message to the King that he should emulate his beloved ancestor and act in the interests of the common people rather than the aristocracy and the clergy.[34]

Indeed, the rhetorical form of the eighteenth-century political pamphlet owes as great a debt to the female speech of the marketplace as it

---

[30]*Receuil Clairambault-Maurepas, chansonnier historique du XVIIIe siècle, publié avec une introduction, commentaire, notes et index par Emile Raumié* (Paris: A Quantin, 1882). I am grateful to Thomas Kaiser for this reference.

[31]See Marion, *The Dames de la Halle,* p. 283.

[32]Jean Tulard, *Nouvelle Histoire de Paris, la révolution,* (Paris: Hachette, 1989), p. 512.

[33]Marion, *The Dames de la Halle,* pp. 310–321.

[34]Moore, *The Genre Poissarde,* p. 349.

does to the *mémoire judiciaire* or the pornographic tract.[35] In the closing years of the Old Regime the production of political *poissardes*, written mostly by lawyers in the voices of fishwives, became increasingly widespread.[36] The *Bouquet*, for example, became a popular satirical pamphlet genre for offering ironic compliments to the King, and the *Cri* a genre for offering invective and correction. The adoption of this voice became a sign of popular legitimacy for the newly emergent political classes of the revolutionary period.[37]

The *poissarde* was also a central figure of Carnival, both as a theatrical persona and as a written form. The literary transvestism of men appropriating women's voices, and the rhetorical masquerade of pseudophonetic representations of speech in written form were given religious legitimation at Mardi Gras, and as post-Lenten forms of comic release. Because of the association of the fishwife with Lenten observance, the *poissarde* genre was also appropriated, in carnivalesque form, by church leaders, to militate against efforts to reform the Church along Jansenist lines.[38]

After 1789 the monarchy and the aristocracy could no longer control the sites of legitimate free speech within French society. The collapse of the Bourbon monarchy after 1789 sent the cultural institutions formed during the last several centuries of its reign into total disarray, not least of all the salons of the aristocracy and the rituals of the market women of Paris. New sites of cultural power, like the revolutionary salons of Mme Roland and Mme de Staël were constituted along political lines, reflecting the shifting force fields within the new National Assembly rather than the hierarchical channeling of patronage through networks controlled by the court and the higher aristocracy.[39] Now it was the politics

---

[35]For recent work on the contribution of the *mémoire judiciaire* to late eighteenth-century political rhetoric, see Sarah Maza, *Private Lives and Public Affairs: The Causes Célèbres of Pre-revolutionary France* (Berkeley: University of California Press, 1993). For work on political pornography, see Robert Darnton, *Forbidden Best-sellers of Pre-revolutionary France* (New York: Norton, 1995); Antoine de Baecque, "Pamphlets: Libel and Political Mythology," in Robert Darnton and Daniel Roche, eds., *Revolution in Print: The Press in France, 1775–1800* (Berkeley: University of California Press, 1989), pp. 165–176; and Lynn Hunt, "Pornography in the French Revolution," in Lynn Hunt, ed., *The Invention of Pornography* (New York: Zone Books, 1993), pp. 301–340.

[36]See Moore, *The Genre Poissarde*; see also, Farge, *Le Dire et le mal dire.*

[37]See Ferdinand Brunot, *Histoire de la langue française des origines à 1900. Tome X: La Langue classique dans la tourmente* (Paris: Armand Colin, 1939), pp. 259–270.

[38]See Alain Fauré, *Paris Carême-Prenant: du carnaval à Paris au XIXe siècle, 1800–1914* (Paris: Hachette, 1978), and Pierre Frantz, "Travestis Poissards," *Revue des Sciences Humaines*, vol. LXI, no. 190 (Avril–Juin 1983): 7–20.

[39]Regarding the new revolutionary salons, see May, *Madame Roland*, pp. 180–199.

of political faction, rather than those of court intrigue that would determine the influence of eloquent elite women in the world of public affairs.

The monarchy was also rapidly losing its grip on popular political expression. On July 14, 1789, the King's cherished fishwives were central participants in the Parisian crowd that brought down the Bastille. Women from the market of the district of St. Paul went in delegation to the new municipal officers on July 20, 1789, in order to make their opinions on events known.[40] In late August, the King made clear to the mayor of Paris, Jean Sylvain Bailly, that he did not want to receive any unauthorized delegations of market women at Versailles on his Saint's day, because of a fear of popular demonstrations.[41] No one listened.

On October 5, 1789, processions of market women led the massive march to Versailles that brought the King and the royal family back to Paris and ensured the ratification of the *Declaration of the Rights of Man* (Figure 1.3).[42] This overt break of the fishwives of Paris with the Crown was looked upon with horror by that acute observer of popular culture, the writer Antoine Rivarol, who noted in disbelief that people confused the *poissardes* who marched on Versailles with the fish sellers of Paris. Those who betrayed the King, were, in fact, in his words "false *poissardes*," mere impostors.[43] Fish sellers had, inconceivably, become revolutionaries.

On November 2, 1789, the royally privileged fishwives of Les Halles, the main Parisian marketplace, made a patriotic contribution to the National Assembly to help the new nation. And in 1791 when the National Assembly abolished all corporations, they dissolved the "Confraternity of Saint-Louis" and made a further donation of its remaining funds to the nation.[44] With the dissolution of this corporation, the last formal ties between the monarchy and the fishwives of Paris were broken.

---

[40]*Discours adressé à l'assemblée des électeurs par les dames poissardes du marché de St. Paul le 20 juillet 1789*, in *Procès-verbal de l'assemblée des électeurs de Paris*, Bailly et Duveyrier, eds., vol. II (Paris: Baudouin, 1790), p. 228.

[41]AN: O1 500, fol. 440, "*Lettre du ministre de la maison du Roi, à M. Bailly, le priant de s'opposer à la venue des femmes du marché Saint-Martin à Versailles, pour éviter les manifestations populaires, le Roi ne voulant recevoir que les dames de la Halle, 20 août 1789.*"

[42]See Paule Marie Duhet, *Les Femmes et la Révolution française, 1789–1794* (Paris: Juillard, 1971), and Dominique Godineau, *The Women of Paris and Their French Revolution*, Katharine Streip, trans. (Berkeley: University of California Press, 1998; original French edition, 1988).

[43]Antoine Rivarol, *Memoires de Rivarol* (Original edition: Paris: Baudouin, 1824; reedited by Editions GALIC, Paris, 1962), p. 263.

[44]*Adresse des dames de la halle à l'assemblée nationale, séance du 27 août 1791.* (Paris: Imprimerie Nationale, 1791).

Figure 1.3 Market Women March to Versailles. "Le départ: Du pain et le roi (The Departure: Bread and the King)." Anonymous engraving, 1789. Bibliothèque Nationale de France, cabinet des estampes, Paris.

The deinstitutionalization of popular female speech heightened the fear of women's words on the street. Which brings us back to the drunken, raving domestic with whom I began. Who could speak, when and where, had ceased to be governed by public authorities, royal or revolutionary. Whatever the political allegiances of market women might actually have been—a much-debated topic—their symbolic bonds with the monarchy had been broken. Political, religious, and economic fissures were everywhere, but nowhere were these more public than in the speech of women selling fish. And men, within both the revolutionary and counterrevolutionary camps, monitored the places of that speech closely in order to detect shifts in the political opinions of women of the popular classes.[45]

While fear of actual women speaking on the streets grew during the Revolution, the *poissarde* pamphlet genre, in both its political and its religious forms, exploded as (mostly) male authors took on the voice of the fishwife to heighten their claims to popular legitimacy: At least sev-

[45]See Godineau, *The Women of Paris*. See also Olwen Hufton, "Women in Revolution, 1789–1796," *Past and Present*, no. 53 (1971): 90–108, and Levy, Applewhite, and Johnson,*Women in Revolutionary Paris*.

enty political pamphlets and an additional dozen literary works—from songs to plays—were written in the voices of market women in the decade of 1789 to 1799; twenty-five in the year 1789 alone. Interestingly, the *poissarde* form knew no political bounds. It was appropriated—as the range of *Mère Duchêne* publications amply illustrates—by clerics and radical *sans-culottes*, royalists and republicans alike (see Figures 1.4 and 1.5).[46] This rhetorical form of popular legitimacy even permeated into petitions sent by popular societies to the National Convention, and were published in the official Bulletin of the Convention to legitimate its policies.[47]

The fishwife persona created in popular song, verse, and theater over the course of the eighteenth century—the stock characters Margot, Merluche, Enguele, Mme Angot, Mère Saumon, Mère Jérôme, and, of course, the Mère Duchêne herself—became such a distinct part of popular consciousness and political dialogue during the Revolution that they even began to shape—indeed to haunt—the perceptions of the police. Hence an undercover police officer offered the following description of a potential counterrevolutionary agitator during a patriotic procession on June 24, 1793—a few months after the execution of Mme Clere:

> As the procession began, an ugly woman, a fat Margot, one of those who sells hotcakes in the market, put herself at the head of the group behind the cavalry. The guards began laughing, but they didn't remove her because she was wearing a cocarde, even though a Jacobin, dressed to look like an executioner, wanted her evicted.[48]

Thus, the line between literary fiction and social actor began to blur. And it was precisely this blurring of the boundary between art and life that made it possible for the authorities to become convinced that the tirades

[46]The *Mère Duchêne* publications have recently been reedited in their entirety: *Lettres bourgrement patriotiques de la Mère Duchêne, suivi de Journal des Femmes*, Ouzi Elyada, ed. (Paris: EDHIS, 1791). For the best study of the political perspectives of the Mère Duchêne, see Ouzi Elyada, "*La Mère Duchêne: masques populaires et guerre pamphletiare, 1789–1791*," *Annales historiques de la Révolution Française*, no. 271 (Janvier–Mars 1988): 1–16. See also Pierre Frantz, "*Travestis poissards*," *Revue des Sciences Humaines*, vol. LXI, no. 190 (Avril–Juin 1983): 7–20.

[47]See Brunot, *Histoire de la langue française*, vol. X, p. 267.

[48]"*Rapport de l'observateur Dutard à Garat, ministre de l'Intérieur*," AN: F1c III Seine, 27, A. D. Schmidt, ed., *Tableaux de la Révolution française*, vol. 2, p. 84; cited in A. Tuetey, *Paris pendant la Révolution*, vol. 9, p. 712.

Figure 1.4 Women and Fish on Top. "The World Turned Upside Down."
Anonymous French engraving, 18th Century. Bibliothèque nationale, Paris.

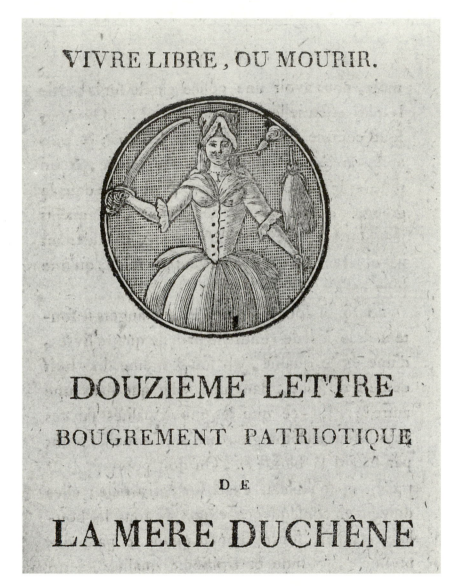

Figure 1.5 A Revolutionary Fishwife. *Douzième Lettre bougrement patriotique de la mère Duchêne* (The Twelfth Fucking Patriotic Letter of Mother Duchêne). 1791. Department of Special Collections, Stanford University Library, Stanford. Palo Alto, California.

of the drunken Mme Clere on the rue Mouffetard were a conscious act of treason rather than a sign of mental derangement.

Recognition and fear of the power of women's speech, when freed from the constraints of ritualized containment, struck into the hearts of political actors on both sides of the revolutionary battle. At the intellectual pinnacle of revolutionary literary culture, Louis Sebastien Mercier, in his treatise *La Néologie*, explicitly invoked market women as a vital source of French linguistic creativity.[49] Popular oral improvisation, which knew none of the constraints of learned culture, and especially the intense poetic energies of the retailer, were the greatest source, Mercier insisted, of new words than kept the French language alive and fecund. But during the crisis of the Year II (1793–1794) such creativity was anathema to political as opposed to cultural authorities. While the republican authorities vigilantly monitored the marketplaces, planting newspapers and broadsides to sway the views of government policy on the street, royalists also agitated to shape the opinions of the popular classes.

Interestingly, despite their opposing political viewpoints, royalists and republicans alike shared a cultural agenda of imposing the authority of the written word against the spoken. As authority came to be embodied in written law rather than personal prerogative, and as printing became the chosen mode of publication, the dangers of illiteracy heightened. The unlucky Mlle Ferrand, an illiterate petty thief, found herself in much bigger trouble than she ever anticipated when she unwittingly defied the laws against emigration by evading the border at Strasbourg, purportedly to get married. Her suspicious comings and goings (probably involving the fencing of stolen goods) led to her arrest and execution for aiding the emigrés.[50] Her inability to read the new laws was not accepted as a defense. Illiteracy created disproportionate danger for women in the Year II (1793–1794).[51] Unable to read the laws now posted with unprecedented rapidity in broadside form on the streets, rather than proclaimed aloud at mass, many women of the popular classes unwittingly fell afoul of the proliferation of emergency measures.

The struggle between the written and the spoken word for cultural

---

[49]This treatise was composed in the 1790s. Louis Sébastien Mercier, *La Néologie* (Paris: Moussard, 1801); cited by Daniel Blake Rosenberg in, "Making Time: Origin, History, and Language in Enlightenment France and Britain," Ph.D. Dissertation, University of California, Berkeley, 1996, see esp., chap. 7.

[50]AN: W 268, dossier, Mlle Ferrand (an II).

[51]Godineau, *Citoyennes tricoteuses*, pp. 215–217.

hegemony in the Parisian popular classes was thematized most explicitly in the royalist *poissarde* pamphlet, *Le Falot du peuple, ou entretiens de Madame Saumon, marchande de marée, sur le procès de Louis XVI*. In this classic argument between two fishwives—Mme Saumon and Mme Doucet—Mme Saumon claims that the King is surely guilty of treason and deserves to die. (The symbolism of Mme Saumon taking up the republican cause would not have been lost on contemporary readers, because salmon was considered a "royal" fish, one upon which the King retained special privileges. In sum, his fish had turned on him.)

Mme Doucet asks her for proof of these serious charges, and she responds that she has heard this at the tribunes of her sections, and she has a cousin in the National Guard from whom she has heard this as well. He was there on August 10, 1792, and watched the massacre of citizens by the King's private guard. Mme Doucet responds that you shouldn't believe everything you hear. She wants written proof. And so Mme Doucet suggests that they visit their local writer, a certain Monsieur du Style who can show them all that has been said in the newspapers. She has the ultimate trust in him to adjudicate the case because he had formerly been a lawyer. Monsieur du Style says:

> I occupy myself reading in order to know what is going on: you don't read anything. So much the better, and so much the worse; better because it doesn't break your brains; and worse because anyone can make you believe anything.[52]

In the end, the written word, the male writer, and the law, triumph in this story, over the insurrectionary words circulated among the old fishwives and their relations. Mme Saumon's eloquence was beginning to fail her. Here, too, as in the cases of Mme Clere and Mme Roland, when the legitimacy of one's political opinions was challenged, the first recourse was to point to what was printed in newspapers as opposed to what was heard either in drawing rooms or on the street.

Indeed, we can detect a shift in the topos of illiteracy in the *poissarde* genre over the course of the revolutionary decade. The *poissarde* plays and verse of the prerevolutionary period always cast the male writer as the butt of the fishwife's wit. Her natural eloquence trumps his literary pretensions. He is reduced to the scribe and this is how the genre produces what we might call its "authenticity effect"—we are meant to be

---

[52][Bellanger] *La Falot du peuple, ou entretiens de Mme Saumon, marchande de Marée, sur le procès du Louis XVI* (Paris: n.p., 1792], p. 12.

hearing the real voice of the market. In Fleury de Lescluse's *Dejeuner de la rapée* of 1755, one of the very early plays presenting the most famous of *poissardes,* Mme Angot, the local fishwives get the better of the literary pretensions of Mme Angot's daughter. The daughter, having married a money changer, now thinks herself important enough to own a library with works like the *"Metaphores d'Olive"* (i.e., Ovid's *Metamorphosis*). The joke is clearly on her, the female character who dares to pretend to read.[53]

By 1792, Mme Saumon, like the King whose fish she represents, saw her authority eclipsed by the author himself, Monsieur du Style. And in 1796, Mme Angot has another go-round with her daughter in the comic opera by Maillot, *Mme Angot, ou une poissarde parvenue.* In this postrevolutionary tale, the illiterate Mme Angot wants her daughter to marry a self-described nobleman named Girard. Her literate daughter, Nanon, wants to marry the humble, but beloved François. The play opens with a figure of female literacy—the daughter writing to her lover. A second daughter defends her sister by citing an exemplary tale she has read in history books, that of the unhappy marriage of Cleopatra to Augustus, in order to counsel her mother about the dangers of arranged marriages. To which Mme Angot replies, *"Mon Dieu, c'est donc beau d'avoir lu comme vous. Mais ça ne s'apprend que de jeunesse."* (Roughly: "My God, it's mighty fine to be able to read like you, but you can only learn when you are young.")[54] With the help of a local notary, Nanon and François unmask the pretender Girard and spare the foolish mother social embarrassment. The literate daughters triumph over their traditionalist mother. The moral of the story, then, is that literacy and self-determination go hand in hand.

No one was more sensitive to the cultural shift from the spoken to the written word as the source of public authority during the revolutionary decade than its greatest woman writer, Germaine de Staël. Nor did any writer better perceive its consequences for eloquent women, of both the popular and the precious kinds. Staël's 1807 novel *Corinne* has most often been read as an autobiographical portrait of the woman writer as a tragically misunderstood genius, who ultimately has no place in the modern era. The woman of genius, whose brilliance is celebrated in courtly aristocratic societies, is unable to conform to the new

[53]Moore, *The Genre Poissard,* pp. 150–152.
[54]Antoine-François-Eve Maillot, *Madame Angot, ou une poissarde parvenue: opéra-comique, en deux actes, joués sur le Théâtre de l'Emulation* (Paris: Barba, an V [1796]), p. 15.

domestic roles being demanded of women in bourgeois society. She is destined to isolation, exile, and ultimately death.

But Staël's heroine, Corinne, is in fact not a writer—even though some of her works are published. She is above all an improvisational oral poet: a performance artist reputed for her spontaneous eloquence. Moreover, she may not even be a figure of aristocratic civility. Her social origins are obscure—she has no patronymic. Here are the words Staël has Corinne speak to her suitor Oswald:

> I take pride in nature's generosity. I particularly like improvisation in men and women of the people; it brings their imagination to light, though everywhere else it is hidden, developing only among us.[55]

Thus, Staël links the spontaneous eloquence of the popular classes with the imaginative wit of the most accomplished of *salonnières*, her heroine. Rising almost to Homeric, indeed mythic, stature, Corinne spontaneously recounts the glories of the Italian republic before enraptured crowds. She is the apotheosis of the traditions of female eloquence (popular and elite) that the Revolution—with its explosion of print— swept into the past.

Though Mme de Staël and Mme Roland held no great regard for one another, Staël, more than anyone else would have understood the plight of Roland—a woman of artisanal origins who had risen to the heights of political society through her wit alone. She, too, would have understood the distinction that Roland had sought to make between a "conversation" and a "meeting"—between the engagement of intellect and political plotting.

The significance of the demise of Mme Roland was not, I suspect, lost upon Staël either, as embittered as she was by her own exile from Napoleonic society. Corinne's story is the story of a world in which female oral genius no longer has a central place in cultural life. Staël has often been interpreted as suggesting that all forms of female literary talent were to be eclipsed in the modern, bourgeois world. But Staël's own career as a writer belies this conclusion. *Corinne,* the novel, was published to extraordinary success, despite the official disapprobation of the Napoleonic regime. The cultural change that Staël recorded in her

---

[55]Germaine de Staël, *Corinne,* Avriel H. Goldberger, trans. (New Brunswick, NJ: Rutgers University Press, 1987; original ed. Paris: Imprimerie des Annales des Arts et Manufactures, 1807), p. 44.

book was the downfall not of women writers, but of women as virtuosi of the spoken word, as *salonnières.*

Staël's prediction that the postrevolutionary world would witness the disappearance of the salon, and the feminine eloquence that animated it, we know in hindsight was premature. The salon as a cultural institution persisted until the opening years of the twentieth century. The ritual reception of the market women of Paris by the King of France was also restored, along with the monarchy, in 1815. But it, too, ultimately, disappeared. The last visit of fishwives to offer a greeting to the Crown occurred with the birth of the Duc de Bordeaux in 1820. A trace of this ritual remains in the republican era in the official presentation of a bouquet to the newly elected president of the French Republic.[56] And so, too, the *poissarde* genre continued until 1875, when the last of the Mme Angot plays, *La Fille de Mme Angot,* was staged in Paris.[57]

The opening of the twentieth century, however, brought with it a series of changes that definitively closed the door on the cultural world of the *précieuse* and the *poissarde.* The destruction of the traditional popular neighborhoods of Paris under Louis Napoleon rid the city of the inns and taverns of the market women and their longshoremen. These locales were supplanted by boulevard cafes. Moreover, with the institution of universal secular education and a mass penny press, female illiteracy conclusively disappeared. With it went the cultural forms that had celebrated feminine oral expression—the *poissarde* and the *précieuse.*

Female speech crimes during the French Revolution occurred at a precise conjuncture within the much broader structural transition in extraparliamentary French political culture from essentially oral to essentially written forms in the period roughly from 1640 to 1910. The era begins with the founding of the French Academy, which sought to regulate speech through written words, and ends with the advent of equal educational opportunities for men and women at the opening of the twentieth century. This transition to literacy, a long cultural *durée,* entailed what we might call a shift from a regime of rhetoric to a regime of philosophy; the transition to literacy and the hegemonic triumph of

---

[56]Pierre Frantz, *"Travestis poissards,"* p. 15.

[57]Louis F.-N. Clairville and Jules Claretie, *La Fille de Mme Angot opéra comique en trois actes. Paroles de Clairville, Sirandan and Koning, musique de Charles Lecoq. Edition illustrée* (Paris: F. Pols, 1875); on the fate of the *poissard* genre, see also Frantz, *"Travestis poissards,"* and Alain Fauré, *Paris Carême-Prenant: du carnaval à Paris au XIXe siècle, 1800–1914* (Paris: Hachette, 1978).

script eclipsed oral performance as the basis of cultural as well as political legitimacy.

In France this transition also coincided with the opening up of a cultural gap between men and women—differential rates of literacy and a differentiation of women's speech from male norms. In the eighteenth century, the improvised spoken word—especially its eloquent excess—was coded as a feminine cultural trait, while the written word and its power to discipline speech was viewed as the masculine rhetorical domain. The power of the written word did not supplant public speech (the theater and the political podium thrived, to be sure); rather, it came increasingly to underwrite its authority.

The spoken word in both popular political life and in popular cultural expression nonetheless remained, until the French Revolution, the more powerful of the two forms of public expression. The salon and the marketplace mirrored the academy and the court as a kind of shadow government where women ruled. This led to the invention of a fascinating set of hybrid cultural forms, most notably the *poissarde,* a means of appropriating the power of speech in written and printed form. Paradoxically, print first heightened the power of the spoken word before it eclipsed it. Thus, in 1789, an anonymous pamphlet titled *Chanson Poissarde,* boasted, "There are more words in their lungs than in the *Encyclopedia.*"[58]

But over the course of the French Revolution, with the advent of legislative democracy and the mass press, as opposed to court intrigue and popular spectacle, the written and the printed word definitively supplanted the spoken word as the source of popular legitimacy. The *poissarde* as a political form flourished, and was then rapidly marginalized as a mere cultural amusement. One now laughed as much at Mme Angot's illiteracy as one formerly had at her eloquence. One now celebrated Staël the writer as opposed to Staël the artist of conversation. The Revolution was thus a critical turning point, not in the history of literacy (which would take a century, still, to fully achieve), but for the triumph of the power of the written over the spoken word in public affairs. Public life would now be governed by writing. And women would have to find their way into literate culture or see their cultural and political power eclipsed. Caught in the scissors of this transition were the *poissardes* and the *précieuses* of the Year II, for whom eloquence had become a perilous art, indeed.

[58]*Chanson poissarde* ([Paris: n.p. 1789]).

CHAPTER TWO

Women into Print

*No other century has begun with such a great number of women
of letters.*
—Fortunée Briquet (1804)[1]

O dd that the postrevolutionary woman of letters Fortunée Briquet
would reflect with such optimism on the French Revolution, when
so much recent historical writing suggests that it silenced women—
both high and low—and relegated them to lives of domestic obscurity.
Their worlds of speech—of the *salonnières* and the fishwives—were destroyed or badly damaged. They were denied the vote in 1789, prohib-
ited from political mobilization during the Terror, denied civil equality
within marriage, and, finally, with the promulgation of the Civil Code
in 1804, legally subordinated to the will of their husbands. Bourgeois
modernity, in short, was not good for women.

Conversely, a long tradition in French cultural history, dating at
least back to the Goncourt brothers in the 1850s, celebrates the prerevolutionary era, the age of absolutism, as an age of greater sexual equality
and freedom for women, when, indeed—thanks to the salon, and to the
rituals of court society—"women ruled."[2] This antirepublican perspective is still alive today, especially in feminist circles.

---

[1]Marguerite Ursule Fortunée Bernier Briquet, *Dictionnaire historique, littéraire et bibliographique des françaises et des étrangères naturalisées en France, connues par leurs écrits, ou par
la protection qu'elles ont accordée aux gens de lettres, depuis l'établissement de la monarchie
jusqu'à nos jours; dédié au premier consul par Mme Fortunée B. Briquet, de la société des belles
lettres, et de l'Athenée des Arts de Paris* (Paris: Gillé, an XII, 1804), p. vi. For a biographical
sketch of Fortunée Briquet, see Nicole Pellegrin, "*Entre local et international, botanique,
poésie et féminisme: Fortunée Briquet, (Niort 1782–1815),*" in *Les Apports de l'histoire des
provinces et des régions à l'histoire nationale: actes des VIIe Assises Nationales de l'Union
Française des Universités de tous ages (13–14–15 mai 1993)* (Versailles: UFUTA, 1995), pp. 97–
110.

The Old Regime, recent scholars argue, sustained institutions—not only the salon, but also the court, the theater, and the provincial political assemblies—which were more inclusive of women than were the determinedly masculine forums of the new republican order. Biological reproduction was at the center of the transmission of social and political power in aristocratic society, with a hereditary monarchy at its apex; women as the bearers of children thus enjoyed, theoretically at least, an essential place in that public order. After the Revolution it would be precisely reproductive biology that would exclude them. The Republic would be understood as held together not by the old bonds of flesh between generations, mediated by the womb, but by a social contract among men alone.[3] In fact, the collapse of patriarchalism, which had paradoxically succored women in its generous embrace, brought with it a sustained assault on public women—most notably the Queen—while fraternity, which took its place, in principle excluded women from a society constituted as a band of brothers.[4]

This story is told to explain the apparently puzzling fact that the legislators of the revolutionary and Napoleonic period (1789–1815)—the supporters and heirs of the rights of man—could so easily justify their denial of equal civil and political rights to women. It is based almost exclusively on an analysis of discursive and visual representations of gender norms generated by a small group of male propagandists and apologists.[5] Crudely put, Old Regime ideologies included women in public life and revolutionary ones did the opposite. Yet little has in fact been said about what women actually did. We have a plausible history of pre-

[2]Edmond and Jules de Goncourt, *La Femme au dix-huitième siècle* (Paris: Charpentier, 1877).

[3]For the French case, see Joan Landes, *Women and the Public Sphere in the Era of the French Revolution* (Ithaca, NY: Cornell University Press, 1988), Dena Goodman, *The Republic of Letters: A Cultural History of the Enlightenment* (Ithaca, NY: Cornell University Press, 1994), esp. p. 11; and Joan Wallach Scott, *Only Paradoxes to Offer: French Feminists and the Rights of Man* (Cambridge, MA: Harvard University Press, 1996). See also, for Germany, Isabel V. Hull, *Sexuality, State and Civil Society in Germany, 1700–1815* (Ithaca, NY: Cornell University Press, 1996).

[4]Lynn Hunt, *The Family Romance in the French Revolution* (Berkeley: University of California Press, 1992); see esp. chap. 6 and conclusion, p. 201.

[5]For the discursive turn in women's history, see, most notably, Joan Wallach Scott, "Gender: a Useful Category of Historical Analysis," in Joan Wallach Scott, ed., *Feminism and History* (Oxford, UK: Oxford University Press, 1996), pp. 152–180. For French examples, see Cécile Dauphin, Arlette Farge, Geneviève Fraisse, et al., "L'Histoire des femmes: culture et pouvoir des femmes, essai d'historiographie," *Annales ESC* no. 2 (Mars–Avril 1986): 271–293; and Geneviève Fraisse, *Muse de la raison: démocratie et exclusion des femmes en France* (Paris: Gallimard, 1995).

scriptive gender roles, but not a history of female participation in the political and cultural upheavals of the late Enlightenment and Revolution.

But what if we take a different point of departure—not that of the doomed institutions of the salon or of market women, nor that of the commentators on the place of women in public, but of a woman doing something that will become, after 1789, immensely important and far more common than ever before: writing. Consider, for example, Louise-Elisabeth Vigée Lebrun's 1784 *Portrait of the Countess de Ceres* (Figure 2.1). It offers a rare depiction in modern Western portraiture: a young woman captured not in the act of reading (a common and highly gendered trope), but at a moment of completing a written text. Is it a letter? To a lover? No matter.[6] She has just set down the pen and she gazes out at the viewer with the satisfaction of someone who has successfully expressed her thoughts. It is a commanding image of literary competence. The picture suggests another story than that of silence and exclusion. It captures a moment of entry into the modern world, a world in which lineage no longer determined identity and the reflective activities of intellectual production—reading and writing—were becoming the primary means of making a self.

How do we reconcile the narrative of women being driven from public life at the end of the eighteenth century with the exuberant intellectual energy captured by Vigée Lebrun in her portrait of the Countess of Ceres? The answer is that, rather than disappearing, women's cultural energies were shifting elsewhere and taking on new public forms. At the very moment that the world of the *salonnière* and the fishwife was being destroyed, a whole new cultural future for women was already in the making.

FRENCH WOMEN IN PRINT

During the French Revolution, women, in unprecedented numbers, found a new public voice in print. To tell this story I begin with first principles: A women writer is a person of the female sex who has pub-

---

[6]This painting is most often titled "Lady Folding a Letter (The Comtesse de Ceres)," but Vigée LeBrun also refers to it in her *Souvenirs* as "A Young Girl Surprised in the Act of Writing"; see Joseph Baillio, *Elisabeth Louise Vigée LeBrun, 1755–1842* (Fort Worth, TX: Kimball Art Museum, 1982), p. 54. On visual representations of women and letters, see Mary Sheriff, "Painted/Penned/Purloined," *Studies in Eighteenth-Century Culture,* Syndy M. Conger and Julie C. Hayes, eds., vol. 26 (Baltimore: Johns Hopkins University Press, 1998).

Figure 2.1 Louise-Elisabeth Vigée Lebrun, "Lady Folding a Letter (Portrait of the Countess of Ceres)." (1784). Toledo Museum of Art, Ohio.

lished her writing; a "publication" is any form of printed writing from a pamphlet or play to a multivolume dictionary, a periodical, or a philosophical treatise.

But "a *French* woman writer" and "a *French* publication" are not so simple to define. Linguistic and legal boundaries are never isomorphic; and, in an era before national citizenship and international copyright laws, these boundaries are even less clear. The national boundaries of France were, moreover, in a continuous state of flux during the wars of 1792 to 1815. Male citizenship was defined during the Revolution, but a woman's legal nationality was determined by the citizenship of her father or husband. So, in strictly legal terms, the most famous woman writing in French during the period, Mme de Staël, would have been considered a Swiss and later a Swedish writer. To avoid this legal morass, I opt for a broader cultural definition of nationality, weighing such factors as residence, language, and location of her principal publishers, booksellers, and readers. I exclude women who wrote originally in languages other than French, even if their works were widely translated into French. But I include—on cultural, rather than juridical, grounds—several Swiss or Dutch women (Etta Palm d'Aelders and Isabelle de Charrière, for example) who wrote in French and had major literary or political careers in France. Finally, I am conservative in attributing anonymous and pseudonymous publication: Certainty is preferable to inclusiveness. More importantly, any woman who never published in her own name or who was not widely known during the period as the author of a publication is not fully part of the "other" Enlightenment whose history I am recounting. It is the public presence of women during the period that changes, and their identity had to be known at the time in order for them to be newly visible.

This raises the question of how being "public" is made manifest. There is to date no definitive bibliographic record of French publications—by men or women—in the eighteenth century that approaches the comprehensiveness of the *Eighteenth-Century English Short Title Catalogue*. And the bibliographic record for the revolutionary decade is even more fragmentary and dispersed than that of the Old Regime. Under the circumstances, my universe from 1750 to 1790 is circumscribed by two sources: the *Année littéraire* (a massive commercial directory of published writers and their publications, which appeared in different guises between 1754 and 1790), and the extraordinary *Bibliographie du genre romanesque (1751–1800)*, recently compiled by a team of bibliographers.[7] From these, the world of prerevolutionary women writers can be recaptured more or less definitively.

[7]For the publishing history of the *Année littéraire* and an assessment of its value, see Robert Darnton, *Gens de lettres, gens du livre* (Paris: Jacob, 1991), pp. 100–118. See also *Index de l'année littéraire*, Danté Lenardon, ed. (Geneva: Slatkine, 1979); and Angus Martin, Vivienne G. Milne, and Richard Frautschi, *Bibliographie du genre romanesque français (1751–1800)* (Paris: France Expansion, 1977; London: Mansell, 1977).

For the revolutionary decade (1789–1800) the *Bibliographie du genre romanesque* continues to be a rich source for novelists, but not for others. For them I searched through Monglond's massive *La France révolutionnaire et impériale: annales de bibliographie;* Martin and Walter's *Catalogue des pamphlets et journaux de la période révolutionnaire à la Bibliothèque Nationale;* the *Catalogue de l'Histoire de France,* which lists holdings at the Bibliothèque Nationale thematically and chronologically; every available collection of documents of women's writing from the period and critical editions of particular women writers; and, finally, every major publisher's trade journal from the revolutionary period. I extracted the names and publications of every "French woman writer." They were then cross-checked systematically in the *Catalogue des imprimés* of the Bibliothèque Nationale, the *British Library Catalogue* and the index of the *Archives biographiques de France* to establish as complete a bibliographic and biographical record for each author as possible.[8] Finally, for the decade of 1811–1821, I relied on the remarkable *Bibliographie de la France,* which, despite its imperfections, does in these decades identify the sex of authors. The names could be cross-checked with the *Archives biographiques.* From all of this a new world comes into focus.

It was a world that, first of all, expanded dramatically at precisely the moment when women were supposedly being driven from public life by the votaries of republican ideology. Fairly firm, but probably conservative, estimates of the number of women who had at least one pub-

---

[8]For the entire record, see Appendix A: Bibliography of French Women, 1789–1800. Sources consulted: *Annonces de Bibliographie Moderne ou catalogue raisonné et analytic des livres nouveaux* (Paris: Habilette, 1790); *Feuille de correspondence du libraire ou notice des ouvrages publiées dans les différents journaux qui circulent en France et dans l'étranger* (Paris: Aubry, 1791–1793); *Opinion des femmes. De la veille au lendemain de la révolution française* (Paris: Des Femmes, 1989); *Bulletin de littérature, des sciences et des arts* (Paris: Lucet, 1796–1803); *Index de l'année littéraire (1754–1790),* Dante Lenardon, ed. (Geneva: Slatkine Reprints: 1979); *Nouvelliste littéraire* (Paris: Marin & Lenoir, 1796–1806); *British Library Catalogue; Bibliographie du genre romanesque français (1750–1800),* Martin, Mylne, and Frautschi, eds. (Paris: Expansion, 1977); *La France révolutionnaire et impériale: annales de bibliographie méthodique et description des livres illustrés,* André Monglond, ed. (Grenoble: B. Arthaud, 1973–1978); *Women in Science: Antiquity Through the Nineteenth Century: A Biographical Dictionary and Annotated Bibliography,* Marilyn Ogilvie, ed. (Cambridge, MA: MIT Press 1986); *Catalogue des pamphlets, journaux et anonymes de la Révolution française à la Bibliothèque Nationale,* Martin and Walter, eds. (Paris: Bibliothèque Nationale, 1941–1951); *Catalogue des imprimés de la Bibliothèque Nationale; Archives Biographique de France (Index); Catalogue de l'histoire de France,* Bibliothèque Nationale.

lication in print, decade by decade, for the period from 1754 to 1820 (except for the 1800s) are specified in Table 2.1.

Table 2.1 French Women in Print, 1750–1820

1754–1765	73
1766–1777	55
1777–1788	78
1789-1800	329
1811–1821	299

Two things become immediately clear from the figures in Table 2.1: (1) Despite the prominence of a few great women writers, in numerical terms women were relatively marginal to the literary culture of the Old Regime, and (2) women's writing flourished once that regime fell.

Robert Darnton's study of writers before the Revolution can help to put these figures into a broader context. Using the same criteria for defining French writers and publications as those elaborated above, he found that the total number of published writers in France nearly tripled during the second half of the eighteenth century, from 1,187 in 1757 to 2,819 in 1784. He calculated the number of women in print in the year 1784 to be 51, which is approximately 2 percent.[9] My figures in Table 2.1 for the entire decade of the 1780s essentially confirm his findings. Women formed a very tiny percentage of published writers during the last decades of the Old Regime. Also worth noting is that while the number of male writers in print nearly tripled, the number of published women increased only slightly (from 73 in the 1750s to 78 in the 1780s).

Unfortunately, there is no study comparable to Robert Darnton's for the revolutionary decade, so it is still not possible to assess the number of women in print after 1789 in relation to the total number of writers (male and female) in the revolutionary decade. Nonetheless, one conclusion is incontrovertibly clear: While the number of women publishing in the last three decades of the Old Regime remained relatively constant, the number of French women in print exploded dramatically (more than tripling) in the decade after 1789. Half again as many women entered the public arena through print in the first revolutionary decade as had been published during the previous thirty-five years. Only 17 of

[9]Darnton, *Gens de Lettres, Gens du Livre*, pp. 107–118.

these 329 writers were no longer living when the Revolution occurred; the table includes reeditions of Renaissance women writers, for example, whose works were still in demand.

And this revolutionary conjuncture was no mere flash in the pan. Two decades later, when pamphleteering and journalism had all but disappeared under the scrutiny of imperial and royal censorship, the number of women writers still remained more than three times as great as it had been in the prerevolutionary period. And, proportionally, they represented a greater part of all literary production as well. In 1820, for example, about 4 percent of published writers were women—81 out of 2,196. The total number of men publishing did not seem to increase substantially from the Old Regime to the new (in fact these years show a decrease from 2,814 in 1784 to 2,196 in 1820). But the number and the percentage of women, by contrast, grew substantially—indeed their proportional presence in the world of print doubled from 2 percent to 4 percent.

The collapse of the old order *was* a critical turning point for female participation in French literary culture and public life, but in precisely the opposite sense from that implied by the current historiography: As with other social groups, 1789—that *annus mirabile*—marked a dramatic and unprecedented moment of entry for women into public life. The Countess of Ceres was a harbinger of great things to come.

In 1804 Fortunée Briquet, with whom I began, compiled a *Dictionnaire historique, littéraire et bibliographique des françaises et des étrangères naturalisées en France.*[10] In her dedication of the work to the First Consul, Napoleon Bonaparte, Briquet reflected on the tumultuous fifteen years since the Old Regime had fallen. She exulted that "No other century has begun with such a great number of women of letters." To prove it, her *Dictionnaire* offered the literary records of 583 women from the age of Clovis to the present, culled from a very impressive range of bibliographic sources. Cumulatively, they revealed nothing short of a literary explosion at the end of the eighteenth century: Though they had some eminent predecessors, well over half the women she documented came from the revolutionary generation!

Just how dramatic a change the French Revolution wrought is made even clearer if we compare the history of female publication in England with that of France during the same period (see Table 2.2).[11] Across the

---

[10]Fortunée Briquet, *Dictionnaire historique.*
[11]Judith Phillip Stanton, "Statistical Profile of Women Writing in English from 1660

Table 2.2 English Women in Print, 1750–1799

1750–1759	28
1760–1769	76
1770–1779	119
1780-1789	166
1790–1799	191

channel, the numbers of women increased steadily for the whole second half of the century, buoyed no doubt by the general tide of commercial literary expansion. In France, by contrast, numbers remained steady— and low (fifty to less than eighty)—decade after decade; then, in just ten years from 1789 the number quadrupled to over three hundred. For most of the period, England had proportionally more women writers than did France; after 1789, the proportions evened out. So while, in both countries, more and more women were published, the differences in the pattern and rate of their entry into the world of commercial print culture was striking.

The liberalization of political life after 1789—new freedoms of the press, the ferments around the Estates General, and elections for the various assemblies and conventions—does not provide a sufficient explanation. The number of publications by women did not decline significantly after the end of the Revolution's liberal phase and renewed repression of the press. What really mattered was the freeing of cultural and commercial life more generally: the collapse of court and aristocratic patronage and the deregulation of the printing and publishing world with the demise of the system of literary privileges and guild regulation. In fact, incidence of publications by women during the revolutionary decade, year by year, was linked less to the political vicissitudes of the Revolution or the relative tolerance or repressiveness of the successive revolutionary governments, than it was to the expansion and contraction of commercial publishing after the collapse of state regulation. Table 2.3 shows the figures.

Women writers were clearly carried along by the outpouring of printed matter after the declaration of the freedom of the press in 1789, and the dramatic political mobilization of the early years of the Revo-

to 1800," in *Eighteenth-Century Women and the Arts*, Fredrich M. Keener and Susan E. Lorsch, eds. (New York: Greenwood Press, 1988), p. 251. Stanton does not include pamphlet publications in her study, but the findings are nonetheless comparable.

Table 2.3 Incidence of Publication by French Women, 1789–1800

1789	85	1795	32
1790	79	1796	20
1791	68	1787	48
1792	39	1798	43
1793	49	1799	43
1794	50	1800	36
		Undated	65
		Total	657

lution. But more interesting is the fact that publication by women did not decrease dramatically at the height of political repression during the Terror (1793–1794), or, more relevant to the immediate subject, during the moment of the emergency revolutionary legislation prohibiting public assemblies of women. Women remained in print, and remained (as we shall see in a moment) both politically and culturally active through their publications during these desperate years.

The decline in the numbers of publications by women during the thermidorian period (1795–1796), after the fall of Robespierre, when laws on the press and public speech were once again relatively liberal, and then the steady increase afterwards until 1800, when censorship was again ascendant, mirror the contours of what we know about the commercial, rather than the legal, history of publishing during the period, and the trajectory of French commerce more generally: decline during the crisis after Thermidor, increase during the boomlet of the Directorate, and then a second crisis beginning in 1800.[12] This is a pattern determined by the demands of the literary marketplace, not legal restrictions or relaxations. The figures for the 1810s in Table 2.1 further confirm this point by showing that the reimposition of censorship under the Napoleonic regime and the restoration of the monarchy did little to diminish the number of women in print.

French women thus experienced something like a literary awakening during the decade of the Revolution. The bibliographic record they have left us permits us to capture something of its social and cultural context as well as its trajectory over time.[13] For women, as for men, Paris

[12]See Carla Hesse, *Publishing and Cultural Politics in Revolutionary Paris, 1789–1810* (Berkeley: University of California Press, 1991), esp. chaps. 4–6.

[13]See Appendix B: Publishers and Publishing Locations of Women Writers: 1789–1800.

was the epicenter of French publishing. Of the 657 imprints they produced, 336 issued from over 200 different publishers in the capital. A few of these, for example, Claude-François Maradan, Pierre-Sebastien Leprieur, and Eugène Onefroy, stand out for their commercial allegiance to new novels—a genre in which women excelled. And one publisher, Guffroy, is memorable for his fearless commitment to publishing the protests of numerous women during the Terror—a commitment that ultimately cost him his life.

Women's literary activity was not, however, an exclusively Parisian phenomenon. Women published in twenty-nine provincial cities, towns, and hamlets—from the major regional centers, like Lyon, Toulouse, Caen, Dijon, and Avignon, to remote villages, such as Pithiviers, Brignoles, and Lisieux. In Toulouse, Avignon, and Pas-de-Calais, women ran the regional newspapers. At Dampierre, in St.-Rémy-Les-Chevreuse, Guyonne-Elisabeth-Josèphe de Lavel, the Duchess of Montmorency, made use of the private presses at her chateau to realize her aspirations as a poet, and to print her translation of *Robinson Crusoe*. She also made her presses available to her friend, the marquise de Lafayette, for her own writings. More modestly, scores of mothers, female merchants, and local administrators employed the power of the press to plead various personal causes, publicly celebrate important familial events, enter provincial academic competitions in both literature and the sciences, and advocate for social or political reforms.

For the attentive reader, a kind of topography of female literary life begins to emerge from what at a first glance appears to be a dry and arcane bibliographic record.[14] At the pinnacle of literary life were eminent women of letters and ladies of the court, such as Mme de Genlis, the Duchess of Polignac, Mme de Staël, Mme de Souza (the Countess of Flahaut), and Mme de Charrière, who saw their works released simultaneously by international publishing groups in all the major cities of Europe. Indeed, eighty-five publications by women during the revolutionary decade commanded international audiences in nearly twenty different European cities. Beneath these cosmopolitan luminaries were constellations of lesser, provincial, lights, who competed for local academic poetry prizes or, like Sophie Cottin, quietly wrote their way into national literary notoriety with best-selling novels. Of course the greatest heat, if not light, emanated from Paris, where militant women on all sides of the Revolution entered full force into the rhetorical fray of political battle.

[14]See Appendix A: Bibliography of French Women, 1789–1800.

This bibliographical investigation of the dimensions of female participation in print culture from the Old Regime through the Revolution tells a radically different story from the one offered by historians of gender ideology and politics during the period. It suggests first of all that, after the great contributions of women to the novel in the late seventeenth and early eighteenth century, female participation in the public cultural life of the Old Regime was not only relatively marginal, it was also relatively static. The period of the high Enlightenment, despite the prominence of a few popular novelists and a few aristocratic *salonnières*, was not a period of significant inclusion of women in the public life of letters. By contrast, the revolutionary decade witnessed a dramatic expansion of female participation in public cultural life and political discourse. It turns out that the cultural institutions of the monarchy and the aristocracy—the salons, the guilds, the system of patronage and privileges—were far less hospitable to female participation—at least as measured by access to print—than was the liberalized commercial publishing world that the Revolution instituted. In contrast to the princes, courtiers, censors, and wealthy patrons of the Old Regime, the commercial publishers of the revolutionary period cared less about whether the female sex was deemed qualified to write, or the literary merits of what they put into print, than whether or not it sold. The Revolution, as it turns out, created unprecedented opportunities for women to enter the public arena.

This is not to deny that the late eighteenth century and the revolutionary period witnessed the increasing elaboration of scientific and philosophical discourses aimed at maintaining sexual hierarchy and the subordination of women to men after the collapse of Aristotelian and biblical justifications.[15] And successive regimes of the revolutionary period deployed this misogynist gender ideology to legislate laws in order to ensure the political and civic subordination of women.

But science, philosophy, law, and politics are not mirrors of the social world. The data on women writers suggests that the economic and commercial vision of the Enlightenment and Revolution opened up possibilities for female participation in an absolutely central arena of modern public life that was at odds with the dominant male conception of appropriate relations between the sexes. And it further suggests that the

---

[15]See, in particular, Thomas Laqueur and Catherine Gallagher, eds., *The Making of the Modern Body* (Berkeley: University of California Press, 1987), and Thomas Laqueur, *Making Sex* (Cambridge, MA: Harvard University Press, 1990).

elaboration of these philosophical, cultural, and ultimately juridical and political gender norms were not so much a reflection of the sociopolitical or cultural realities of the revolutionary period as they were a reactionary response to a sociocultural world that was rapidly and radically challenging and exploding the normative boundaries of gender that these men held dear.

The literary criticism of the postrevolutionary period makes clear just how much friction there was between masculine gender norms and the realities of female cultural participation. On the one hand, Jean-François De la Harpe's *Lycée ou cours de littérature ancienne et moderne* (1797–1803) effectively wrote women out of French literary history.[16] On the other hand, Marie-Joseph Chénier, in his *Tableau historique de l'état et des progrès de la littérature française depuis 1789* (1816), offered the radically different judgment that "Women figure with the greatest distinction among modern novelists."[17] These conflicting viewpoints on the literary achievements of women attest to the social tension created by the emergence of women as major players in the print culture of the postrevolutionary world. Normative assumptions about women came into sharp conflict with sociocultural realities.

THE SOCIOCULTURAL WORLD OF WOMEN WRITERS DURING THE REVOLUTIONARY ERA

The Social Spaces of Women Writers

There has been much written about the history of the stereotyping of the woman of letters—in fiction and in the world—as socially marginal: Mme de Staël's tragic heroine *Corinne*, George Sand's illusive *Lélia*, or the "blue-stockings" derisively depicted by Honoré Daumier in the 1840s. Images of the woman writer as either an outcast or a rebel, an unmarried sister or a maiden aunt (Austin), a libertine cosmopolitan aristocrat (Staël, Charrière), a bohemian (Sand), or an actress (Colette), permeate modern culture.[18]

---

[16]Joan DeJean, "Classical Rededucation: Decanonizing the Feminine," in *Yale French Studies*, no. 75, Special issue: *The Politics of Tradition*, Nancy K. Miller and Joan DeJean, eds.

[17]Marie-Joseph Chénier, *Tableau historique de l'état et des progrès de la littérature française depuis 1789* (Paris: Maradan, 1816), p. 227, cited in Margaret Cohen, *The Sentimental Education of the Novel* (Princeton, NJ: Princeton University Press, 1999), chap. 1.

[18]Sandra M. Gilbert and Susan Gubar, *The Madwoman in the Attic: The Woman Writer in the Nineteenth-Century Imagination* (New Haven, CT: Yale University Press, 1979).

It is difficult to dig beneath these stereotypes, in part for practical reasons: Women's lives are less well-documented than men's. And because their civil status and even their names depended on their relationship to men, the same woman may appear in the historical record under many different names over a lifetime. So women are more difficult to track: Amélie Julie Candeille, to take one example, became Mme la Roche, and then Mme Simons, and later still Mme Périe de Senovert (1767–1834).[19] Moreover, the social spaces and economic trajectories of women's lives don't map easily onto the classificatory grids of class and profession employed by traditional social historians.[20] Their social positions have been seen as largely contingent on their relations to men (fathers, husbands, and lovers). And here too the trajectories of women's lives elude social fixity. Germaine de Staël was both the daughter of a Swiss bourgeois and the wife of a Swedish aristocrat. Olympe de Gouges was the daughter of a butcher, the widow of a banker, and a courtesan. Clearly, they played multiple social roles over their lifetimes.

This does not mean that we have to abandon the possibility of locating women in the social world, because, in fact, they did this themselves. When women, like men, chose to publish their writings, no law compelled them to identify themselves—but they did. They were not compelled to use a given legal name, or the same name on all their publications, nor were they required to identify their social or civil status, but a great many of them did. Thus the constitution of an authorial signature was an act of public self-constitution, relatively independent of the normative stereotypes that circulated about them and sought to fix them. Tables 2.4 and 2.5 specify the published authorial signatures of French women writers between 1789 and 1800, based on their social and civil status. If we are to believe what these women say about themselves—and we have no reason not to—the social backgrounds of women in print during the period were remarkably diverse, but socially marginal they were not. Few identifiable "madwomen in the attic" here. Their circumstances ranged from the most modest, even desperate, (Parisian flower girls, who signed their petitions collectively) to the pin-

---

[19]See entry for her name in Appendix A. Candeille wrote for the opera. For an extensive analysis of women in the opera during the revolutionary period, see Jacqueline Letzter and Robert Adelson, *A Drama of Disappointed Ambitions: French Revolutionary Opera by Women* (forthcoming). I am grateful to the authors for making this manuscript available to me.

[20]Joan Wallach Scott, *Gender and the Politics of History* (New York: Columbia University Press, 1989).

Table 2.4 Social Status of French Women Writers, 1789–1800

Titled Aristocracy	109
Commoners	220
Total	329

nacle of court society (Mme de Genlis). Not surprisingly, a very high proportion (one-third) came from the aristocracy (either by birth or through marriage). They were manifestly not marginal.

No less significant, however, is how many of them didn't come from this exclusive caste: a full two-thirds. Access to print, after the fall of the Bastille, was not the near-exclusive privilege of those with access to court patronage. It was access to commercial publishers that mattered. A closer look at the numerous nonaristocratic women writers for whom we have biographical information further confirms this. For the most part, they were solidly bourgeois in circumstances, tending to come from the higher echelons of the professional classes. As in our own times, these were the women who had the education and the time to write, and no doubt greater access to the world of publishers and printers.

The record of their familial status is also revealing. Again, we find remarkable signs of both diversity of experience and social integration. By far the majority of women writers were married (198) and had successfully integrated careers as writers with family life. But it is also true that a much higher proportion of women writers than women in the population at large were either unmarried (at the time of writing or throughout their lives) or widowed. Here again, as with social status, there is some evidence of greater independence from the familial regime, but little evidence of social marginality.

Writing and publishing, as difficult as they are, could be adapted more easily to the contingencies of women's lives (married or unmar-

Table 2.5 Marital Status of French Women Writers, 1789–1800

Married	198
Single	43
Widowed	44
Status unidentified	44
Total	329

ried) than any other profession that was as intellectually satisfying and as economically remunerative. It could be done at home, at any time of day or night, with or without children, or a husband or family. As George Sand remarked in her autobiography, with her tongue only partly in her cheek, she found herself at home alone with the children and in need of money. She had two choices, make dresses or write novels. She chose the latter.[21] And so did many others, who not only wrote novels, but also engaged in related activities, like the Countess Legroing de la Maisonneuve, who ran the *Mercure* and the *Etoile,* two major journals, out of her drawing room.[22] As Germaine de Staël noted, you didn't even need a study or a desk to do it, just pen and paper.[23]

There were many rebellious women writers in the revolutionary era, who, through their writings, challenged the social and cultural or political norms of their times, sometimes at the cost of becoming outcasts or exiles, like Mme de Staël, and sometimes, as in the case of Olympe de Gouges, even at the cost of their lives.[24] But becoming a women writer was not an inherently marginalizing form of social activity. Writing remained one of the few bourgeois professions that could still feasibly be conducted at home, one of the last forms of aristocratic, and then bourgeois, enterprise that in modern times has remained within the realm of the domestic.

Motives for writing are inevitably complex. But one motive, in particular, emerges repeatedly from the biographical record, especially of middle- and upper-class women in the postrevolutionary period: money. Wealthy aristocratic women like Madame de Souza (the Countess of Flahaut) or Isabelle de Charrière, for example, who didn't need the money, wrote for charity, mobilizing subscription drives for their books to assist friends in distress who had lost fortunes in the Revolution.[25] Public avowals that one was writing for charity rather than personal profit did not, however, mean that women writers were indiffer-

[21]George Sand, *Story of My Life: The Autobiography of George Sand,* collective trans., Thelma Jurgrau, ed. (Albany: State University of New York Press, 1991), pp. 882–887.

[22]See the biographical entry for Legroing de la Maisonneuve in Michaud, frères, eds. *Biographie universelle, ancienne et moderne* (Paris: Desplaces, 1843).

[23]See Madelyn Gutwirth, *Madame de Staël, Novelist: The Emergence of the Artist as Woman* (Urbana: University of Illinois Press, 1978), pp. 259–260.

[24]On Olympe de Gouges, see Joan Wallach Scott, "The Uses of the Imagination: Olympe de Gouges in the French Revolution," in *Only Paradoxes to Offer: French Feminists and the Rights of Man* (Cambridge, MA: Harvard University Press, 1996), pp. 19–56.

[25]See Isabelle de Charrière, Letter to Henriette Hardy, February 10–14, 1795, in *Oeuvres complètes,* vol. 5, pp. 44, 112, and 285.

ent to the profits generated from their mental labors. Sophie Cottin, a wealthy provincial widow and best-selling novelist, at once publicly disavowed any personal profits from her works, but at the same time could be found, in her private correspondence, to be a very hard business negotiator with her publisher, Maradan. "Her friends counseled her," she wrote, "to demand a higher price" than 4,000 livres for her newest manuscript, or to seek another publisher.[26]

But more common than wealthy ladies who wrote as a form of civic charity were women like Mme Roland and Pauline de Meulan (the future Madame Guizot). Pauline de Meulan was one of two daughters of an Old Regime tax collector who found her family virtually without fortune after the Revolution. She foreswore her claim to a dowry, and, hence to a suitable marriage, in favor of her younger sister, and instead of marrying set about writing novels to restore the family's finances. The critical and financial success of her first two novels, *Les Contradictions* (1799) and *La Chapelle d'Ayton* (1800) launched her into the literary elite of the Consulate and Empire.

It also brought her the admiration and, ultimately, a proposal of marriage from François Guizot (who was almost twenty years younger than she). Writing in Pauline de Meulan's case made it possible for her to move from the margins to the center of the postrevolutionary world. She did stop writing and publishing novels after her marriage, but she did not stop writing and publishing. Over the next several decades she wrote a series of extraordinary moral, educational, and political treatises and, by the 1820s (before her husband achieved his own intellectual eminence), she had emerged as one of the most prominent moral and educational theorists in the nation. She won the prize for moral theory from the *Académie Française* in 1822 and a second prize from the same institution in 1827 for her treatises on education.[27] The private letters and published memoirs left to us by these writers reveal that many, many other women—some famous (like Louise de Kéralio-Robert), others obscure—wrote and published in order to restore their families' fortunes, or to establish a fortune of their own.

The commercial successes of women writers in the postrevolutionary period suggests one particular reason for the increasing circulation of negative stereotypes of them by male journalists and critics in the

[26]BN: Mss. Fr. 12757, Letter from Sophie Cottin to Maradan, 1 germinal, an 12 (March 31, 1804).

[27]See the biographical entry for Elisabeth-Charlotte-Pauline Guizot (née de Meulan) in Michaud, frères, *Biographie universelle.*

1820s and 1830s, depicting women of letters as socially transgressive: They were rivals and competitors for the unprecedented popular reading public that their novels had helped to create. In reconstituting the social identities that women writers constructed, we confront a picture of social experience that flies in the face of the prescriptive literature on gender norms of their period and literature that either vilified or empathized with their transgressions. Many politically, socially, and culturally transgressive women wrote, to be sure, but there is little evidence that either women or men perceived writing and publishing to be a socially transgressive act for women in and of itself. As with men, it depended on what they wrote and published.

Olympe de Gouges was executed for putting specific political views into print because they were perceived to be treasonous by a government in the grips of a civil war. Germaine de Staël was denied citizenship by the government of the nation of her birth, and then exiled specifically for publishing views critical of the Napoleonic regime. These women were made outcasts and condemned for *what* they wrote and published. But they were not condemned for writing and publishing *per se*. Indeed, there is little evidence that the successive regimes of the revolutionary period sought to exclude women from participation in the public life of letters on the basis of their sex. On the contrary, every regime from the constitutional monarchy through the Jacobin Convention and even the Napoleonic Empire was delighted to offer patronage to women who wrote and published works that they found compatible with the literary and political aims of the regime. Women writers came to play strategic roles in every successive regime.

Mademoiselle Marie-Charlotte-Pauline Robert de Lezardière (1754–1835), for example, wrote for the reforming monarchy. She was born into an old noble family of the Vendée with a tradition of military service and a passion for historical erudition. A gifted child, deeply influenced by her readings in Montesquieu, by the age of twenty-four, Mlle de Lézardière had composed a major political treatise defending the constitutional claims of the monarchy (the *Tableau des droits réels et respectifs du monarque et des sujets depuis la fondation de la monarchie jusqu'à nos jours*).[28] The manuscript was presented to the young King Louis XVI by her father in 1778.

[28]For a brief account of her life and writings, see Christine Fauré, "Mlle de Lézardière entre Jeanne d'Arc et Montesquieu?" in *Les Femmes et la Révolution française, actes du colloque internationale, Université de Toulouse–Le Mirail*, vol. 1, Marie France Brive, ed. (Toulouse: Presses Universitaire du Mirail, 1989): 183–190; see also, Elie Carcassonne,

It seems to have lingered in the antechambers of Versailles for over a decade, and then suddenly appeared in print in 1791 under the title *Esprit des lois canoniques et politiques*, along with her other work, *Théorie des lois positives de la monarchie française* in 1792, both under the imprint of the Paris publisher Nyon aîné et fils. Why? Because—as shown by the archives of the Royal Book Trade, and those of the King's famous *Armoire de fer*, which was seized by the National Assembly after the monarchy fell on August 10, 1792—the King, in a last-ditch effort to turn educated public opinion toward his constitutional authority, secretly subsidized its publication. Indeed, it seemed to be of such sensitive and strategic importance that he guarded the documents of the negotiation to publish it among his most private papers.[29] If we are seeking evidence of women's participation in the revolutionary public sphere, here it is.

And during the period of the National Convention (1792–1795), when the Revolution reached its most radical phase, we also find women at the center of the regime's cultural politics—indeed, in disproportionate numbers. The archives of the Committee, and then the Commission, on Public Instruction, which was the key institution of cultural patronage during the period of the Republic, offer striking evidence of women's literary prominence at this time. Of the sixty-six subsidies of publishing projects made by the Convention for which we still have a record, *seventeen* (almost one-third) went to women writers: for translations of classical literature and contemporary philosophy; for grammars, novels, and plays; for poetry and songs.[30] And the Convention did not simply subsidize women's writing; it made considerable efforts to propagate it. So we find that on October 19, 1794, it ordered that the novel, *Triomphe de la saine philosophie, ou la vraie politique des femmes*, by the "citizeness Boosere," "be distributed by her in the various departments of the Republic" at the Convention's expense.[31]

Montesquieu et le problème de la constitution française au XVIIIe siècle (1927; Geneva: Slatkine Reprint, 1970.)

[29]For the royal approbation of Nyon's timely publication of this work, see AN: series VI, carton 552, Letter from Nyon to the Administration of the Book Trade, and response, September 25, 1789. For the negotiations of the subsidy, see AN: series C, carton 183, portfolio 107, nos. 384–393.

[30]For evidence of republican patronage of women of letters, see M. J. Guillaume, ed., *Procès-verbaux du Comité d'Instruction Publique de la Convention Nationale*, 7 vols. (Paris: Imprimerie Nationale, 1889): vol. IV, pp. 240, 430, 447, 558 (and note 3), 592, 618, 629, 938; vol. V, pp. 20, 119, 138, 175, 359–360, 402, 432, 450–451, 457, 481–482; vol. VI, pp. 76, 106, 426–427, 431–433, 447–448, 550, 591–593, 629, 675, 722.

[31]AN: Series F4, carton 2554, doss. 4, Boosère, 28 vendémiaire, an III (October 19, 1794). See also Guillaume, ed., *Procès-Verbaux*, vol. V, p. 138.

"Women are writing more than men these days," or so it seemed to Isabelle de Charrière upon hearing of the publication of Sophie de Condorcet's French translation of Adam Smith's *Moral Sentiments* (with a government subsidy) in 1798.[32] This, at the very moment when the ideologue Pierre-Jean-Georges Cabanis and his disciples were propounding biological theories supposedly proving the intellectual inferiority of women.[33]

Under the Empire—when the Civil Code legally subordinated women to men—there is further evidence that Napoleon courted as many women writers as he persecuted. In 1804 the First Consul agreed to receive the dedication of Mme Fortunée Briquet's *Dictionnaire historique, littéraire et bibliographique des françaises et des étrangères naturalisées en France.* She celebrated his great patronage of belles lettres generally, and pointed to the additional glory he garnered by "permitting my *Dictionnaire* to appear under his auspices."[34] Individual stories of Napoleonic patronage of women of letters abound. Françoise Thérèse Antoinette, Countess Legroing de Maisonneuve (1764–1837), for example, entered a convent at the age of sixteen and rapidly proved herself to be a distinguished classical linguist through her translations of Homer, Virgil, and Cicero. By the age of eighteen she also showed herself to be a person of extraordinary administrative vision and skill when she was charged with revising the constitution of one of the most reputable women's religious communities in France.

From her religious retreat, she began to write fiction, which was published with great success, at first without her permission. Legroing de la Maisionneuve emigrated during the Revolution, but continued her literary pursuits, publishing an *Essai sur le genre d'instruction le plus analogue à la destination des femmes* (1799). This work, in tune with the new regime's views of what were appropriate roles for the two sexes, drew the attention of Napoleon, who invited her to become the superintendent of two major educational institutions under the auspices of the Legion of Honor. She declined on political grounds. But after the restoration of the Bourbons, she returned to France, edited two major journals,

[32]Isabelle de Charrière, Letter to Benjamin Constant, August 3, 1798, in *Oeuvres complètes*, 10 vols., Jean Daniel Candaux, C. P. Courtney, Pierre H. Dubois, Simon Dubois-De Bruyn, Patrice Thompson, Jeroom Vercruysse, and Dennis M. Wood, eds. (Geneva: Slatkine, 1981), vol 5. p. 466.

[33]See Lynn Hunt, *The Family Romance of the French Revolution* (Berkeley: University of California Press, 1992), p. 157.

[34]Fortunée Briquet, *Dictionnaire historique*, p. v.

wrote a history of the Gauls, and was granted and accepted a literary pension from Louis XVIII.[35]

Patronage by officials was not wielded exclusively for the purpose of shaping public morals. It could also be exercised, more covertly, to satisfy the private tastes of men in power. Thus, in the archives of the Napoleonic Ministry of the Interior we discover that Félicité de Choiseul-Meuse, was dependent on official patronage for her survival.[36] Remembered today as the author of the infamously pornographic pastiche of Rousseau's *Nouvelle Heloïse*, titled, *Julie, ou j'ai sauvée ma Rose* (1807), among many other works, Choiseul-Meuse clearly found an audience for her literary productions, not only in the marketplace, but in the corridors of power as well.[37]

There is also considerable evidence of the sustained inclusion and recognition of women of letters by the major literary and scientific academies—for example, Louise de Kéralio (history), Pauline Guizot (moral theory), Fanny de Beauharnais (novels), Charlotte de Bournon, Countess of Malarme (novels), Claudine Guyton de Morveau (natural sciences), Anne Marie de Montgergoult de Coutances, Countess de Beaufort d'Hautpol (poetry), and Sophie Bacquié (poetry). After years of patronage from the Napoleonic regime, in 1815, Mme Dufrénoy became the poet laureate of the Française Académie, its highest literary honor.[38] Similarly, in the new publishing and literary societies of the revolutionary period, like the *Cercle Social* and La Harpe's *Lycée*, women found themselves welcomed among the men.

The number of women writing and publishing in France during the revolutionary era may have been few, both in relation to the total number of writers and the population at large, but they were hardly marginal in social, cultural, or even political life. And their numbers, as we have seen, increased dramatically over this period. Not even at the moments of greatest public anxiety about the public influence of women

[35]See biographical entry for Legroing de la Maisonneuve in Michaud, frères, *Biographie universelle*.

[36]AN: series AA, carton 63, doc. 196, Letter from the dame Choiseul-Meuse to the Minister of the Interior, March 29, 1810.

[37]On Choiseul-Meuse, see Kathryn Norberg, "Making Sex Public: Félicité de Choiseul-Meuse and the Lewd Novel," in *Going Public: Women and Publishing in Early Modern France*, Elizabeth C. Goldsmith and Dena Goodman, eds. (Ithaca, NY: Cornell University Press, 1995), pp. 161–175.

[38]Edmond Biré and Emile Grimaud, eds., *Les Poètes lauréats de L'Académie Française, recueil des poèmes couronnés depuis 1800, avec une introduction (1671–1800)*, 2 vols. (Paris: A. Bray, 1864), vol. 1, pp. 155–187.

(especially during the Terror and under Napoleon), is there evidence of systematic discrimination against writers on the basis of sex. It was content not gender that mattered. It was *what* they wrote and published, rather than *who* wrote and published, that mattered. Thus, while the market opened up the possibility of expressing viewpoints that were independent of, and even in conflict with, the values of the successive regimes of the period, the regimes themselves sought at the same time to capture the newly awakened literary talents of women and deploy them toward their own ends.

Women and Genres

Women wrote novels. This prevailing normative view has a long tradition in French literary history and criticism, dating back to the beginnings of the modern novel itself in the classical age (Boileau) and reverberating, in both denigrating and laudatory terms, down to our own time.[39] There is no doubt that, from Mme de Scudéry and Mme de Lafayette to Marguerite Yourcenar, women writers played a central role in the invention of the modern novel and continued to be noted as practitioners of the genre.

Women writers have thus come to be seen as the great chroniclers of private, rather than public life; as fabricators of fictions rather than producers of truth; as prophets of eros rather than shapers of our political world. But if we look at what women actually published at the opening of the modern era this characterization seems superficial, at best (see Table 2.6). Indeed, we encounter an intriguing tension between the literary practices of women and the cultural representation of them as writers.

A few towering female intellectual figures emerge from the bibliographical record of female publication during the revolutionary decade, and their names come as no surprise to those familiar with the period: Stéphanie de Genlis, Olympe de Gouges, Germaine de Staël, Isabelle de Charrière, and Louise de Kéralio. Their literary careers had no generic boundaries. They published everything from political pam-

---

[39]See Georges May, *Le Dilemme du roman au XVIIIe siècle; étude sur les rapports du roman et de la critique, 1715–1761* (New Haven, CT: Yale University Press, 1963); Joan DeJean, *Tender Geographies: Women and the Origins of the Novel* (New York: Columbia University Press, 1991); Joan DeJean, *Ancients Against Moderns: Culture Wars and the Making of a Fin de Siècle* (Chicago: University of Chicago Press, 1997); and Joan DeJean and Nancy K. Miller, eds., *Displacements: Women, Tradition, Literatures in French* (Baltimore: Johns Hopkins University Press, 1991).

Table 2.6 Publications, by Genre, of French Women Writers, 1789–1800

Original Works

Politics	251	Law/Philo.	14
Novels	96	Almanacs	5
Plays	49	Health	5
Education	39	History	4
Poetry	28	Literature	22
Journalism	23	Music	5
Commercial	17	Travel	5
Memoirs	15	Stories	3
Letters	20	Nat. Sci.	1
Songs	13	Cooking	1
Religion	10		
		Total:	626

Translations

Novels	22	Nat. Sci.	1
History	2	Poetry	1
Law/Philo.	4		
Theater	1	Total:	31

TOTAL PUBLICATIONS:	657

phlets, history, philosophy, and educational treatises to novels, plays and poetry.

More generally, there were no specifically "feminine genres" during the Revolution. Women wrote and published in every literary and political form of the period: from the pious prognostications of Clothilde Labrousse to the erotic poetry collections of Suzanne Giroux; from the erudite legal treatises of Mlle de Lézardière and the educational treatises of Mme de Genlis and Countess Legroing de la Maisonneuve to the translation of a treatise on fossil formation by Claudine Guyton de Morveau and the songs of the market women of the district of St. Paul.[40]

Novels were a cherished form of self-expression for women (they produced almost one hundred of them over the revolutionary decade), but by no means a predominant one. Women were also central to the explosion of journalism during the Revolution, founding and editing over twenty periodicals, a striking figure in proportion to their small num-

[40]See name entries in Appendix A.

bers. But by far the most common form of publication by women was the political pamphlet, especially petitions to public authorities.[41] Indeed, the most striking, and moving, voices to emerge from the bibliographic record are those of over two hundred women, both eminent and obscure, who at great personal risk sought publicly to redress what they perceived to be political and financial injustices by the authorities against themselves, their families, and their communities.

It is perhaps not surprising that women asserted the new and unprecedented right to participate in public political discourse after the collapse of royal regulation and censorship of the publishing and printing world. But there is no common "women's perspective" on the massive social, cultural, and political possibilities that the Revolution opened up. Instead, we find an extraordinary diversity of political and social views, ranging from *sans-culotte* pamphleteers to royalist apologists, feminists calling for equal rights and antifeminists calling women back to the home, defenders of the Queen (Staël) and vilifiers of the Queen (Kéralio-Robert), abolitionists (Gouges) and slave traders (the widow Grégoire).[42] It is easy, especially for literary historians, to dismiss this proliferation of political ephemera and to focus instead on the literary masterpieces of Germaine de Staël or Isabelle de Charrière. But the journals and pamphlets of the revolutionary period ultimately did more to change the world and are a more powerful testament to the invention of democratic cultural life.

When we shift our perspective from the history of gender ideology to the study of the literary practices of women during the Enlightenment and the French Revolution, three points become clear: (1) The French Revolution marked the advent of unprecedented female participation in public debate, not its suppression; (2) women who wrote were not socially marginalized as outcasts or rebels; rather, they were at the very center of their social and political worlds, as diverse as those worlds were; and (3) there were no typical "feminine" forms of literary self-expression or "feminine" perspectives on the political and social world. Women wrote in every genre and from all sides of the political spectrum.

[41]Suzanne Desan has pointed to the centrality of petitioning in the repertoire of women's political activities during the Revolution in her paper "Rewriting Family and Nation: Women's Political Pamphlets in the Early Revolution," delivered at the American Historical Association annual meeting, San Francisco, January 7, 1992.

[42]See name entries in Appendix A.

There was no "women's revolution" in 1789, but, through the commercialization of cultural life, the French Revolution opened up the unprecedented opportunity for women to participate in public political discourse and debate, and indeed to debate the appropriate place for women within a democratic polity. And women did so in dramatic numbers. And these revolutionary gains in public representation were not ephemeral. The increased number of women in print was sustained well into the nineteenth century. Though it denied women equal political and civil rights, the French Revolution, in opening up the possibility for this debate through the democratization of cultural life, made it possible for the first time in history for almost any woman or man to appeal publicly to the reason of fellow citizens and, ultimately, to win civil and political equality for women—even if it took more than a century to do so. The "other Enlightenment," the public exercise of female reason, began in full with the commercialization of French cultural life after 1789.

CHAPTER THREE

Female Authorship
in the New Regime

*Half of the human species is deprived of its natural rights. . . . Their
rights and their property—as saintly and as sacred as those of men—
must be restored to them.*
—Mme Cambis (1791)[1]

The French Revolution created the modern author. But it did not do
so equally for men and women. It established that a writer of either
sex was the author of his or her own ideas because they were the mani-
festation of a unique inner self. To make the dimensions of that self public, however—to publish a work—entailed entry into a dense web of
property and family law where they were treated very differently indeed. Men could publish at will; women could not. There was for men
no disjuncture between their ownership of ideas, in a moral sense, and
the public, legal recognition of these ideas as their property. It is precisely
the gap between the moral ownership of ideas, and the power to determine their public fate that distinguishes the modern woman author.

In France, before the Revolution of 1789, ideas and their forms of expression were not legally considered property. Ideas were a gift from
God, revealed through the writer—God's chosen messenger.[2] The
power to determine what constituted God's knowledge and to desig-
nate who would enjoy the *privilège* of its *jouissance* (enjoyment) belonged

[1]Mme de Cambis, *Du Sort actuel des femmes* (Paris: Cercle Social, 1791), pp. 3, 8.

[2]For a full discussion of *privilèges en librairie* under the Old Regime, see Augustin-
Charles Renouard, *Traité des droits d'auteur* (Paris: Renouard, 1838), vol. 1, pp. 106–193. For
discussion of the origins of legal theories of the claims upon texts and upon their transmission under the Old Regime, see Gaines Post et al., "The Medieval Heritage of a Hu-
manistic Ideal: *Scientia Donum Die Est, Unde Vendi Non Potest*," *Traditio*, vol. XI (1955): 195–
234; Natalie Zemon Davis, "Beyond the Market: Books as Gifts in Sixteenth-Century
France," *Transactions of the Royal Historical Society*, fifth series, vol. 33 (1983): 69–88; and
Raymond Birn, "The Profit in Ideas: '*Privilèges en librairie*' in Eighteenth-Century France,"
Eighteenth Century Studies, vol. 4, no. 2 (Winter 1971): 131–68.

to God's first representative in the kingdom, the King, and his administration. It was by the King's "grace" and "pleasure" that authors or publishers might materially exploit the dissemination of ideas. Thus, in the
arrêt of August 30, 1777, concerning the duration of royal *privilèges* in the
book trade, the King's Council of State explained:

> His majesty has recognized that a privilege for a text is a grace
> founded in Justice. . . . The perfection of the work requires that
> one allow the publisher to enjoy this exclusive claim during the
> lifetime of the author . . . but to grant a longer term than this
> would be to convert the enjoyment of a grace into a property
> right.[3]

The legal conceptions of the author as an individual creator of ideas and
of written texts as forms of property only emerged at the end of the eighteenth century, and were established in law only after the collapse of the
monarchy during the French Revolution.

On July 19, 1793, revolutionary legislators, for the first time, recognized authors as the unique originators of their ideas and hence the
owners of their work. Drawing on John Locke's theory that a person has
an inviolable property right in the fruits of his labor, the deputy to the
National Convention, Isaac-René-Guy LeChapelier wrote:

> Of all the forms of property, the least susceptible to contest is
> without exception that produced by the genius of the mind; and,
> what is astonishing, is that it was necessary to recognize this
> property, to assure its exercise by positive law.[4]

With this law, the doctrine of divine revelation ceased to guide thinking
about authorship. The property rights of authors were guaranteed and
these rights were conferred to their heirs and editors for ten years after
their death. Authors thus became self-determining actors in the public
world—free, for the first time, to control the publication of their works
during their lifetime, and to enjoy the profits from their work.[5]

---

[3] *Arrêt* of August 30, 1777: AN: F18, carton 1.

[4] Cited in Claude Colombet, *Propriété littéraire et artistique* (Paris: Dalloz, 1980), p. 6.
For a complete discussion of this law, see Carla Hesse, "Enlightenment Epistemology and
the Laws of Authorship in Revolutionary France, 1777–1793," *Representations*, vol. 30
(Spring 1990): 109–137. For the Lockean roots of modern theories of literary property, see
Mark Rose, *Authors and Owners: The Invention of Copyright* (Cambridge, MA: Harvard Uni-
versity Press, 1993).

[5] While it is true that the legislation of 1793 acknowledged the author as a right-bear-
ing individual and the text as property for the first time, claims upon texts as property

This was not the case for one particular category of author: women.[6] Their legal status did not evolve parallel to that of their male counterparts from the Old Regime to the new. This legal contingency, the contingency of female authorship in the modern era, constrained and enabled the self-fashioning of women as participants in the postrevolutionary public sphere.[7]

---

were never absolute. In fact the authors' (and their heirs') claims were limited to ten years after the author's death. Unlike all other forms of property, after this period a text fell into the public domain. Thus, while acknowledging the text as property, the legislation of 1793 significantly limited the author's claim in comparison with the terms of the *arrêt* of 1777. The *arrêt* of 1777 limited publishers' *privilèges* to the life of the author, but treated authors' *privilèges* as inheritable in perpetuity. Author's claims were further limited to publication in the country of their citizenship or the country in which the contract was signed. It was not until the first International Copyright Conference in Berne, Switzerland, in 1886, that the individual male author and the text acquired international protection.

[6]Despite the recent renewal of interest in the history of authorship and publishing in France, there has been surprisingly little research devoted to the legal status of women writers and their relationship to their works. While we have a few precious studies of the legal situations of individual French women writers, as yet there has been no systematic effort to assess the extent to which the legal realities ensuing from the revolutionary law on authorship and literary property differed for men and women. A beginning has been made by Annie Prassoloff in *"Le statut juridique de la femme auteur," Romantisme*, vol. 77 (1992): 9–14. For a more general discussion of the social status of women writers in nineteenth-century France, see Christine Planté, *La Petite Soeur de Balzac* (Paris: Seuil, 1989). Three extremely valuable studies offer concrete treatment of the legal question: Michèle Blin Sarde, "The First Steps in a Writer's Career," in *Colette: The Woman, the Writer*, Erica Mendelson Eisinger and Mari Ward McCarty, eds. (University Park: Pennsylvania State University Press, 1981), pp. 16–21; English Showalter, *"Les Lettres d'une Péruvienne: composition, publication, suites,"* *Archives et Bibliothèques de Belgique*, vol. LIV, no. 1–4 (1983): 14–28; and Nina Ratner Gelbart, "The *Journal des Dames* and its Female Editors: Politics Censorship and Feminism in the Old Regime Press," in *Press and Politics in Pre-Revolutionary France*, Jack R. Censer and Jeremy D. Popkin, eds. (Berkeley: University of California Press, 1987), pp. 24–74.

[7]French historians and literary critics have written profusely about the rise of the modern author in Western democracies at the end of the eighteenth century, but they have largely ignored this question. See, for example, Roland Barthes, "The Death of the Author," in *Image-Music-Text*, Stephen Heath, ed and trans. (New York: Wang and Hill, 1977), first published in French in *Mantéia*, vol. 5 (1968), and Michel Foucault, "What is an Author?" in *Textual Strategies, Perspectives in Post-Structuralist Criticism*, Josue V. Harari, ed. (Ithaca, NY: Cornell University Press, 1979), pp. 141–59, first published in French in 1969 in the *Bulletin de la Société Française de Philosophie*, no. 63. For an example of the explicit assumption of a parallel between male and female experience, rather than a total lack of consideration of the question, see Molly Nesbit, "What Was an Author?" in *Yale French Studies*, no. 73 (1987): 229–257, esp. p. 230. Gérard Genette is an exception to this general trend. In his work, *Seuils* (Paris: Seuils, 1984) he points to the potential difference in the status of female authorial signatures and notes the paucity of research on the question (see p. 41). Students of British literature have given considerably greater attention to the subject. See, in particular, Catherine Gallagher, *Nobody's Story: The Vanishing Acts of Women Writers in the Marketplace, 1670–1820* (Berkeley: University of California Press, 1994).

Olympe de Gouges is perhaps best known for her *Declaration of the Rights of Women*, presented without success to the National Assembly in 1791.[8] A year earlier, however, Gouges had made an appeal specifically on behalf of literary women to the committee of writers formed by Pierre-Augustin Caron de Beaumarchais to plead the cause of authors' rights before the revolutionary assembly. Thus in her *Lettre aux littérateurs françois* (Letter to French Writers), she wrote:

> It is to you only that I have recourse, knowing that you have formed a committee of all men of letters, especially to take charge of the complaints that they have to lodge. . . . ; you know that women, particularly in this last century, have sought to become your equals in the arts. With pleasure you have seen them enter into competition with you. Far from discouraging this timid sex, you have encouraged them . . . ; you cannot cease now to concern yourselves with their glory; you cannot, above all, abandon them in a circumstance in which there is a common cause.[9]

Thus, as male writers mobilized to claim their own texts as property, their female compatriots asked not to be left behind.[10]

In identifying the cause of women writers with that of their male counterparts, Gouges had been right about one thing: During the eighteenth century their fortunes had slowly risen together and in the new regime they shared the same "complaints" about property rights. Gouges was also to discover that she—just like her male colleagues—could be tried and guillotined for a crime of the pen—sedition. Under these circumstances, she—like them—owned, and was held morally and legally responsible for, her written words. But unlike men, Gouges, as a woman, did not enjoy any political standing in the state that executed her.[11] As a women she was not seen to be responsible enough to

---

[8]Olympe de Gouges, *Déclaration des droits de la femme et de la citoyenne* (1791), reprinted in: *Cahiers de doléance des femmes et autres textes*, Paule-Marie Duhet, ed. (Paris: Editions des femmes, 1981), pp. 205–223. For an English translation, see Darlene Levy, Harriet B. Applewite and Mary B. Johnson, eds., *Women in Revolutionary Paris* (Urbana: University of Illinois Press, 1979), pp. 87–96.

[9]BN: in 8 Ln 27.8955, Olympe de Gouges, *Lettre aux littérateurs françois par Madame de Gouges* (n.p., n.d. [Paris: 1790]), p. [1].

[10]For the mobilization of male writers in the opening years of the Revolution, see, for example: Jean-François de La Harpe, *Adresse des auteurs dramatiques à l'Assemblée Nationale* (n.p., n.d. [Paris: 1790]) and Pierre-Augustin Caron de Beaumarchais, *Pétition à l'Assemblée Nationale* (n.p., n.d. [Paris: 1791]).

[11]See, Olivier Blanc, *Olympe de Gouges* (Paris: Syros, 1981), pp. 199–200. For the complete dossier of the trial of Olympe de Gouges, see also Alexandre Tuetey, *Répertoire général*

hold political rights, but she was held accountable for her political views. And sexual difference made a legal difference with regard to the literary property claims of women as well as their claims to political rights.

Women came to the revolutionary cause of author's rights from a different legal position than that of men under the Old Regime. Generally, in the eighteenth century, never-married women who reached their majority (age twenty-five) had the right to manage their own financial affairs and thus to sign contracts freely and to represent themselves in court. Widows shared this status and, further, regained their dowry and a share of the communal property from their marriage. Married women, however, were effectively not legal individuals, and ceased to be such if they had ever enjoyed this status. Property and assets acquired by a woman during marriage were fully controlled by her husband. She could do nothing legally without his consent. Moreover, there was no divorce. A married woman could legally effect a physical separation from her husband (a *séparation de corps*) only if she could prove that she was the victim of life-endangering abuse at his hands. Legal separation of property (a *séparation de biens*) was possible but could occur at the woman's initiation only if she could prove that her husband had willfully dissipated her fortune. Even after a legal separation, a woman still had to have her husband's consent in order to sell or mortgage property. However, a woman who brought no dowry to a marriage but had earned money during the marriage had a right upon separation of property to have her earnings after separation protected from the liability of her husband's debts.[12]

As we have seen, few women wrote and published under the Old Regime, and many of those who did were legally separated, unmarried, or widowed. Perhaps the two most widely read women writers of the eighteenth century, Mme de Gaffigny and Mme Riccoboni, for example, did not in fact begin their literary careers until after they were separated from their husbands.[13] We find traces, too, in the archives, of never-

---

des sources manuscrites de l'histoire de Paris pendant la Révolution française (Paris: Imprimerie Nouvelle, 1890–1894), vol. 10, entry nos. 812–846.

[12]Adrienne Rogers, "Women and the Law," in *French Women in the Age of Enlightenment* (Bloomington: Indiana University Press, 1984), pp. 35–37; see also Elisabeth Guibert-Sleziewski, "Naissance de la femme civile. La Révolution, la femme, le droit," *La Pensée*, no. 238 (Mars–Avril 1984): 34–48; and by the same author, "La Femme, objet de la Révolution," *Annales historiques de la Révolution française*, no. 267 (Janvier–Mars 1987): 1–16.

[13]For the case of Mme de Gaffigny, see Showalter, "Les Lettres d'une Péruvienne, pp.

married women, like sister Marguerite-Emannuelle Le Fréron, Superior of the Order of the Visitation, acting on their own behalf, in this case to defend the exclusive privilege of her religious order to publish the works of Saint Francis of Sales.[14] When the young writer Louise de Kéralio reached her majority, unmarried in 1783, she applied for and received two *privilèges d'auteur* in her own name—for her biography of Queen Elizabeth and for a collected edition of great French women writers.[15]

It was another story for married women. Marie-Elizabeth Le Gendre, who sought to defend her literary privileges against the encroachments of an unauthorized publisher at the beginning of the eighteenth century, is specified by the royal officials who oversaw the book trades, as "a wife authorized by her husband, M. Estienne de Galice," to pursue the affair.[16] Suzanne Necker, the wife of the famous minister of finances, Jacques Necker, and the mother of the future Mme de Staël, was an acclaimed *salonnière* with ambitions to be a published writer. Her husband apparently disapproved of her seeking literary notoriety and bullied her into abandoning her ambitions to publish.[17] She continued to write, however, and after her death her husband published five volumes of her works as a posthumous homage to her intellectual legacy![18] Thus it was M. Necker who had the legal right to determine whether or not, and when, his wife's works would be published.

Further evidence is offered by Gabriel de Broglie, the biographer of

---

1–4 (1983), pp. 14–28. Concerning Mme Riccoboni, see James Nicholls, ed., "Mme de Riccoboni's Letters to David Hume . . . ," *Studies on Voltaire and the Eighteenth Century*, vol. CXLIX (1976): 12; and Joan Hinde Stewart's introduction to Riccoboni's *Lettres de Mistress Fanni Butlerd* (Geneva: Droz, 1979), p. xxxiii.

[14]BN: Mss. fr. 22149, fols. 11–12, Collection Anisson Duperron, Letter from Marguerite-Emannuelle Le Fréron, Superior of the Order of the Visitation to the Director of the Book Trade, April 26, 1746. See also fols. 13–17 for the denouement of this affair.

[15]For evidence of her *privilèges*, see her bankruptcy papers, found under the name Lagrange, in the *Archives départementales de la Seine* (hereafter AD), Fond faillite: D4B6, carton 105, dossier 7454, March 30, 1789.

[16]BN: Mss. fr. 22108, fol. 180, Collection Anisson Duperron, *Mémoire pour dame Marie-Elizabeth Le Gendre, épouse autorisé du sieur Estienne de Galice, écuyer, sieur de Chasteauneuf, . . . contre Antoine Alibert et sa femme, marchand libraire, et ses enfants mineurs, légataires et successeurs et ayant repris l'instance au lieu de feu Noëlle-Léonarde Pierre, connue sous le nom de la dame d'Orival* (Paris: Jollet, n.d.).

[17]Madelyn Gutwirth, *Madame de Staël, Novelist* (Urbana: University of Illinois Press, 1978), pp. 39–42.

[18]Suzanne Necker died in 1794. Some of her manuscripts were first edited and published by her husband, Jacques Necker, in 1798. See *Catalogue général des livres imprimés de la Bibliothèque Nationale* (Paris: Imprimerie Nationale, 1933), vol. CXXIII, p. 285.

yet another famous eighteenth-century woman of letters, Mme de Genlis. Broglie felt compelled to note that her first publication, even though anonymous, had her husband's consent and that he financed it.[19] Another, yet more explicit, example of a husband's power to determine the fate of literary property within the marital regime is offered by the *Journal des Dames*. Even though legally separated "in property" from her husband, the journal's last editor, Mme de Montanlos, still thought it necessary to insist that her husband explicitly restore her authorial privileges: He thus

> declares . . . and irrevocably authorizes Dame Marie Mayon, my wife . . . to give and hand over to whatever person she chooses, for whatever price, terms and conditions she judges appropriate, the privilege of the *Journal des Dames*. . . . She may receive payment, give receipts, contract whatever obligations, sign and witness whatever acts are necessary, and generally do whatever she deems correct, fair and fitting.[20]

Under the Old Regime, in short, a married woman's right to publish her work was contingent on her husband's consent. She was not permitted to sign any contracts without her husband's consent, she could not, on her own, make a legally binding arrangement with a publisher. And, if she did publish, the legal claim to her work belonged to him unless he explicitly authorized his wife to act on her own behalf.

While women may have made few gains in political rights during the French Revolution, their civil standing did improve significantly, if only in the short run. By abolishing in 1791 guild restrictions imposed by the former regime, revolutionary legislators opened all professions, including publishing and printing, to women, as long as their husbands (if they were married) consented. Prescriptive primogeniture was abolished and divorce legalized in September of 1792.[21] By the same law women were admitted for the first time as witnesses in the courts. By a law promulgated on June 10, 1793, all women were allowed to sign contracts in a variety of business and commercial circumstances.[22] And women gained a more equal role in the administration of community property.[23] Legal reform, however, did not go so far as to render the civil

---

[19]Gabriel de Broglie, *Mme de Genlis* (Paris: Perrin, 1985), pp. 104–105.
[20]Gelbart, "The *Journal des Dames* and Its Female Editors," p. 69.
[21]Marcel Garaud, *La Révolution française et la famille* (Paris: PUF, 1978), p. 44.
[22]Ibid., p. 173
[23]Ibid.

status of married women equal to that of their husbands. This radical proposal, initiated by the legislator Jean-Jacques-Régis de Cambacérès, was definitively rejected by the Convention in 1793.[24] So even at the revolutionary high water mark, the legal standing of married women still remained contingent to a certain extent on the will and consent of their husbands.

The Revolution did seem to make it possible for women to act with greater autonomy in the world of printing and publishing. The case of the novelist Mme Mérard de Saint-Just and her dealings with her Paris publisher Louis Maradan reveal just how far the commercial realities of the publishing world had moved beyond the formal legal rules of the Old Regime by the eve of the Revolution. It also testifies to the exuberant expectations of women writers at the opening of the revolutionary era, and the consequent limitations that revolutionary legislation imposed.

In 1790 Mme Mérard de Saint-Just sent Maradan a copy of the terms of a contract he had signed with her in 1787.

> [Maradan had written:] I recognize having received from Madame de St.-Just, a manuscript with the title *Histoire de la Baronne d'Alvigny* . . . on the condition that it will be published at my cost and, my expenses deducted, the profits of the sales divided with her. The property right to the work remains that of the author, Mme de St.-Just . . . I agree to publish the work during the course of November 1787 . . . at 1000 copies and to remunerate her within six months.[25]

By 1790 Mme Mérard de Saint-Just had still not seen the fruits of her labor. Thus she queries, "Given that [M. Maradan] is far from fulfilling his engagements with Mme de Saint-Just, she demands to know how he wishes to conclude with her."[26] Clearly Mérard de Saint-Just had no hesitation about transacting her own business affairs.

The outcome of this particular dispute is unknown, except that the novel did indeed appear under Maradan's imprint. But the significance of the letter is this: It reveals that, though married, Mme de Saint-Just (perhaps with her husband's consent) was, by 1787, dealing with Maradan on her own terms and, most interestingly, asserting her literary

[24]Ibid.
[25]BN: Nouv. acq. fr. 2766, no. 6, Letter from Mme Mérard de Saint-Just to Louis Maradan, Paris, September 29, 1790.
[26]Ibid.

"property rights" several years before such rights were offically recognized by the law of 1793.

Relations between Mme Mérard de Saint-Just and Maradan remained turbulent throughout the revolutionary era. The records of the Civil Tribunal of Paris leave us this evidence: In February of 1799, Maradan took the liberty of producing a second edition of the *Mémoires de la Baronne d'Alvigny* without the consent of Mme Mérard de Saint-Just. When the case against Maradan for piracy went to court, however, it was her husband who represented "her" claim to "her property." Free to sign contracts, married women were not free to defend those contracts in the courts. Legally, her claim was mediated by his right and obligation to defend any legal engagements made in his name.[27] Literary creation within the marital regime became community property and therefore fell under the husband's governance. The Mérard de Saint-Just case gives us some sense of the ambiguities and uncertainties of revolutionary civil law with regard to female autonomy within the marital regime.

Unmarried adult women and widows acquired the same literary property rights as those enjoyed by adult men in consequence of the copyright law of 1793. Thus we find the widowed Sophie Cottin, one of the most successful novelists of the revolutionary period, also dealing directly with the publisher Maradan. Cottin, as we have seen in the last chapter, had no qualms about asserting her clout within the literary market and threatening to negotiate with another publisher if Maradan did not assent to the price she demanded for the rights to her manuscripts.[28]

The legal claims of women writers upon their literary productions continued to depend not only on the authorization and consent of their husbands; the government, too, could intercede, even against the desires of the husband. Such was the case of the most noted woman writer of the period, Mme de Staël. A little-known dossier extant in the archives of the Ministry of Justice discloses her situation. In the fall of 1796, Mme de Staël returned to France from her chateau in Switzerland. Upon her entry into France, the Directorate government, wary of her inordinate political influence, issued an *arrêt* to have her deported without judg-

---

[27] Aristide Dourache, ed., *Les Tribunaux civils de Paris pendant la Révolution (1791–1800)* (Paris: L. Cerf, 1905–1907), vol. II, p. 618, session of February 25, 1799.

[28] BN: Mss. fr. 12757, Letter from Sophie Cottin to Louis Maradan, 1 germinal, an XII (1802).

ment as a foreigner on French soil.[29] An appeal in the hand of her husband, but probably drafted by Staël herself, was submitted to the Minister of Justice in her defense. The Baron de Staël argued that his wife was a French citizen and therefore could not be deported without a trial. He wrote:

> French women, or any being at all, born and residing in France, who know no other country, who speak the same language, who have need of the same air, who have been shaped by the same customs, who demonstrate, in a word, all that constitutes patriotism, and all that binds to the soil which saw us born, cannot be put . . . outside of the law.[30]

Her husband's plea was followed by her own.[31] These pleas were further bolstered by two more letters on her behalf from her influential lover, the politician and novelist Benjamin Constant.[32] All to no avail.

On what ground was Staël found by the revolutionary government to be a foreigner? The answer was clear in the response sent to Mme de Staël by the Minister of Justice:

> I find myself obliged, Madame, to tell you that you do not appear to have the status of *Citoyenne Française*. It is true that you were born in France . . . but [your father] was at that time a foreigner . . . you were married in your minority to a Swede, and by this act you became, if one can speak thus, even more foreign still: that is to say that there is not one single instant in which you could have, in free majority, declared your will *to be French*.[33]

Married as a minor, Staël had never experienced her "free majority," and therefore had never had the legal power to exercise her "will to be French." A woman's nationality, like her name, was legally determined first by her father's nationality and then by that of her husband.

Benjamin Constant's letter on behalf of Staël had not focused on her particular claim to "Frenchness." He argued, rather, that from a prag-

[29]J. Christopher Herold, *Mistress to an Age: A Life of Madame de Staël* (New York: Bobbs-Merrill, 1958), pp. 168–178.

[30]AN: BB16, carton 709, dossier 518, Ministère de la Justice. Letter from the Baron de Staël-Holstein to the Directorate, Coppet, December 15, 1796.

[31]AN: BB16, carton 709, dossier 518, Ministère de la Justice, Letter from Mme de Staël to the Directorate, December 18, 1796.

[32]Ibid., two letters from Benjamin Constant to the Directorate, both dated December 31, 1796.

[33]Ibid., draft of a letter to Mme de Staël from the Minister of Justice, undated.

matic perspective of political economy and state interest, to deny a woman citizenship on the basis of her husband's nationality would open up a dangerous legal loophole in the laws against emigration and, particularly, the emigration of wealth. By giving fathers the opportunity to sign the family estate over to a daughter and then marry her to a foreigner, he observed, this policy would open a floodgate for the flight of aristocratic capital from France. The Ministry of Justice nonetheless affirmed patriarchal lineage over both nativity and political economy.

Mme de Staël, a writer *of* French, born in France, was thus legally declared to be Swedish. In this case, the express wishes of both her husband and her lover, as well as that of Staël herself, were overridden by the government. The legal consequences of this decision for Staël as a writer were considerable: Until the middle of the next century, authors —male or female—who were not French citizens had limited legal power to control the circumstances of the publication of their works in France.[34] Thus denied the status of French citizen, and hence that of "French writer," Staël technically had no legal claim or control over the publication of her works in France.[35] She would have to rely on her French publishers to protect her interests, which she did by holding onto her copyrights and negotiating bilateral agreements with publishers in each separate country where an edition appeared.[36]

In 1804, the Napoleonic Code embodied and reaffirmed the position articulated by the Minister of Justice under the Directorate. According to the Code, a woman's citizenship, and thus her legal claim upon her work were determined by the nationality of her husband.[37] The question of nationality and marriage remained a concern of women writers like the Baroness of Montaran throughout the nineteenth century. Proposals of marriage from foreigners put French women in the position of having to choose between the love of their nation and that of their suitors.[38]

[34]Claude Colombet, *Propriété littéraire et artistique* (Paris: Dalloz, 1980), pp. 335–336.

[35]A foreign author could contract with a French publisher, and Staël did. But, then, the legal power to protect the property was in the hands of the French publisher. Foreign publishers did not have rights in France until 1886. See the decision of the French *Cour de Cassation* of March 23, 1810 in AN: F17, carton 2652, Undated report titled "*Convention Nationale. 1793. Législation et jurisprudence qui régissent la propriété littéraire.*"

[36]See, for example, her correspondence with Louis Maradan of March 17, 1803, concerning the second edition of *Delphine*, in Germaine de Staël-Holstein, *Correspondance générale*, 5 vols. (Paris: Pauvert, 1962), vol. 4, p. 572.

[37]See Isidore Alauzet, *De la Qualité de français et de la naturalisation* (Paris: Cosse-Marchel, 1867), pp. 17, 20.

[38]Baronne de Montaran, *Mes Loisirs* (Paris: Amyot, 1846), vol. 1, pp. 160–163. She de-

The Napoleonic Code went further in eroding the legal position of women generally and, perforce, women writers. Divorce was made nearly impossible and then abolished completely in 1816.[39] While a legal separation was still possible, it became even more difficult for women to obtain than under the Old Regime.[40] The Code denied married women any separate legal personality or the right to sell off or give away property without their husband's consent.[41] It stipulated in article 215 that married women could not plead in court in their own names even if they were in business or separated from their husbands.[42] Two of the most distinguished historians of French private law, Paul Ourliac and Jehan de Malafosse, have been led to the sober conclusion that from the point of view of civil law, "the revolutionary parenthesis closed without any true amelioration of the condition of women."[43] If anything, their civil rights were even more circumscribed.

Under the new regimes of the nineteenth century, married women writers who had not separated their property from their husbands were required to receive a signed authorization from them in order to negotiate with a publisher. The archives of the Lavocat publishing house in Paris leave us the trace, for example, of Josephine-Henriette Fanny Arnaud, femme Reynaud, who signed a contract for the sale of the rights of several novels on February 12, 1836. The contract specifies that Mme Reynaud was "contracting in her name, and is authorized to this effect

---

cided not to marry a Russian in order to retain her citizenship. See also chap. 5 for a further discussion of how the citizenship question haunted non-French francophone women writers.

[39]Garaud, *La Révolution française et le famille*, pp. 174–187. For the most complete assessment of the section of the Code pertaining to divorce, see Roderick Phillips, *Putting Asunder: a History of Divorce in Western Society* (Cambridge, UK: Cambridge University Press, 1988).

[40]Articles 108–214 of the Code. See Mäité Albistur and Daniel Armogathe, *Histoire du féminisme français* (Paris: Editions des femmes, 1977), p. 241.

[41]James F. Traer, *Marriage and the Family in Eighteenth-Century France* (Ithaca, NY: Cornell University Press, 1980), pp. 172–190.

[42]Ibid., p. 190.

[43]Paul Ourliac and Jehan de Malafosse, *Histoire du droit privée: le droit de famille* (Paris: PUF, 1968), vol. 3, p. 154. It is worth noting that, while not disputing these facts, this traditionally negative assessment of the civil status of women during the Revolution has recently been challenged by Elizabeth Guibert-Sledziewski, "*Naissance de la femme civile*," *La Pensée*, no. 238 (Mars–Avril 1984): 34–48. She stresses that the early years of the Revolution, 1789–1794, saw gains for women that were only to be recovered in the twentieth century. In her view, it was not the Revolution, but the counterrevolution, that deprived women of equal civil status.

by her husband."[44] The authorization in this contract would serve as a cover for all her later transactions. This standard formulation can be found at the head of most contracts signed in the nineteenth century by married women writers.

George Sand's literary career commenced after her separation from her husband. She thus signed her first major contract with her editor François Buzot in December of 1834 in her own name.[45] It was a disadvantageous agreement, made in a moment of financial desperation, and she later tried, unsuccessfully, to have it invalidated in the courts on the grounds that it had not been signed by her husband![46] The doctrine of the *paterfamilias*, so pervasively governed married women's literary affairs throughout the nineteenth and twentieth centuries that Sand's claim was not absurd, even if it was ultimately not convincing to the judges.

As Sand's case suggests, however, this doctrine did not go uncontested in the nineteenth century on either commercial or moral grounds. The problem of authors' moral right to control how their works were edited brought the question of woman's intellectual autonomy to the forefront of legal debate. By the middle of the nineteenth century, the French copyright law of 1793 was coming under new scrutiny. The law combined two different legal principles that were constantly at odds with one another: On the one hand, the author had a "natural right" to his (or her) productions, which were perceived to be almost sacred emanations of the individual personality and therefore indisputably the author's; on the other hand, the "public interest" dictated that this natural property right should be limited to the lifetime of the author, plus ten years, after which time anyone should be free to publish the work. Over the course of the first half of the nineteenth century, authors and publishers sought ceaselessly to strengthen the doctrine of the "natural rights" of authors in order to extend the duration of their exclusive publishing rights and, moreover, to ensure that the intentions of authors were respected by posthumous editors.

The doctrine of authors' "natural rights" was amplified by nineteenth century legal theorists into a broader theory of "moral rights,"

[44]Archives of the Calmann-Levy Publishing House, Paris: *"Traité entre Mme Charles Reynaud et Pierre-François Lavocat, 12 février 1836"; "Traité entre Mme Charles Reynaud et MM Michel Levy frères, 27 mars 1844."* I am grateful to Jean-Yves Mollier for making these sources available to me.

[45]George Sand, *Correspondence*, Georges Lubin, ed. (Paris: Garnier, 1966), vol. 2, pp. 757–758, and note 3: *"Traité avec François Buzot, 5 décembre 1834"*; see also Prassoloff, *"Le Statut juridique,"* p. 11.

[46]Sand, *Correspondence*, ibid.

rooted in their natural possession of their ideas, in order to protect authors' works from editorial distortions or public misuse. In the late 1830s, a proposal for a new law on literary property was passed by the French Senate. The law proposed for the first time to acknowledge the "moral right" to have the integrity of an author's work preserved in perpetuity, regardless of who controlled the publication rights. At the same time that it recognized this eternal "moral right," it proposed extending the duration of exclusive "property rights" in a literary work from the ten years after the author's death, stipulated in the law of 1793, to fifty years—thereby greatly enhancing the private commercial value of the author's creation to his or her heirs, or to the publishers to whom these rights had been ceded.[47] Even after the work entered the "public domain," the public was never to have the right to violate the personality of the author by publishing his or her work in an edition that distorted the author's intended meaning. The law was sent to the Chamber of Deputies for final approval in 1841.

The general question of moral autonomy opened up the specific question of the moral independence of women writers within the marital regime. It was article 3 of the proposed law that put the question directly before the deputies. It stipulated that:

> After the death of the author, the exclusive right, for the extent of its duration, will be transmitted, according to the rules of civil law, to the heirs, designated at the moment of succession. With regard to the surviving spouse, the exclusive right will be regarded as community property, in the absence of contrary matrimonial conventions.[48]

If literary property after the dissolution of a marriage by death was community property, then was it also community property during the marriage? And if so should it be governed by the same rules as those for other forms of community property? The deputy Auguste Vivien put the question squarely:

> If a married woman is an author, does the exclusive [authorial] right become part of the community property? . . . If it is community property, the husband has the right to dispose of it or to sell it; he has, finally, all the attributes of a true proprietor.[49]

[47]*Gazette des Tribunaux*, no. 4843, March 15 and 16, 1841.
[48]*Moniteur Universel*, March 25, 1841.
[49]Ibid.

The deputy's questions would not seem to be terribly problematic. The general principles of the Napoleonic Code seem unambiguous: Yes, a woman author's right—like the rest of her property—belongs to the community and as such is at the disposal of the *paterfamilias* as a "true proprietor." But, clearly, matters were not so simple or Vivien would not have posed the alternative:

> Can a wife publish a work without her husband's authorization?
> . . . I demand that the law define the right of the wife in matters of literary property.[50]

The notion of the inviolable moral integrity of the creator did not square well, in the minds of more progressive-minded legislators, with the legal submission of married women authors to their husbands' will. If she has an inviolable natural right to determine the shape and fate of her ideas, how can a husband treat her creations as community property at his disposal—to publish, even against her will, or to edit in whatever form he chooses?

Any resolution of this tension depended, as contemporaries realized, on distinguishing three aspects of authorship: the composition of the work; the publication of the work; and the management of the profits that were a consequence of its publication. The deputies—a majority at any rate—seemed sympathetic to the notion that the "inviolability of the person, the intelligence, and the imagination" of the married woman should be respected. A husband, thus, could not prohibit his wife from thinking or writing. Moreover, the works of a wife should not be published without her consent.

It seemed clear to many, as well, that the husband should control the management of his wife's commercial profits from her work. That left the middle term: Who could determine whether a work should be published? Could a wife publish a work without her husband's consent? "What, in effect," queried the deputy Augustin-Charles Renouard,

> is publication? Is it an act by which the author, after having conceived and composed his thoughts, puts himself into communication with the public . . . ? Can one say that this communication of the author with the public belongs to anyone other than the author?

He thought yes: While, on the one hand, "persons charged with managing the affairs of a legal incompetent cannot publish without the con-

[50]Ibid.

sent of the author," on the other hand, "the author, if they do not have full civil competence, cannot publish without the consent of the persons charged with the legal guardianship of their will."[51] Though he did not accept the premise that women were legal minors, the deputy Vivien, for the sake of debate, presented a revision of article 3 that incorporated Renouard's interpretation of the Civil Code. While, he argued, a married woman had a "moral right" over what she created, she could not publish those works without her husband's consent. The new version of the article thus read: "In the absence of contrary matrimonial conventions, the publication and rights ceded by the husband, *or by the wife with the permission of the husband*, will alone enter into community property."[52] In other words, as long as a woman did not attempt to publish a work it remained hers, and not part of the community property. Once it became a commodity (i.e., through publication by spousal authorization), it devolved to the community and thus to the husband's control. The deputy Pascalis concurred with this amendment. As he saw it, nothing less that the honor of the patronym was at risk: "The wife, in effect, bears the name of her husband: as she can bring honor to this name, she can compromise it through publications that she might engage in."[53] It was his name, he was responsible for defending its honor, and, therefore, he, not his wife, should control its fate. Outraged, feminist deputies, called for a "total emancipation" of women writers from the marital regime. "Women of genius won't marry," they chided.[54] The deputy Vivien vividly invoked the potential consequences of the law for French letters more generally:

> Wouldn't you regret it if an author like Mme de Staël, whose writings have so enriched our literature, could not have made them available to the public, because an ignorant or hostile husband refused his consent to the publication of her works?
>
> And to take an example that is closer to us, need I speak to you of the works of George Sand, whose works are so diverse and so well appreciated . . . and which sparkle with such brilliance in our contemporary literature? Would it not be regrettable if George Sand, who certainly wouldn't have obtained the consent of such an unsympathetic husband, had been reduced to powerlessness

[51]*Moniteur Universel*, March 26, 1841.
[52]Ibid (my emphasis).
[53]Ibid.
[54]Ibid.

and had found it impossible to make her works (so well known to you) available to the public?

I say that the intelligence of women was not put into tutelage by our legislation, that she conserves her freedom of thought, like her husband, and that, when her thoughts are useful to society, she has the right to publish them.[55]

The majority of deputies disagreed.

The question of the legal autonomy of women writers within the marital regime opened up a whole series of questions regarding women's testamentary rights and freedom to exercise other professions. French legislators, even those sympathetic with the idea of female moral autonomy within marriage, were not prepared to bring down the whole edifice of the doctrine of the "male head of household," to make the world safe for future Staëls and Sands. Efforts to delete the clause of article 3 specifying the requirement of "husband's consent" were defeated, and the husband's control over the right to publish upheld.

But even though article 3 passed, the law on literary property as a whole ultimately broke down on the shoals of the elusive legal distinction between "moral rights" and "property rights" in intellectual property. If the two were, in fact, separable, moral rights could be held to be absolute, while property rights could be limited in duration. But drawing that legal line proved to be beyond the conceptual and legislative skills of the deputies in 1841. Over the course of the late nineteenth and twentieth centuries, this problematic distinction would be repeatedly challenged in the courts.[56]

In the absence of a clear legal resolution, the situation of married women writers remained uncertain. The late nineteenth century saw at least one successful example of a spiteful husband publishing a book by his wife against her will.[57] But the trend of the courts was to prohibit such actions. Rather, they moved increasingly toward the protection of the moral rights of women authors, while at the same time maintaining the control of the husband over publication and community property—including literary property.

In fact, the special circumstances of women gave added impetus to the increasing acceptance by the courts of the dualist theory of literary

---

[55]Ibid.
[56]Claude Colombet, *Propriété littéraire et artistique* (Paris: Dalloz, 1980), pp. 213–225.
[57]Prassoloff, "Le Statut juridique," pp. 9–10.

property rights more generally. The case of Colette's *Claudine* novels is illustrative. When she and Henry Gauthier-Villars (a.k.a. Willy) divorced in 1909, Colette was acknowledged to be the "moral" author of the novels (i.e., her name had to appear on the title page of their publication), while Gauthier-Villars, as her husband, was free to sell the publication rights to the novel without her consent—which he did.[58]

French copyright law remained unrevised until 1957. The new law of 1957 embraced the dualist theory of literary property, sustaining the distinction between moral and property rights. It also still upheld the doctrine of the husband's consent as necessary to publication by married women. Even after French women gained the vote in 1945, as citizens, as women, and as writers, they were still legally subsumed under the signature of a husband's name. The law of 1957 thus more or less accepted wholesale the doctrines of a century earlier. In his legal treatise on literary and artistic property (1879), the French legal theorist Eugene Pouillet wrote: "It is clear that a woman cannot publish her works, whatever they may be, without the authorization of her husband. He is the guardian of the honor of his name."[59] It was his family name. She had no legal power to determine its fate. It was only with the revision of the laws concerning governance of community property within marriage in 1965 that married French women were granted full financial independence—the freedom to sign contracts and to publish at their own will, without authorization from their husbands.

Male and female authorship in France thus took divergent legal paths into the modern era. In the case of adult men, by the end of the eighteenth century the authorial signature, rather than royal grace, became the legal basis by which the origins, claims, limits, meaning, and fate of the text were to be determined. By the 1880s, this inviolable relationship between text and author was encoded, universally, in international law, ensuring male writers global control over the circumstances of the publication of their writings.[60]

The story of women's authorial signatures evolved along different

---

[58]Many years later, Colette was ultimately able to recover her property rights to these novels in the courts. For the most accurate account of Colette's publishing history to date, and this episode in particular, see Claude Francis and Fernande Gontier, *Creating Colette* (South Royalton, VT: Steerforth Press, 1999), pp. 265–279.

[59]Eugene Pouillet, *Traité théorique et pratique de la propriété littéraire et artistique* (Paris: Marchel-Billard, 1879), p. 233.

[60]For a general discussion of the legal and commercial aspects of authorship in the nineteenth century, see Jean-Yves Mollier, *L'Argent et les lettres: histoire du capitalisme d'édition* (Paris: Fayard, 1988).

lines. Because of the contingencies of a woman's legal status as either an unmarried adult, a wife, or a widow, her legal authorship, and thus her relationship to both her signature and her texts, did not become fully integrated along with that of her male compatriots. While the state and the Church were removed as intermediaries between male authors, their publishers, and their public, women writers saw the power of the state and the Church delegated to their husbands. Permission to publish, once a privilege of the state, was transmitted with the so-called "Declaration of the Rights of Genius" in 1793 not to the individual female author, but in the case of married women to the "head of the household." Her text became property but, for a married woman, the fate of that property remained in the hands of her husband—unless, like Flora Tristan, George Sand, and, ultimately, Colette, she sued for a legal separation of her property.

During the French Revolution, male authors succeeded in redefining themselves as Lockean individuals: self-determining creators of their own literary works, and property owners free to control their public identities. The legal identity of married women writers, by contrast, evolved over the same period along Kantian, as opposed to Lockean lines. It was a dual identity, recognized as at once morally autonomous and juridically subordinate. Free to write, they were not free to make their writings public, or to create independent public identities. French women writers would no doubt have readily recognized their marital situation in Kant's famous dictum about the appropriate relationship of citizens to the enlightened sovereign: "Criticize but obey."[61]

The particular constraints on women writers within the marital regime suggest a reinterpretation of the meaning of pseudonymity and anonymity as female signatures of authorship from the Old Regime to the late twentieth century.[62] In *A Room of One's Own*, Virginia Woolf wrote:

[61]Immanuel Kant, "An Answer to the Question: What is Enlightenment?" (Berlin: Berlinishe Monatschrift, 1784), in *Perpetual Peace and Other Essays*, Ted Humphrey, trans. (Indianapolis: Hackett Publishing, 1983), pp. 41–48.

[62]My argument here parallels the extremely interesting discussion of the differences in women's uses of pseudonyms in nineteenth century France presented by Roger Bellet, "*Masculin et féminin dans les pseudonyms des femmes de lettres au XIXe siècle*," in *Femmes de lettres au XIXe siècle: Autour de Louise Colet*, Roger Bellet, ed. (Lyon: Presses Universitaires de Lyon, 1982), p. 251. I am also indebted to Joan DeJean's analysis of how anonymity as a female signature may function as a strategy of self-empowerment rather than self-effacement in "Lafayette's Ellipses: The Privileges of Anonymity," *PMLA* vol. 99, no. 5 (October 1984): 884–902.

It was a relic of chastity that dictated anonymity to women, even so late as the nineteenth century. Currer Bell, George Eliot, George Sand, all victims of inner strife as their writings prove, sought effectively to veil themselves by using the name of a man. . . . Anonymity runs in their blood. The desire to be veiled still possesses them.[63]

Yet it was hardly vestiges of "feminine" modesty or chastity that inspired most French women of the postrevolutionary era to take on pseudonyms—and most frequently masculine ones. Male signatures controlled women's access to literary power. Women thus appropriated male names and spoke through them. While some women employed male signatures, like George Sand, Daniel Stern, or André Léo, others developed strategies for working around them.[64] Every pseudonym taken by a woman writer resulted in a multiplication rather than a consolidation of her public identities. To her inherited identities as daughter and wife, she added a self-chosen identity of author and created a name to mark the difference between them.

The Countess d'Agoult, who came to write under the name Daniel Stern, recounts the following conversation with her publisher over her first published article in his journal *La Presse*, in June of 1837:

You have not signed it, said M. de Girardin. No. You must sign. I cannot. Why not? [he responded] I cannot make use of a name that does not belong to me alone. I do not want to ask for authorization. . . . I do not want to engage anyone to defend me. That is just! cried M. de Girardin. So then, take a pseudonym. What? Try a name . . . I picked up the pencil and mechanically wrote Daniel . . . Daniel Stern! The name was found.[65]

So, too, Aurore Dudevant, who became George Sand, recollected a similar conversation with her mother-in-law in her autobiography:

She asked me why I was staying in Paris so long without my husband. I told her that my husband consented to this arrangement. But, she asked, Is it true that you intend to print a book? Yes Madame. Well! she cried, . . . what a strange idea. . . . I hope you

[63]Virginia Woolf, *A Room of One's Own* (New York: Harcourt Brace and World, 1957), p. 52.

[64]On André Léo's authorial strategy, see Roger Bellet, "*André Léo écrivain-idéologue*," *Romantisme*, vol. 77 (1992): 61–66.

[65]Countess d'Agoult, *Mémoires (1822–1854)* (Paris: Calmann-Levy, 1927), p. 212.

do not put the name that I bear on the cover of printed books. Oh, certainly not, madame, there is no danger of that.[66]

Pseudonymity was thus not necessarily an act of modest self-effacement. For married women writers, it could become a gesture of self-invention, a declaration of independence from the patriarchal signifier. And sometimes they succeeded in transforming literary fictions into legal realities. The children of George Sand took the name Sand as opposed to Dudevant. Sand thus succeeded in imposing her pseudonym as a patronymic.[67]

Other women were less successful. In 1858, for example, Juliette La Massine published a work, greatly admired by George Sand, titled *Idées antiproudhonniennes sur l'amour, la femme et le mariage* (*Anti-Proudhonian Ideas on Love, Women and Marriage*). The work proved a success, and her husband remarked: "Not bad for a beginning, I will be glad to sign it with my own name when the first printing is exhausted." Juliette replied, "That's an unpleasant joke." To which her husband responded, "Perhaps for you, but not for me. The law authorizes it. . . . The work of a wife belongs to her husband." And he did sign the second edition.[68]

Pseudonyms could represent a social compromise between the desire of an individual woman to have a public career, and a husband's or his relations' interests in retaining control over the family name. The pseudonym could, alternatively, be a gesture of rebellion against the constraints of the familial regime. The story of French women and literary property discloses repeated gestures of self-distancing from the name of the father or the spouse. St. Simonian women journalists suppressed their surnames altogether.[69] So, too, the socialist writer Flora Tristan, in blatant disregard of the Civil Code, left both her husband and his name, returning to that of her birth: Tristan.[70] After initial prevarication about signing and publicly acknowledging the authorship of her works, Colette, like Tristan before her, ultimately sued for literary inde-

---

[66]George Sand, *Oeuvres autobiographiques*, 2 vols. (Paris: Gallimard, 1970), vol. 2, p. 138.

[67]Nicole Mozet, "La Femme-auteur comme symptôme," in *34/44 Cahier de Recherches, Paris 7, no. 13: Femmes et institutions littéraires* (Paris: U.E.R., 1984), p. 38.

[68]Juliette La Messine-Adam, *Mes premières Armes littéraires et politiques* (Paris: n.p., 1904), pp. 80–82. Cited in Joseph Barry, *Infamous Woman: The Life of George Sand* (New York: Doubleday, 1977), p. 356. (Barry's translation).

[69]Laure Adler, *A l'Aube du féminisme: les premières journalistes (1830–1850)* (Paris: Payot, 1979), p. 49.

[70]Jean Baëlen, *La Vie de Flora Tristan* (Paris: Seuil, 1972), pp. 65–87.

pendence from the marital regime and definitively affixed her maiden name, rather than her married name, to her works.[71]

If, by the 1880s, the European male authorial identity was tightly secured within the horizons of a single name that functioned as a "single center of truth," as some literary critics have claimed, such was not the case for his female counterparts.[72] The modern public sphere was thus opened to French women writers on differential terms. Free to think, write, and imagine, they were free to publish only with the contingent consent of their husbands, if they had them. For French women, the new regimes of the modern era amounted to a kind of enlightened absolutism in which the husband replaced the sovereign as the arbiter of the fate of their ideas.

This did not mean, as we have seen in the last chapter, that women were not able to take up the opportunities that the new commercial literary world of the nineteenth century offered. Despite the constraints of the Napoleonic Code, women became increasingly literate in the nineteenth century and they entered print in droves. But their participation in the modern public sphere was marked by their sexual difference.

While they were free to *think* critically, in order to *publish* they still had to reckon with their sexual subordination in civil law, either by marrying approving husbands, by living beyond the marital regime, or by devising artful strategies such as pseudonymity in order to reconcile their desire for independent public identities with the demands of patriarchal lineage. One way or another, female authors were conscious that they were entering the modern public world on different terms. Unlike men, women of letters had to conceive of their identities as doubled: They were at once private beings who were subordinated within the web of civil society, and at the same time public figures, capable of transcending those constraints in order to participate in a universal life of the mind. The consciousness of this duality, as we shall see in the chapters that follow, meant that they would have to shape a distinctive path into the modern world, and that sometimes-tortuous path indelibly marked their creative lives with signs of that difference.

[71]Claude Francis and Fernande Gontier, *Creating Colette* (South Royalton, VT: Steerforth Press, 1999), esp. pp. 62, 94, 201, 204, 211. See also Michèle Blin Sarde, "The First Steps in a Writer's Career," in *Colette, the Woman, the Writer,* Erica Mendelson Eisinger and Mary Ward McCarty, eds. (University Park: Pennsylvania State University Press, 1981), pp. 16–21; and Susan D. Cohen, "An Onomastic Double Bind: Colette's Gigi and the Politics of Naming," *PMLA,* vol. 100, no. 5 (1985): 793–809.

[72]See, for example, Peggy Kamuf, "Criticism," *Diacritics,* vol. 12, no. 2 (Summer 1982): 42–47.

In legal terms, the Old Regime thus ended for women of letters not in 1789 or 1793, or even with the achievement of the suffrage in 1946, but in 1965 when they finally achieved legal and financial independence within marriage.[73] This domestic revolution of the 1960s is still within the living memory of women writing in France today. Shortly before her death in 1999, the "new novelist" Natalie Sarraute remarked, "Until 1965 I had to have my husband's authorization to publish. That is our legacy from the Napoleonic Code." "Ironically," she added, "it took Charles de Gaulle to liberate us."[74]

[73]Mäité Albistur and Daniel Armogathe, *Histoire du féminisme français* (Paris: Editions des femmes, 1977), p. 438; see also Mariette Sineau, "Law and Democracy," in *A History of Women, Volume 4: Toward a Cultural Identity in the Twentieth Century,* Georges Duby and Michelle Perrot, eds. (Cambridge, MA: Harvard University Press, 1994), p. 508.

[74]In conversation with the author, Cherence, France, Summer 1984.

PART TWO

Self-Making
Politics, Ethics, Poetics

CHAPTER FOUR
Becoming Republican

Quid foemina possit.
(What couldn't a woman do.)
—Louise de Kéralio, citing the *Aeneid,* Book V (1786).[1]

M en did not confront the problem of rethinking political sovereignty alone in 1789. As the French people assembled for the first
time in over 150 years, women as well as men began to imagine new
possibilities for how the nation might be governed. Today, the best
known of these women is Olympe de Gouges (1748–1793), butcher's
daughter, banker's widow, playwright, and author of a 1791 pamphlet
titled the *Declaration of the Rights of Women.*[2] Gouges, more forcefully
than any other woman, deployed the language of natural rights to call
for political and civil rights for women in the new regime.

But radical as these political claims were, Gouges, it should be noted,
dedicated her pamphlet to the Queen, Marie-Antoinette, and argued that
the recognition of women's equality was the best means to strengthen
the French monarchy. She was an ardent and active monarchist until the
King's flight in 1791. After the King's execution, she became a vociferous
critic of the National Convention and she was put to death for treason by

[1]Cited by Louise de Kéralio in the *discours préliminaire,* to her *Histoire d'Elisabeth, reine
d'Angleterre,* 5 vols. (Paris: Lagrange, 1786–1788), vol. I, p. iv, note. Kéralio miscites the
passage as appearing in Book II of the *Aeneid,* and adds an interrogatory. (I am grateful to
Shaun Marmon for this observation and to Ann Blair for her assistance with the Latin
translation.)

[2]See Olivier Blanc, *Olympe de Gouges* (Paris: Syros, 1981); Olympe de Gouges, *Oeuvres,* Benoîte Groult, ed. (Paris: Mercure de France, 1986); Darline Gay Levy, Harriet Bran-
son Applewhite, and Mary Durham Johnson, eds., *Women in Revolutionary Paris* (Urbana:
University of Illinois Press, 1979); and Joan Wallach Scott, "The Uses of Imagination:
Olympe de Gouges in the French Revolution," in *Only Paradoxes to Offer: French Feminists
and the Rights of Man* (Cambridge, MA: Harvard University Press, 1996), pp. 19–56.

the republican government in 1793. While Olympe de Gouges engaged the language of rights to rethink constitutional relations between male and female citizens, in her *Declaration of Rights* she never challenged the notion of patrilineal political sovereignty—the King was to remain the ultimate source of sovereign will; the Queen, his partner.

It fell to another woman writer of the revolutionary era, Louise-Félicité Guynement de Kéralio-Robert (1758–1822), to take on seriously the problem of monarchical political authority itself and to imagine a future for women under a republican form of governance. Rigorously trained in the dominant form of political argumentation of the late eighteenth century—historical analysis—Louise de Kéralio-Robert was well-suited to the task. Her intellectual engagements over the course of the revolutionary era with the problem of political authority, and especially the authority of queens, offer an opportunity, unique in French women's history, to recapture what it entailed to become a modern republican, as a women.

Kéralio was famous before the collapse of the Old Regime. In June of 1787, one of France's most noted journalists, Jacques Mallet du Pan announced in the *Mercure de France* that

> There exist an overwhelming number of Histories and Historiographers, but very few Historians. Up until now we have not seen in France a *Historienne;* Mlle de Kéralio, I think, is the first . . . And yet another singularity is joined to this one, the Author's choice to trace the lives of two Women.[3]

Mallet du Pan thus credited Kéralio, the author of the newly published *Histoire d'Elisabeth,* with more than the composition of an admirable history; he thought that she had invented a new authorial identity, that of the woman historian. In fact, there had been histories of women written in France for several centuries before the publication of Kéralio's *Histoire d'Elisabeth, reine d'Angleterre* in 1787. And there had been many women writers of history as well.[4] Moreover, Mallet du Pan was a man of considerable learning and no doubt well aware of these facts.

[3]Jacques Mallet du Pan, review of the *Histoire d'Elisabeth, reine d'Angleterre,* by Louise de Kéralio in the *Mercure de France,* June 23, 1787, pp. 151–165.

[4]See Natalie Z. Davis, "Women's History in Transition: The European Case," *Feminist Studies,* vol. III (Spring–Summer 1976): 83–103; and Ian Maclean, *Women Triumphant: Feminism in French Literature 1610–1652,* (Oxford, UK: Clarendon Press, 1977). For a discussion of the precedents for women writing history, see Faith Evelyn Beasley, *Revising Memory: Women's Fiction and Memoirs in Seventeenth-Century France* (New Brunswick, NJ: Rutgers University Press, 1990).

In what, then, did he perceive her innovation to consist? By what light did she cast all those who came before her into shadow?[5] How did Louise de Kéralio come to be recognized as France's first and only *historienne* on the eve of the French Revolution? And in her hands what fate awaited the history of women in the Revolution itself? In her struggles as a revolutionary historian attempting to overthrow past models of female authority and to shape a new future for women, Kéralio charted an political trajectory from queenship to sisterhood.

THE MAKING OF A *HISTORIENNE*

Louise-Félicité Guynement de Kéralio was born in Paris in 1758, into an old noble Breton family that exemplified, in its anglophilia and reform-mindedness, the enlightened liberal aristocratic literati in the latter half of the eighteenth century. The intellectual world of Louise de Kéralio's parents was sharply delineated along gender lines.[6] Her father, Louis-Félix Guynement de Kéralio, wrote erudite military histories and was a member of the Royal Academy of Inscriptions and Belles-Lettres.[7] Her mother, Marie-Françoise-Abeille, wrote and translated fic-

---

[5]For a discussion of the etymology of the term *historienne*, see Michel Delon, "*Les Historiennes de Silling*," in *Actes du Colloque: L'Histoire au XVIIIe siècle*, Centre Aixois d'Etudes et de Recherches sur le XVIIIe siècle, May 1–3, 1975 (Aix: EDISUD, 1980), p. 102.

[6]The classic study of the association of writing and reading novels with women in the eighteenth century, and with feminism in particular, is Georges May, *Le Dilemme du roman au XVIII siècle*, (Paris: PUF, 1963), see, esp., chap. 8. The most pathbreaking recent work on gender and literary culture in eighteenth-century France has been accomplished by Nancy K. Miller. See Nancy K. Miller, ed., *The Poetics of Gender* (New York: Columbia University Press, 1986); Nancy K. Miller and Joan DeJean, eds., *The Politics of Tradition: Placing Women in French Literature* (New Haven, CT: Yale University Press, 1988); and Nancy K. Miller, *Subject to Change: Reading Feminist Writing* (New York: Columbia University Press, 1988). For the most recent synthesis of the gender issues in eighteenth-century literary culture, see the relevant sections of *A New History of French Literature*, Denis Hollier et al., eds. (Cambridge, MA: Harvard University Press, 1989). For a sociocultural history of men of letters in the eighteenth century, see Daniel Roche, *Le Siècle des lumières en province, académies et académiciens provinciaux, 1680–1789*, 2 vols. (Paris: Editions EHSSS, 1989; orig., 1978).

[7]See Roger Chartier, "Historiography in the Age of Absolutism" in *A New History of French Literature*, Hollier et al., eds., pp. 345–350. For further discussion of official historical writing in the eighteenth century, see Blandine Barret-Kriegel, *Les Historiens et la monarchie*, 4 vols. (Paris: PUF, 1988), see esp. vol. 2 and vol. 3, pp. 261, 284. For explorations of other uses of history and historical writing, see the *Actes du Colloque: L'Histoire au dix-huitème siècle*, (Aix: EDISUD, 1980); and Michel de Certeau, *L'Ecriture de l'histoire* (Paris: Gallimard, 1975), esp. pp. 182–196.

tion. But like most women writers of her generation, she published her works anonymously, declining to sign or to publicly acknowledge her literary achievements.[8] An only child, Louise de Kéralio can, in many respects, be seen as a woman struggling to come to terms with this dual inheritance of paternal historical erudition and her mother's passion for writing and translating fiction.

Indeed, Kéralio proved from the very start to be a virtuoso at bending the rules of both gender and genre as far as they could bend. Her parents had set the pattern at her christening when she received her father's names (Louis-Félix) but with the endings feminized: Louise-Félicité; it was her father, rather than her mother, who took charge of her education.[9] And though Kéralio's first published works appear to descend directly from her maternal side—a series of translations from Italian and English and a novel published anonymously in 1782—here already she had elaborated a more complex configuration of her gender identity than might at first appear. Her first work, *Adélaïde ou les mémoirs de la marquise de* *** may have been a novel, but it was a memoir-novel—an extremely unusual form for an eighteenth-century woman writer, much less for a woman who was only twenty-four years old when the book appeared in 1782. This genre was almost entirely the province of men.[10] Thus by writing an anonymous memoir-novel, even if it is writ-

---

[8]On the complexities of female literary anonymity during the period under consideration, see Roger Bellet, "*Masculin et féminin dans les pseudonymes des femmes de lettres au XIX siècle*," *Femmes de lettres au XIXe siècle: Autour de Louise Colet*, Roger Bellet, ed. (Lyon: Presses Universitaires de Lyon, 1982), esp. p. 251; Nancy K. Miller, "A Feminist Critic and her Fictions," *Diacritics*, vol. 12, no. 2 (Summer 1982): 48–53; Joan DeJean, "Lafayette's Ellipses: The Privileges on Anonymity," *PMLA*, vol. 99, no. 5 (October 1984): 884–902; Carla Hesse, "Reading Signatures: Female Authorship and Revolutionary Law in France, 1750–1850," *Eighteenth-Century Studies*, vol. 22, no. 3 (Spring 1989): 469–487; and Nancy K. Miller, "The Gender of the Memoir-Novel," in *A New History of French Literature*, Hollier et al., eds., pp. 437–438.

[9]The essential biographical information on Louise de Kéralio has been compiled by L. Antheunis, *Le conventionnel Belge François Robert (1763–1826) et sa femme Louise de Kéralio (1758–1822)* (Wetteren, Belgium: Editions Bracke, 1955), esp. pp. 11–13. According to contemporaries, Kéralio read Greek and reportedly spoke and read Latin, English, and Italian fluently. For evidence that her father was responsible for her education, see Antheunis, *ibid.* See also Louise de Kéralio, *Histoire d'Elisabeth, reine d'Angleterre*, vol. I, p. ii; and *Collection des meilleurs ouvrages français, composés par les femmes*, 12 vols. (Paris: Lagrange, 1786–1788), vol. I, p. vii; and Joseph-François Michaud and Louis Gabriel Michaud, eds., *Biographie universelle, ancienne et moderne nouvelle édition*, 45 vols. (Paris: Desplaces, 1843–1865), vol. 21, pp. 535–536.

[10]Miller, "The Gender of the Memoir-Novel," pp. 437–438. The following discussion is indebted to Miller's interpretation of the gender politics behind Mme de Tencin's *Mémoires du comte de Comminges*, which was published anonymously in 1735.

ten in the first-person feminine, Kéralio was in fact adopting a public authorial persona that was coded male.

Moreover, *Adélaïde* proves to be a violently antimaternal novel. In the opening pages, the young heroine introduces her mother as a haughty and vain woman, whose

> pride of birth—the kind that is inspired by rare beauty—and the sentiment of her superior enlightenment heightened her passions to an extreme vivaciousness; and my mother submitted to their empire, imagining not that either her equals or her inferiors should ever resist her. My father, who had experienced all the inconveniences of this kind character, gave me an education which was completely opposed to it. Through wise precepts and useful examples he rendered me capable of thinking and feeling.[11]

The tragic story of Adélaïde begins when she falls madly in love with a young count Rofaure who loves her in return; her father delights in her choice. But he dies before they can be wed, and Adélaïde soon discovers that her mother has been secretly seeking the affections of the young count for herself. Revealed as the thwarted rival, her mother determines never to allow the lovers to marry. The plot of mother-daughter rivalry, jealousy, and persecution grinds relentlessly through a gruesome forced marriage and repeated unsuccessful attempts by the lovers to reunite. The book ends tragically, with the triumph of the mother's will and an unbridgeable separation of the two lovers.

Kéralio's first novel reveals four themes that were to be reworked continuously throughout her literary career: (1) Her identification with her paternal inheritance, (2) the adoption of an authorial persona that was at once recognized as feminine, but typically associated with men, (3) the creation of an *oeuvre* populated almost entirely by powerful female figures, and (4) a central preoccupation with the problem of female rivalry.

In 1786, four years after the publication of *Adélaïde,* Mlle de Kéralio, began publishing openly under her own name the first volumes of what were to be her two greatest intellectual projects: a five-volume *Histoire d'Elisabeth, reine d'Angleterre* (*History of Elizabeth, Queen of England*), which she prefaced with an effusive dedication to her father, and twelve volumes of a *Collection des meilleurs ouvrages français composés par des femmes*

---

[11][Louise de Kéralio], *Adélaïde, ou les mémoires de la marquise de ***. Ecrits par elle-même* (Neuchâtel: n.p., 1782), p. 2.

(*Collection of the Best Works Written in French by Women*), dedicated to her mother. These two publications marked an inversion of the configuration of gender identification and literary genre that she had established in her earlier work. Kéralio now publicly claimed authorship of her work as an unmarried young woman. But at the same time as she abandoned her anonymity, she also abandoned the novel for an unambiguously masculine genre: history.

Of course, the term *histoire,* was slippery in the eighteenth century, and the boundaries between history and the novel were not as clearly fixed as they would become in the nineteenth century. *Histoire* could mean either history or story, or both—as, for example, in English, Henry Fielding's *History of Joseph Andrews.* Indeed, the standard eighteenth-century French dictionary, edited by Antoine Furetière, gives two definitions of the term, one referring to an official record of public political events, and the other referring to *histoire particulière,* which recorded private lives and events that could just as well be invented as not.[12]

By the end of the seventeenth century, these two different genres of *histoire* were also clearly coded in gender terms. Public histories were written almost exclusively by men about the political and military actions that were documented in official records. *Histoires particulières*— stories of private lives—by contrast, were written largely by women to advance their own, often feminist interpretations of the social, moral, and even political order of the Old Regime.[13]

Louise de Kéralio left no room for doubt as to where her own works stood within contemporary understandings of historical practice. The aim of history, she asserted in the preface to the *Histoire d'Elisabeth,* is to reconstruct the truth found in public records.[14] Her histories, she announced, like those of her erudite father, were to be histories of public lives, based on a verifiable public record of historical fact. They were, however, histories of *women:* women in public life.

Though both were historical works in our modern sense of the term, the *Collection* and the *History of Elizabeth* represented two distinctive

---

[12]See Roger Chartier, "Historiography in the Age of Absolutism," *A New History of French Literature,* Denis Hollier et al., eds., pp. 345–350; May, *Le Dilemme du roman,* esp. chap. 5; Suzanne Gearhart, *The Open Boundary of History and Fiction: A Critical Approach to the Enlightenment* (Princeton, NJ: Princeton University Press, 1984); and Michel de Certeau, *Heterologies,* Brian Massumi, trans. (Minneapolis: University of Minnesota Press, 1986), esp. chap. 15, "History: Science and Fiction," pp. 199–221.

[13]See Beasley, *Revising Memory.*

[14]See, in particular, her preface to the *Histoire d'Elisabeth, reine d'Angleterre,* vol. I, p. i.

paths toward a public historical identity for women: one literary, the other political; one separatist, the other integrationist. The *Collection* was an explicitly feminist attempt to construct a separate literary tradition for women writers, from Héloïse to the eighteenth century. But as extraordinary as this work is, it was not especially innovative. Working strictly within the traditional conventions of historical writing about women established by the renaissance histories of *femmes fortes* (worthy women), the *Collection* presented a series of portraits of exceptional women, followed by a selection of each author's works.[15] Although the work is organized chronologically, it retains the structure of a series of timeless exemplary portraits, offered as models to the women writers of her own age.

The *History of Elizabeth,* by contrast, is both innovative and monumental. Here Kéralio departs radically from the *femme forte* histories by situating Elizabeth's reign squarely within the history of male political sovereignty: "Under Titus, Trajan, Marcus Aurelius, Gustavus Adolphus, Henry IV, and Elizabeth, virtue dared to reappear" (II:3). The history of the Queen is thus not specifically a history of a woman, as such, but of a ruler among rulers. It is a bold project to integrate a woman into the history of men.

Moreover, by explicitly following the historiographic path paved by Voltaire in his *Siècle de Louis XIV*, Kéralio made great claims for her subject. It was to be the history of "a celebrated era" rather than an exceptional individual ruler (I:i). A woman too could define an era of public time. The achievements of Elizabeth's reign could be understood, she insists, only within the wider context of the European Reformation. Finally, citing Locke and Montesquieu as her authorities, she wrote that her ultimate aim was "to assess Elizabeth's contribution to the progress of the law" (I:vii).[16] And it is here that her historiographic goal became clear: to establish Elizabeth's reign as a linchpin in the development of English constitutional law, whose history had issued from the pens of David Hume and William Blackstone following the English Revolution of 1688.[17]

---

[15]See Natalie Z. Davis, "Women's History in Transition: The European Case," *Feminist Studies,* vol. III (1976): 83–103; Beasley, *Revising Memory;* and Ian Maclean, *Women Triumphant.*

[16]She cites John Locke, *The Second Treatise on Government,* and Charles Louis de Secondat, baron de la Brède et de Montesquieu, *The Spirit of the Laws.*

[17]The two works she cites most frequently are: (1) David Hume, *The History of England,* the first volumes of which were published in Edinburgh in 1754 (The completed six-

Thus she argued that the real founder of the modern—by which she meant secular—constitutional state was not Henry VII, as past histories had claimed (and, one might add, as current histories now do), but rather Elizabeth. Why? Because Elizabeth believed in religious tolerance and was the first ruler to successfully establish secular over religious rule. Kéralio acknowledges that the Queen ruled too much by prerogative and too little through Parliament. But she nevertheless maintains that the reign of Elizabeth marked the critical turning point in the path toward a secular constitutional monarchy, which would only be fully, or nearly (she hedged here), embodied by the liberal constitutional principles of the Revolution of 1688.

Kéralio knew that she was working against received ideas so, in anticipation of her critics, she deployed the entire arsenal of skills she had inherited from her father, the *érudit*, to make her case. "If I am daring to raise my voice against the opinion of the majority, who still attribute to Henry VII the present government of England," she wrote, "it is not without proof for what I am advancing" (I:4, note 1). Her history, she announced, was the result of ten years of research, extensive consultation of previously unexamined archival material, an exhaustive reading of all available histories, and scrupulously critical cross-examination of the documentary evidence (I:i). She copiously footnoted every point, and published a fifth volume devoted entirely to *pièces justificatives*, (supporting documents), along with a critical bibliography of existing sources. Even Mallet du Pan found this was excessive. But it was effective!

This critical, erudite, and magisterial synthesis of English constitutional history, issuing from the hands of a twenty-eight–year–old woman, became one of the literary sensations of the French pre-Revolution. Mallet du Pan's fourteen-page review in the *Mercure de France* was not the only one to laud Mlle de Kéralio as the "premier" woman historian of her age.[18] The royal censor charged with evaluating the book wrote in the official approbation that he was

> astounded that a refined woman would devote herself from the first years of her youth to such a demanding work; she has con-

volume edition appeared in 1762. A French translation of the complete work, by Mme Octavie Belot, was published in 1769); and (2) Sir William Blackstone, *Commentaries on the Laws of England*, 4 vols. The first edition of this work was published by Clarendon Press in Oxford, between 1765 and 1769, and went through ten editions before 1785. There was no French translation until the nineteenth century.

sulted all the original sources, and all the men of Queen Elizabeth's reign; and her discussions, her reflections, and her style
merit praise.[19]

In 1787 she became one of only three women ever elected to the Academy of Arras.[20] The *History of Elizabeth* had succeeded in translating the
history of female sovereignty from the Renaissance genre of the *femme
forte* into the Enlightenment idiom of a critical history of the law. Herein
lay the innovation that Mallet du Pan recognized as singular and without precedent.

But Mallet du Pan did not find Kéralio's work without flaws. Most
centrally, he was perplexed by her preoccupation with the relationship
between Elizabeth and Mary Stuart. Indeed, he observed, it was really
a "history of two women"; she had devoted almost half of the four volumes to documenting their relationship. And he acutely observed that
this extended narrative of female rivalry worked like a kind of riptide
against the dominant movement of the work. While Kéralio's overarch-
ing thesis celebrated the Queen and seemed to ally her firmly with the
Humean, pro-Elizabeth historiography, when it came to Mary Stuart,
Kéralio parted company with her respected English predecessor. In
her estimation, Mary Stuart was the innocent victim of plotting male
courtiers, and of a Queen who was blinded by her own narcissistic jealousy of Mary's greater beauty and feminine charm. But despite copious
archival documentation of Scottish court intrigue, Mallet du Pan found
this depiction of Elizabeth as Mary's jealous rival implausible. Hume's

---

[18]Reviews of the work appeared in the *Journal encyclopédique*, no. 8 (1787), pp. 267–
278, 436, 447; Jacques Mallet du Pan, *Mercure de France* (June 23, 1787): 151–165; and Lans
de Boissy, *Journal Littéraire*, Nancy, vol. XXXIV (1787): 106–119.

[19]See the *approbation du roi*, signed by the royal censor Démeunier, December 7, 1786,
and printed at the end of volume five of the *Histoire d'Elisabeth, reine d'Angleterre*.

[20]None of the 116 regular members of the Academy of Arras in the eighteenth century were women. Of the 124 honorary members, only three were women, and all of them
single. Mlle de Kéralio and Mlle de Masson le Golft were both admitted as honorary members on February 3, 1787, and Mlle du Chastellier was admitted as an honorary member
on October 16, 1789. See E. Van Drival, *Histoire de l'Académie d'Arras depuis sa fondation, en
1737, jusqu'à nos jours* (Arras: Courtin, 1872), pp. 223–255. It was typical for academicians
to come from the older nobility, but Mlle de Kéralio was unusually young (twenty-nine)
at the time of her election. For a sociocultural profile of the Academy of Arras in the eighteenth century, see Daniel Roche, *Le Siècle des lumières en province*, vol. I, pp. 189–210; and
vol. II, pp. 209, 213. Roche also documents an increasing academic interest in historical
subjects in the last two decades of the century, see ibid., vol. II, pp. 295. Unfortunately,
Roche does not offer any figures for the number of women admitted to the provincial
academies in the eighteenth century.

less equivocal portrait of the Queen, he judged, was more coherent and hence more convincing.

While Kéralio depicted Elizabeth the Queen as the nearest thing to an enlightened constitutional monarch that the sixteenth century could have possibly produced, she presented Elizabeth the woman in profoundly ambiguous terms. Indeed, at the very heart of Kéralio's history was a war between two differently, yet equally flawed and equally tragic, conceptions of womanhood, embodied on the one hand by Elizabeth and on the other by Mary Stuart. The book ends with the following double portrait of the two Queens. Of Elizabeth, she wrote,

> When one sees such great achievements accomplished by the genius of a women, all the defects, all the weaknesses of her sex, of her character, disappear even in face of the most severe judges. . . . One can almost pardon her exercise of absolute power. . . . If all of these male characteristics place her amongst the ranks of great kings, one cannot credit her with having united them with the charms of a refined woman. But it should be observed that gentleness, weakness even, which are the real charms of a woman in private society, would have marred her virtues as a sovereign; and Mary Stuart, who possessed all the graces and the charms of her sex, would perhaps have been able successfully to resist her formidable rival, if she had been, like her, less amiable, and if she had had her strength, her power, and her greatness of character. The death of this princess is the only blemish that cannot be removed from the life of Elizabeth; it is inexcusable.[21]

Mary Stuart was successful as a woman, and by virtue of this success failed as a ruler and was destined to be dominated by her rival. Elizabeth, by contrast, abandoned womanhood to become a successful ruler. And in the one moment in her career when she permitted her desire to be loved as a woman to express itself (in her jealous rivalry with Mary), she failed as a ruler.

In these two painfully tragic portraits, Kéralio exposed the inherently paradoxical nature of the concept of female sovereignty in a political culture that coded public virtue as masculine and private virtue in the feminine.[22] In fact, a history that begins as a celebration of female

---

[21]Louise de Kéralio, *Histoire d'Elisabeth, reine d'Angleterre*, vol. IV, pp. 666–667.

[22]For further discussion on the gendering of public virtue as masculine, see Joan Landes, *Women and the Public Sphere in the Age of the French Revolution* (Ithaca, NY: Cornell

rule ends as a poignant testimony to its impossibility. It also ends with the repetition of the warning to women that the author had first sounded in her novel *Adélaïde:* Women in positions of absolute power (for example, widowed mothers or sovereign queens) are dangerous not so much to the men, whose equals they become, as to other women, over whom they come to reign.

FROM HISTORIAN TO ANTIHISTORIAN

The dilemmas of taking on male characteristics in order to acquire public power were not abstract intellectual issues for Kéralio. By the time the Revolution erupted in 1789, Kéralio had proven herself to be extremely adept at forms of covert literary cross-dressing in order to acquire male cultural privileges and prerogatives. Despite the laws prohibiting women from becoming publishers, in 1785 she launched a publishing business behind a man's name by providing capital to a Paris guild publisher, Jean Lagrange, who in effect served as her front man.[23] In 1789 she went a step further. Two weeks before the National Assembly officially declared freedom of the press in August of 1789, she threw herself openly into a new career as a revolutionary journalist-printer, founding her *Journal de l'Etat et du Citoyen.* The Revolution, she an-

University Press, 1988); Dorinda Outram, *"Le Language mâle de la vertu:* Women and the Discourse of the French Revolution," in *The Social History of Language,* Peter Burke and Roy Porter, eds. (Cambridge, UK: Cambridge University Press, 1987), pp. 120–135; and Dorinda Outram, *The Body in the French Revolution: Sex, Class, and Political Culture* (New Haven, CT: Yale University Press, 1989), esp. chap. 8.

[23]On the complexities of the relationship between the legal and familial status of women in the eighteenth century, see Adrienne Rogers, "Women and the Law" in *French Women in the Age of Enlightenment,* Samia Spencer, ed. (Bloomington: Indiana University Press, 1984), pp. 35–37; Elisabeth Guibert-Sledziewski, *"Naissance de la femme civile. La Révolution, la femme, le droit,"* *La Pensée,* no. 238 (Mars–Avril 1984): 34–48; Michèle Bordeaux, *"Droit et femmes seules. Les pièges de la discrimination,"* in *Madame ou Mademoiselle? Itinéraires de la solitude féminine 18e–20e siècle,* Arlette Farge and Christiane Klapisch-Zuber, eds. (Paris: Montabla, 1984), pp. 19–57; and Carla Hesse, "Reading Signatures: Female Authorship and Revolutionary Law in France, 1750–1850," *Eighteenth-Century Studies,* vol. 22, no. 3 (1989): 469–487. By contemporary accounts, Kéralio's business did spectacularly well, especially with her history of Elizabeth, and by 1789 the publishing house had gained notoriety in Parisian cultural circles as an important source of enlightenment philosophy and new novels. See BN: mss fr., 6687, *"Mes Loisirs,"* the journal of Siméon-Prosper Hardy, vol. VIII, entry for January 21, 1789; AN: V1 553, memorandum of the office of the book trade concerning Mlle de Kéralio, November 12, 1789; Joseph-François Michaud and Louis-Gabriel Michaud, eds., *Biographie universelle,* vol. 21, pp. 535–36; and AD: fond faillites, D4B6, cart. 105, doss. 7454, March 30, 1789.

nounced, not only offered, but also demanded, a new role for the author in French society:

> A new order has been established in the nation; the great work of French liberty has been accomplished in a week . . . But it is a small thing to build ramparts, you must defend them. . . . this is without doubt the most worthy employment of literary talent.[24]

During the fall of 1789, Kéralio deployed her pen and her presses in the service of the political and cultural vanguard of the Revolution.[25]

But in moving from history to political journalism, Kéralio began to encounter firsthand the limits of the gender-genre system she had so painfully analyzed in her *History of Elizabeth*. By the end of October 1789 she found herself publicly characterized by radical journalists as a *"phenomène politique,"* and an *"amazone."*[26] Moreover, by 1789 Kéralio was thirty-one years old and still single. She was thus becoming increasingly vulnerable to the threat of social marginalization as a *"vieille fille"* (old maid). Indeed, hostile pamphleteers were already beginning to attach the stereotypical attributes of the *"vieille fille"*—*"laide"* (ugly), *"susceptible aux fureurs utérines"* (prone to uterine hysteria)—to her name.[27]

Kéralio had been an intellectual innovator under the Old Regime, but, as her views on Mary Stuart suggest, she had not been a social rebel.

---

[24]See the *Prospectus du journal de l'état et du citoyen proposé par souscription, chez mademoiselle de Kéralio, rue de Grammont, no. 17*. The *Prospectus* is undated, but appeared shortly after August 6, 1789. The first issue of the journal appeared on August 13, 1789. On the founding of her publishing house, see her memorandum to this effect of November 12, 1789, which she addressed to the royal administration of the book trade: AN: V1 553.

[25]For examples of the radicalism of her ideas, see her comments on Jean-Joseph Mounier and Jean-Paul Marat in the *Journal de l'Etat et du Citoyen*, no. 4, September 1789, and the supplement to no. 14, October 22, 1789; and her *Observations sur quelques articles du projet de constitution de M. Mounier* (signed Mlle de Kéralio) (Paris: Imprimerie de N.-H. Nyon, n.d.[1789]).

[26]*Journal de l'Etat et du Citoyen*, supplement to no. 14, October 22, 1789, p. 229. These accusations originally appeared in the *Révolutions de Paris*, no. XVI, p. 32.

[27]On the social realities and the stereotype of the *"vieille fille,"* in eighteenth-century France, see Cécile Dauphin, *"Histoire d'un stereotype, la vieille fille,"* in *Madame ou Mademoiselle?* Farge and Klapisch-Zuber, eds., pp. 207–231. On the medical belief in the particular susceptibility of single women to *"fureurs utérines,"* see, Arlette Farge, *"Les Temps fragiles de la solitude des femmes à travers le discours médical du XVIIIe siècle,"* in *Madame ou Mademoiselle*, pp. 251–263. For the attribution of *laideur* and *fureurs utérines*, to Louise de Kéralio, see the anonymous pamphlet, *Les Crimes constitutionels de France, ou la désolation française, décrétée par l'assemblée dite Nationale Constituante, aux années 1789, 1790, et 1791. Accepté par l'esclave Louis XVI, le 14 septembre 1791* (Paris: Chez Le Petit et Guillemard, 1792), cited by Lynn Hunt, "The Many Bodies of Marie-Antoinette," in *Eroticism and the Body Politic*, Lynn Hunt, ed. (Baltimore: Johns Hopkins University Press, 1991), p. 120, note 42.

And, in response to such public vituperation, her views on the appropriate roles for women in the new regime began to take a decidedly domestic turn. Privately, in a letter to Jacques Pierre Brissot de Warville, dating most likely from October 1789, she attempted to distinguish her own views on the role of women in the new society from those whom she described as "little amphibious beings," who were dressing as men and taking to the streets of Paris. She, in contrast, believed that in women "the love of publicity destroys modesty, and that the loss of this great good leads to a distaste for domestic occupations, [and] from this disorganization . . . all forms of public disorder are born." Women should remain in the home, and receive men there, she concludes, à la Rousseau, rather than seeking to meet them in public spaces.[28]

In December of 1789, Kéralio announced that her *Journal du Citoyen* was folding, and that a new journal, the *Mercure National,* would serve as its successor. Significantly, the prospectus of the *Mercure* announced that the journal was to be edited by three soldiers of the National Guard—Louis-Félix Guynement (ci-devant de Kéralio) (her father), Hugou de Basseville, and François Robert (her husband)—and by "a citoyenne, daughter, and wife of two of them."[29] Denounced as a "political amazon," and *"vieille fille,"* Kéralio at last married at the age of thirty-two, and took refuge behind the names of her father and her new husband, the Belgian Jacobin, François Robert.

Madame Robert did continue to contribute articles to the *Mercure.* But she now had to contend with the emergence of women as a central element of popular counterrevolutionary political mobilization.[30] Initially she attempted to rescue the political reputation of women as a voice in radical politics by publicly denouncing counterrevolutionary women in the *Mercure.* But within an increasingly antifeminist revolutionary environment, her public role as a revolutionary writer became more and more untenable, even as a denouncer of other political women.[31] She steadily withdrew not only from politics, but from writing and publishing as well—at least in her own name.

[28]AN: Papiers Brissot, 446 AP7, doc. 188, Letter from Louise de Kéralio to Jacques Pierre Brissot de Warville, October 10, [1789].

[29]Prospectus for the *Mercure National,* (n.p., n.d. [1790]).

[30]For the counterrevolutionary mobilization of women, see, in particular, Olwen Hufton, "Women in Revolution 1789–1796," *Past and Present,* no. 53 (1971): 90–108; and Suzanne Desan, "Redefining Revolutionary Liberty: The Rhetoric of Religious Revival during the French Revolution," *Journal of Modern History,* vol. 60, no. 1 (1988): 1–27.

[31]For Kéralio's efforts to distance herself from counterrevolutionary women, see her *"Adresse aux femmes de Montauban"* in *Mercure National,* no. 6, May 23, 1790, p. 429; also

In 1791 a new work of women's history, titled *Les Crimes des reines de la France depuis le commencement de la monarchie jusqu'à Marie Antoinette* (*The Crimes of the Queens of France from the Beginning of the Monarchy to Marie Antoinette*), appeared anonymously, from the Parisian publisher Louis Prudhomme. It was immediately—and rightly—attributed to Kéralio.[32] This work is frequently cited as part of the flurry of anonymous anti–Marie-Antoinette polemics of the early revolutionary period, and the publisher clearly intended the book for just this market.[33] He adorned the volume with a licentious, engraved frontispiece, depicting a sexually voracious queen reigning triumphantly over her consort, exhausted from excessive venery (see Figure 4.1). But because of its length and its substantive character, the book stands apart from the many porno-polemical tracts that attacked the Queen. Whatever else it is, the *Crimes of the Queens* is a work of history and not just a polemical tract, if only because it poses two crucial questions: What sort of history can be written in a revolutionary moment? And, more particularly, How can a political history of women be written in a moment in which women were being driven from direct involvement in politics?

The *Crimes of the Queens of France* was a generic inversion of her *History of Elizabeth*. And just as the *History of Elizabeth* had taken the genre of the *femme forte* and reworked it, transforming it from a series of portraits of exemplary queens into an institutional history of female sovereignty, so *The Crimes of the Queens of France* attempted to perform a similar revision of the evil twin of the *femme forte* histories, the histories of bad queens.

There were numerous models for this kind of generic inversion dating from earlier political crises. In both the Wars of Religion of the sixteenth century and the *Fronde*, a century earlier, histories of bad queens

---

published separately as the *Adresse aux femmes de Montauban . . . par Mme Robert* (n.p., 1790).

[32]For the contemporary attribution of this work to Kéralio, see Hunt, "The Many Bodies of Marie-Antoinette," pp. 120–122, esp. note 42.

[33]See Hunt, "The Many Bodies of Marie-Antoinette," pp. 120–122. For further discussion of the pamphlet literature attacking Marie-Antoinette, see also Robert Darnton, "The High Enlightenment and the Low-life of Literature," reprinted in *The Literary Underground of the Old Regime* (Cambridge, MA: Harvard University Press, 1982), pp. 1–40; Chantal Thomas, *La Reine scélérate: Marie-Antoinette dans les pamphlets* (Paris: Seuils, 1989); Sarah Maza, "The Diamond Necklace Affair Revisited (1785–1786): The Case of the Missing Queen," in Hunt, ed., *Eroticism and the Body Politic*, pp. 63–89; and Elizabeth Colwill, "Just Another Citoyenne? Marie-Antoinette on Trial, 1790–1793," *History Workshop*, no. 28 (Autumn 1989): 63–87.

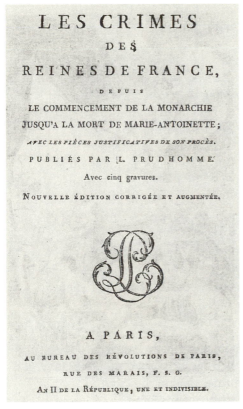

Un peuple est sans honneur, et mérite ses chaînes,
Quand il baisse le front sous le sceptre des Reines.

Figure 4.1 Frontispiece of Louise de Kéralio's *Crimes des reines de la France.*
Paris: Prudhomme, an II [1793–1774], Private Collection.

were deployed by opponents of the French monarchy who felt that
Catherine de Medicis and Anne of Austria had overstepped the appropriate political roles prescribed for queen-regents.[34] Indeed, on the eve
of the Revolution of 1789, there was an established cast of bad French
queens (Clotilde, Frédégunde, Brunhaut, and Catherine de Medicis)
readily available to any polemicist who needed historical illustrations
of the sorry consequences of permitting women an equal role in public

[34]See Rachel Weil, "The Crown Has Fallen to Distaff: Gender and Politics in the Age
of Catherine de Medicis, 1560–1589," *Critical Matrix*, vol. 1, no. 4 (1985): 14–31, esp. pp.
17–19; and Elizabeth Dudrow, "Anne of Austria and Political Rebellion: Depictions of the
Queen during the Fronde," Unpublished seminar paper, University of California, Berkeley, Spring 1990, esp. pp. 17–19, 22–23, 34, 38–39. I would like to thank Elizabeth Dudrow
for her permission to cite this paper.

life. *The Crimes of the Queens of France* drew heavily on these past models, but broke with them in ways that merit further consideration.

First, earlier black histories of queenship had been written with the purpose of restoring the monarchy to what the authors regarded as its proper course. The histories of bad examples, put before Catherine de Medicis and Anne of Austria, in particular, were intended as attempts to rein in these bad queens, who had overstepped their authority, and bring them "back into order." They were reformist narratives. *The Crimes of the Queens,* by contrast, had a revolutionary purpose: to condemn the institution of queenship itself. This gives the narrative an overdetermined and vertiginous quality: In the end, it implies, all queens, by the very fact of being queens, are bad. Like the *History of Elizabeth, The Crimes* is not a history of exemplars, but rather a history of the institution of queenship itself.

Madame Robert advanced two different arguments against queenship. On the one hand, she argued that the problem with queens was that they were women. And here she deployed traditional rhetoric about women's greater passions and their lesser capacity for self-control:

> Drunkenness from wine produces greater vice in women than in men; so too, the inebriation of power, the lust for domination, is more hideous and deadly in the former than in the latter. . . . a woman who can do anything is capable of anything.[35]

She went on quickly to advance a kind of corollary principle: As women deformed politics, so, too, did politics deform women. She writes, "A woman who becomes a queen changes sex, she thinks everything is permitted to her, and defers to nothing." This line of argument, however, simply returned her to the problems of male monarchy itself, the absence of checks on absolute power. To get back to the problem of queens, in particular, she then took another turn, this time toward a Rousseauvian critique of the institution of queenship. She writes,

[35][Louise de Kéralio-Robert], *Les Crimes des reines de la France depuis le commencement de la monarchie jusqu'à Marie Antoinette, publiés par Prudhomme* (Paris: Prudhomme, 1791), pp. vi–vii. For a historical perspective on these stereotypes, see Natalie Zemon Davis, "Women on Top," in *Society and Culture in Early Modern France,* (Palo Alto, CA: Stanford University Press, 1975), pp. 124–151; Ian Maclean, *The Renaissance Notion of Woman* (New York: Cambridge University Press, 1980); Paul Hoffmann, *La Femme dans la pensée des lumières* (Paris: Ophrys, 1977); Landes, *Women and the Public Sphere in the Era of the French Revolution;* Outram, *The Body in the French Revolution;* and Hunt, "The Many Bodies of Marie-Antoinette," pp. 108–130.

> The queens who have held the scepter in their own names are not
> those who have done the most evil; they were accountable, if not
> to the law, then at least to opinion, which sometimes condemns
> more quickly than the law: it is the wives of kings, who insist on
> being called queens, who have had the most damaging influence
> on the destiny of empires and the happiness of peoples. . . . These
> queens have only escaped public resentment because they have
> known how to hide their intrigues behind the dignity of their
> marital status. (vii)

French Salic law, which forbade women to rule in their own right, far
from restraining French queens, made them worse than any others, precisely because it put their power outside the law and beyond the reach
of public opinion. French queens ruled through deception because they
were not allowed to rule as men, that is, in their own names.

It is difficult to read these lines without wondering if Robert also
meant to sound a warning to republicans who sought to exclude women
from public life, and who drove them to act through men. She momen-
tarily strayed toward such musings, invoking an even earlier, premonar-
chic past under the Gauls, when, she wrote, "several *gauloises* took seats
in the senate and voted and deliberated the same as the men." (x–xi).
One wonders where this text might have gone, in another political cli-
mate, or in the hands of a less misogynist editor than Louis Prudhomme.
Perhaps Mme Robert might have found a historical model for women's
political inclusion in the new regime. But she did not. This was a text
written against the past. In fact, it was not history, but antihistory. She
pursued the narrower, negative course taken by the broader revolutionary movement toward the Queen: to write her out of public life.

Thus, when Robert came to Marie-Antoinette, she deviated from the
tactics of the porno-polemicists. The problem was not that her private
life distorted and corrupted politics. The Queen's personal vices should
be of interest to the Queen's conscience alone. Unlike the revolutionary
prosecutor, Antoine-Quentin Fouquier-Tinville, Robert insisted that the
ex-Queen should be tried only for her political crimes, her conspiracy,
her waste of public funds. These acts she committed as a public person.
Her solution to the threat of Marie-Antoinette was to remove the issue
of her sexuality and her sex from public discussion; to declare an end to
the monarchy and thus reduce the Queen to a private woman. *The
Crimes of the Queens of France* wrote an end to the public history of
women insofar as that history had been understood as a chronicle of the

political actions of the kingdom's only public woman—the Queen. This negation of the history of women was, for its author, also an act of self-negation. The end of the history of queens represented the end of the career of their historian. With the *Crimes*, Robert's career as a historian ended. In 1793 Louise Robert published an open letter announcing her retreat from public life. She published nothing further for fifteen years.[36]

POST-REVOLUTIONARY FICTION: HISTORY BY OTHER MEANS

If the revolutionary Terror of 1793–1794 had attempted to purge the nation of a corrupted past, Thermidor precipitated a recovery of memory, and, on the part of male cultural elites, a return to the writing of history. The French nation needs a "new history," Henri Grégoire proclaimed upon the floor of the National Convention in 1795.[37] But for the former historian of queens, Mme Robert, the problem of coming to terms with the past would demand the invention of new forms of historical writing. In 1808, a five-volume novel titled *Amélia et Caroline, ou l'amour et l'amitié* appeared under a new authorial identity, Mme Kéralio-Robert.[38] This third revision of her public signature was itself an expression of a desire to recover a sense of historical continuity across the rupture of the revolutionary period, which was, in her case, also a passage from the name of her father to that of her husband. Mme Kéralio-Robert acknowledged as much in the dedication of the novel:

> In former times I dedicated the first work that I published in my name to my father. For twenty years I have published nothing. For twenty years I have been yours, and it is to conjugal love that I dedicate this work.

This new work was presented to her husband. But if the hyphen between Kéralio and Robert sought to create a continuity, it also betrayed a discontinuity, and the need to erase that brief revolutionary moment in the fall of 1789 when she had been neither daughter nor wife but

---

[36]Louise Robert, *A Monsieur Louvet, député à la Convention Nationale par le Département du Loiret* (Paris: Baudouin, n.d. [1793]).

[37]Henri Grégoire, *Rapport sur les encouragements, récompenses et pensions à accorder aux savants, aux gens de lettres et aux artistes* (Paris: Imp. Nat., an III [1794–1795]), pp. 15–20.

[38]Louise de Kéralio-Robert, *Amélia et Caroline, ou l'amour et l'amitié*, 5 vols. (Paris: Leopold Collin, 1808).

rather an amazon, a *"phenomène politique,"* as well as the succeeding period in which she had written women out of public life. Indeed, in stating that she had published nothing for twenty years, that is, since 1788, she denied authorship of all her publications during the revolutionary period.

In the preface to her novel, Kéralio-Robert expanded more openly on the problem of postrevolutionary lineage as a literary problem. She acknowledged that in former times she had written a history of Queen Elizabeth. The success of that work, she now wrote, had given her the courage to embark on publishing a collection of women writers, but the Revolution had forced her to abandon it (vii). And since the Revolution, she continued, French literary "taste has been deformed," so that there is no market for these women writers of the past: "The French imagination has gone off to distract and lose itself in catacombs and tombs." (ix–x). Kéralio-Robert was not a great partisan of the Gothic novels that had come into vogue after the Revolution. She found their lack of *vraisemblance* (plausibility) dissatisfying. Moreover, she found their representations of women undignified. It was difficult for her to believe that women wrote them (xiii). Of course, it was true, she continued, that every historical moment has its own style and its own mores, and that it was the job of the novelist to capture the specificity of each era. Novels were in their own way a record of their era. Indeed, the novel, she wrote, "is the history of private life" (xvii).

Mme Kéralio-Robert thus reworked her own literary past and created a new lineage for herself, descending this time through the maternal, rather than the paternal line, from her mother's novel rather than from her father's academic history; from her *Collection des meilleurs ouvrages*, rather than the *Histoire d'Elisabeth*. Yet, at the same time as she re-identified herself with the novel, Kéralio-Robert also assigned the novel the status of a historical genre, albeit a "history of private life." Thus, the novel, in her hands, became a pursuit of history by other means, a history written from within the feminine register of fiction.[39] Like many

[39]Kéralio-Robert's definition of the novel as *histoire* was not unprecedented. Indeed, it can be located in a tradition of feminist literary invention dating back to at least the seventeenth century. As Faith Evelyn Beasley has shown, feminist writers after the *Fronde*, and most notably Mme de Lafayette, also exploited the double meanings of *histoire* as public history and as *histoire particulière*, in order to write their own versions of history. See Beasley, *Revising Memory*. It would be interesting to explore further the association of this narrative strategy with moments of political reaction, i.e., the post-*Fronde* world of Mme de Lafayette, and the postrevolutionary world of Mme Kéralio-Robert. For further reflections on the relationship of women's writing to history in the revolutionary period, see

women writers of the postrevolutionary era, Kéralio-Robert began to use allegory as a fictional means to pursue her interest in political and historical themes.[40] Thus, the two senses of the word *histoire* converged.

Amélia and Caroline confronts the problem of historical writing and historical identity on a number of different levels. It is a work of historical fiction in the sense that it is set in the past: the English Revolution of 1640–1660. This was manifestly not an innocent or random choice of period. Contemporary readers would have immediately recognized this setting as an allegory for their own revolution and, at one moment in the text, Kéralio-Robert explicitly echoes the common contemporary analogy between Cromwell and Robespierre (I:197). But the choice of period had a more particular meaning within the *oeuvre* of Kéralio-Robert. It is difficult not to see this work both chronologically and thematically as a continuation of the *History of Elizabeth*. And it too is a "history of two women."

Further, *Amélia and Caroline* is not simply the story of private lives set against a historical backdrop. Rather, it unfolds as a double narrative, tacking back and forth between two generic registers, one recounting the public history of the English Revolution and the other detailing the fictional story of the private lives of its two heroines, Amélia and Caroline. The novel thus plays continuously with the *double entendre, histoire-histoire*, history-story. Moreover, this double narrative is clearly marked in gender terms.

The public history is that of men in revolution. Here Kéralio-Robert meticulously reconstructs the events of the English Revolution, replete with direct quotations from primary sources and footnotes to key authorities. She quotes from a letter Cromwell wrote to Parliament, outlining his religious views (II:6), and offers careful descriptions of the battles of Naseby and Maarston Moor, based on citations to the best historians—Clarendon, Gumble, and especially, Hume (III: 126, 140–141, 168–69).[41] This political history is interwoven with the fictional narra-

---

Marie-Claire Hoock-Demarle, *La Rage d'écrire: femmes-écrivains en Allemagne de 1790 à 1815* (Aix-en-Provence: Alinea, 1990), esp. pp. 99–104, 243–250.

[40]There is much more that needs to be written about women and political allegory in the revolutionary period, but, for a beginning, see Doris Y. Kadish, *Politicizing Gender: Narrative Strategies in the Aftermath of the French Revolution* (New Brunswick, NJ: Rutgers University Press, 1991).

[41]The sources for her historical account are Edward Hyde, first Earl of Clarendon, *The History of the Rebellion and Civil Wars in England, Begun in 1641, with the Precedent Passages and Actions that Contributed Thereto, and the Happy End and Conclusion Thereof by the King's Blessed Restoration* (Oxford: Printed at the Theater, 1704); Thomas Gumble, *The Life*

tive recounting an intergenerational struggle—not between fathers and sons but, rather, between mothers and daughters.

This political narrative of the Revolution was no mere historical backdrop for a romance. Indeed, the whole interest of the novel lies is showing how the histories of public and private life, and the histories of men and women, do not simply parallel one another, but, rather, are profoundly and inextricably implicated in one another. Thus, as the novel closes, a minor character remarks philosophically, "The troubles of state, traversed everyday life . . . and opened up different vistas in the affairs of private individuals who found themselves wounded in the wars between competing factions" (V: 109). Kéralio-Robert's novel thus quietly rebelled against the masculinist postrevolutionary ideology of separate spheres. Indeed, the whole point of the book was to reveal that the histories of public and private life are profoundly implicated in one another.

The dilemmas of postrevolutionary lineage and the determination of social identity offer the premise for the plot. Charles, the émigré son of a cavalier, rescues a girl named Caroline from robbers who have killed her guardian. Caroline does not know who she is, though she has retained a jewel box that she has been told contains the secret of her identity. Charles and Caroline fall in love. His mother consents to their marriage, because, as she says, in revolutionary times, all lineage is called into doubt. Suddenly the daughter of Oliver Cromwell, Adélina, and her daughter Amélia (Cromwell's granddaughter), arrive at the neighboring chateau. The shrewish and vain Adélina becomes the young Caroline's persecutor, first attempting to seduce her beloved Charles, then, when that fails, trying to have the two lovers captured and put to death as counterrevolutionary traitors.

But, Adélina's daughter Amélia becomes Caroline's best friend and protector. After volumes detailing the horrible persecutions of the two girls by the bad mother, who, like a queen, manipulates her father's men and thus turns the whole political world against Caroline and Amélia, we finally discover that Caroline is, in fact, the daughter of the wicked Adélina's husband by his first marriage. Caroline's mother was the source of the entire family fortune and so Caroline is hence to be the true heiress

---

of General Monck, Duke of Albemarle, etc., with Remarks upon his Actions (London: T. Basset, 1671) (French editions of this work appeared in London 1672 and in Cologne in 1712); and David Hume, *The History of England, from the Invasion of Julius Caesar to the Revolution in 1688* (London: A. Millar, 1762).

to the family fortune. Thus, Caroline and Amélia are not only friends, but half-sisters. When these truths of their identities finally come to light, Adélina, the wicked mother, attempts first to kill Caroline and then Amélia, and, finally, failing in both these attempts, she kills herself.

The novel could have ended with the marriage of Charles and Caroline—and indeed, precisely this denouement is implied—but it does not end that way. The closing pages are concerned rather with the problem of settling the inheritance of the two half-sisters, Caroline and Amélia. Their father announces that, by the terms of the maternal will, Caroline, her natural daughter and the eldest of the two, is to receive the entire fortune. But Caroline rebels. No, she insists, she will not accept the inheritance, unless it is divided equally between herself and her sister Amélia:

> You have two daughters, Milord, and my mother's fortune is in your hands; let it be shared between both of them. At this price, I will accept the inheritance of my mother, when it has been dispensed as I desire it to be." (V:167)

And, she continues, these two sisters, "were united by unhappiness; wealth shall not have the deadly power to divide them." (V:168–169). This revolt by the daughters against the inequities of the maternal will at last put an end to the deadly inheritance of maternal tyranny, female rivalry, and domination.

Amélia and Caroline was not a continuation of *Adélaïde*, nor of the *History of Elizabeth*, nor of *The Crimes of the Queens*. It was a postrevolutionary rewriting of their female plots. Through fiction, Mme Kéralio-Robert was, at last, able to write a truly revolutionary—indeed a utopian—plot, in which the problem of female rivalry is resolved through the suicide of the wicked queen mother, and the daughter's rebellion in the name of equality and sisterly love.

The reshaping of political consciousness along modern, republican lines during the French Revolution entailed a reworking of public symbols and collective narratives. As lineage gave way to individual talent as the foundation of identity and authority, the symbolic universe of the nation was recast in a new mold. The aristocratic *femme forte* and queens —good and bad—were to be replaced in republican propaganda by the domesticated republican mother as a new social ideal for women.[42]

---

[42]See Lynn Hunt, *The Family Romance in the French Revolution* (Berkeley: University of California Press, 1992).

But by symbolically killing off the queen, Louise de Kéralio-Robert asserted something more affirmative than the downfall and domestication of public women: She took a critical step in the political coming of age of modern French women. Kéralio-Robert's histories had cast a dark light on the political possibilities for women under the Old Regime. They record the cruelty of an absolutist political culture toward women who sought, or who found themselves, in public roles. Moreover, she revealed the ways in which absolutist modes of power—as surely in the hands of women as in those of men—pitted mothers against daughters and sisters against one another. The exceptional woman, like the absolutist queen, was someone who lived beyond the law—an exception to the rule—and thus was dangerously unaccountable to anyone beyond herself and her own desire.[43] Kéralio's histories thus made manifest why it was necessary for revolutionary women, and not just for revolutionary men, to kill off the queen. If women were to have a real revolution—to achieve the power of self-determination and the power to enact more equitable laws in their own names—the tyranny of mothers would have to go, as well as that of the absolutist fathers.

The Revolution imposed a normative gender order—one that sought to relegate women more strictly to the private realm than they had been under the Old Regime. The consequences of this for women's history are clear. Insofar as the writing of history continued to be conceived as a task of recording the events of public life, women were not to be its subject. But they were not written out of *histoire* in its other sense. Having abandoned the legal-historical analysis of queens, Kéralio-Robert turned to prose fiction. Her postrevolutionary novel, however, suggests that this change of genre, in fact, represented an opportunity to move beyond the constraints of past models for writing women's history and to write a truly revolutionary and republican plot. Needless to say, this fictional plot of contractual equality and sisterly love, this daughter's revolution, was not the kind of plot that the Napoleonic censors would have been on the lookout for.

---

[43]For some very interesting theoretical reflections on the problem of female exceptionalism and history writing, see Christine Planté, *"Femmes exceptionelles: des exceptions pour quelle règle?"* in the special issue of *Les Cahiers du Grif: Le Genre de l'histoire*, no. 37/38 (Spring 1988): 91–111.

CHAPTER FIVE

The Ethics of Unequals

I have no other mentor to give you than yourself.
—Isabelle de Charrière (1795)[1]

In 1794, the Swiss writer Isabelle de Charrière Bell van Zuylen (1740–1805) read Immanuel Kant's essay *On the Proverb: That May Be True in Theory But Is of No Practical Use* (1793). This short treatise on ethical obligation inspired her to write a novel titled *Trois Femmes* (*Three Women*), which explored the problem of moral duty for women in the postrevolutionary world.[2] Charrière was quick to see that the sudden entry of women into the modern world of moral autonomy would combine uneasily with their continued juridical subordination.

She was not alone in her philosophical preoccupations. In the winter of 1794–1795 a debate about the nature of moral duty swept through French intellectual circles. The fall of Robespierre and the end of the Ter-

---

[1]Isabelle de Charrière, *Trois Femmes*, in *Oeuvres complètes*, tome IX, Jean-Daniel Candaux et al., eds. (Geneva: Slatkine, 1981), p. 48.

[2]Immanuel Kant, "On the Proverb: That May Be True in Theory But Is of No Practical Use," in *Perpetual Peace and Other Essays*, Ted Humphrey, ed. and trans. (Indianapolis: Hackett, 1983), pp. 61–92 (original edition: Berlin: Berlinische Monatschrift 1793). Isabelle de Charrière's novel *Trois Femmes* first appeared under the pseudonym of the Abbé de la Tour in a German translation by Louis-Ferdinand Huber, *Drei Weiber* (Leipzig: Pet. Phil. Wolfischen Buchhandlung, 1795). The first (mutilated) French edition was published in London in 1796. A second French edition appeared in Lausanne in 1797, and the first definitive illustrated edition, *Trois Femmes. Nouvelle de l'Abbé de la Tour,* appeared in Leipzig, published by Pierre Philippe Wolf in 1798. The essential details of the publishing history of the novel are to be found in the editors' introduction to the superb critical edition of *Trois Femmes* in Isabelle de Charrière Belle de Zuylen, *Oeuvres complètes*, 10 vols., Jean-Daniel Candaux, C. P. Courtney, Pierre H. Dubois, Simone Dubois-De Bruyn, Patrice Thompson, Jeroom Vercruysse, and Dennis M. Wood, eds. (Geneva: Slatkine, 1981), vol. IX, pp. 38–125. All further references are to this edition.

ror left the nation's cultural elite to ponder the devastation that civil war had wrought on the social bond. Two moral maxims—enshrined in the new *Declaration of the Rights and Duties of the Citizen*, promulgated by the French Republic in August of 1795—were meant to reassert social solidarity as the essential foundation on which the Republic would be rebuilt: "Do only unto others as you would have them do unto you; always do the good for others that you would like to receive."[3] These maxims were easy to express and easy to sanction as law. But they left crucial questions—one practical, the other philosophical—unanswered: How was moral regeneration to be achieved in a nation still suffering from the paroxysms of fratricidal violence? And where did seemingly self-evident moral ideas come from—Divine revelation? Innate faculties? Upbringing and education? After Thermidor, moral duty became the order of the day, and moral philosophy the *lingua franca* of thermidorian cultural life.[4]

The moralists of the eighteenth century had been centrally preoccupied by the relationship between "happiness" and "virtue." But Robespierre's rhetorical obsession with "public virtue" irremediably contaminated the word "virtue" for the foreseeable future. "Moral duty" took its place as a more politically benign means of expressing the same idea, but it did not resolve the old question of whether the goals of public morality and personal happiness were, in fact, reconcilable. The pursuit of the one might—as Robespierre feared—inevitably compromise the other. The moral legitimation of the new regime depended on a successful reconciliation of the public and the private good. The resolution to this moral debate was to determine the shape and the direction of thermidorian intellectual and educational policies, from the curriculum of the primary schools to the research agenda of the nation's greatest scientists. Two schools—materialist and Christian—faced off.

Many thermidorians, shaken by the revolutionary experience, returned to the pastoral fold of the Church.[5] They took the view that only the Christian idea of original sin could explain the horrors France had witnessed; moreover, the Terror proved that, without some fear of di-

[3] *Les Constitutions de la France depuis 1789* (Paris: Flammarion, 1979), p. 102.

[4] François Picavet, *Les Idéologues* (Paris: Alcan, 1891), p. 27.

[5] On the neo-Christian revival under Thermidor, see George Boas, *French Philosophies of the Romantic Period* (Baltimore: Johns Hopkins University Press, 1925), p. 70; and Martyn Lyons, *France Under the Directory* (Cambridge, UK: Cambridge University Press), pp. 100–115. See also Claude Langlois, *"Le Renouveau religieux au lendemain de la Révolution,"* in *Histoire de la France religieuse,* Jacques Le Goff and René Rémond, eds. (Paris: Seuil, 1991), vol. 3, pp. 415–423.

vine retribution, people's essential wickedness—their destructive and selfish passions—would triumph over any possible benign moral impulses. Without the support of religion, people would inevitably lose their way, again and again. Thus, a rechristianization of France would be the only possible successful path to renewal of social peace and public morality. Institutionally, these neo-Christians argued for a return of the Republic's educational resources to the hands of the Church.

A majority of French men of letters in 1795 were probably at least deists in their private faith; that is, they still saw some role for God in the larger order of things. But those who inherited cultural power in the newly restored National Convention—the members of the Committee on Public Instruction—were also men of the Enlightenment, bent on discovering a secular basis for moral reasoning.[6] The government's *Declaration of Rights and Duties* had been careful to assert only that these moral duties were "engraved by nature in the hearts of citizens."[7] How nature was to do its work was another question.

In their search for a secular moral foundation, the Enlightenment philosophers of the thermidorian period picked up the threads of the eighteenth-century debate between the sensationalist tradition of Etienne Bonnot de Condillac, Claude-Adrien Helvetius, and Marie-Jean-Antoine Caritat, Marquis de Condorcet, on the one hand, and Rousseau and the sentimentalists, on the other. The sensationalists, represented most notably after 1795 by Antoine Destutt de Tracy and Constantin-François de Chasseboeuf, comte de Volney, argued that the true source of moral ideas was to be found in the rational calculation of self-interest based on information derived from the senses. Rational self-interest, Volney asserted, would inevitably lead men to the conclusion that their higher interest was to be found in the maxim: "Live for your fellow man so that he will live for you."[8] No notion of original sin, nor any fear of eternal damnation, was necessary for man to arrive at this

---

[6]Martin Staum, *"Volney et l'idée d'une science morale à l'Institut,"* in *Volney et les idéologues: Actes du colloque d'Angers, textes réunies par Jean Roussel* (Angers: Presse Universitaire d'Anger, 1988), pp. 131, 134. See also Martin Staum, "The Enlightenment Transformed: The Institute Prize Contests," *Eighteenth-Century Studies,* vol. 19 (1985–1986), pp. 153–179, esp. p. 157; and J.-R. Suratteau, *"Le Directoire avait-il une politique religieuse?"* *Annales historiques de la Révolution française,* vol. 238 (1991): 79–92.

[7]*Les Constitutions de la France,* p. 102.

[8]Staum, *"Volney et l'idée d'une science morale à l'Institut,"* p. 133. For a general history of sensationalist theory and the origins of the postrevolutionary debate, see John C. O'Neal, *The Authority of Experience: Sensationalist Theory and the French Enlightenment* (University Park: Pennsylvania State University Press, 1996), esp. chap. 9.

self-interested conclusion. Personal happiness and public good thus harmonized happily in the sensationalist model.

The argument that moral universals derived from individual sensations and simple perceptions was vulnerable from the start to criticism: How, without some innate social instinct—sympathy, for example—could one make the mental leap from particular experiences to general ideas?[9] Pierre Cabanis, following Rousseau, thus argued that there must be some physiological basis for a sympathetic moral sentiment in the workings of the nervous system.[10] Differences in moral development could be linked, he argued, to physiological differences, and especially those between men and women. Men, he held, because of their more robust tissue structure, were physically predisposed to intellectual and moral superiority over women—they were capable of greater firmness and rectitude.[11] Cabanis's theories promised an alternative, but equally materialist and secular, account of how moral principles are generated from physical sensations.

In both the sensationalist and the sentimental accounts, personal happiness would prove to be compatible with public morality. Either by physiological predisposition or through acquired experience, men would come to understand the relationship between individual happiness and the greater social good. Moreover, neither theory relied on a universal moral dictum. Moral rules were *a posteriori* findings—the result of investigation, just as would be any other generalization about the natural world. They were tested by experience; that is, by the consequences that follow from their adoption.

Materialist philosophy thus led to a consequentialist moral logic. As a key member of this group, Benjamin Constant would argue that lying could thus be endorsed, if it resulted in a higher good, such as preventing the unjust sacrifice of a life. No general moral dictum against lying could be sustained in the face of contingent circumstances.[12]

---

[9]Boas, *French Philosophies of the Romantic Period*, p. 176.

[10]Staum, "*Volney et l'idée d'une science morale à l'Institut*," p. 134.

[11]Anne C. Vila, *Enlightenment and Pathology: Sensibility in the Literature and Medicine of Eighteenth-Century France* (Baltimore: Johns Hopkins University Press, 1998), esp. chap. 7, and Anne-Marie Jaton, "*La définition de la féminité dans 'Les Rapports du physique et du moral,' de Cabanis et dans 'La Loi naturelle,' de Volney*," in *Volney et les idéologues: Actes du colloque d'Angers, textes réunies par Jean Roussel* (Angers: Presse Universitaire d'Angers, 1988), pp. 183–191. See also Geneviève Fraisse, *Muse de la raison* (Paris: Gallimard, 1995).

[12]Ernst Behler, "Kant vu par le groupe de Coppet: la formation de l'image staëlienne de Kant," *Groupe de Coppet: Actes et documents du deuxième colloque de Coppet*, Simone Balayé and Daniel Candaux, eds. (Geneva: Slatkine: 1977).

In the end, the secular philosophers of Thermidor decided that the research agendas of the proponents of the theories of "interest" and "sympathy" were not incompatible. They could be combined into a single "moral science," which investigated the origin of moral reasoning in mental and physical development. Moreover, both schools agreed that, if there was to be a regeneration of public morality, individuals could not simply be abandoned to their own particular experiences, even if directed by physiologicially grounded sentiments. Citizens needed a moral and political education to come to a full understanding of their "best interest" in relation to the larger public good. They also needed a course in physical education to ensure that their bodies developed in a healthy way. Finally, some policing of private passions by public authorities inevitably would be necessary to ensure the moral health of the public as a whole. Civic institutions, good legislation, and rational educational institutions would guide individual impulses toward their natural moral end.[13]

Even before the *Declaration of Rights and Duties* promulgated a new moral basis for the postrevolutionary regime, this group of secular philosophers had been busy formulating the social policies that were to effect the much-needed regeneration of both individual and society. Meeting regularly at the salon of Mme de Helvétius in Auteuil and for weekly dinners at a restaurant on the rue de Bac in Paris, a group of materialist philosophers, including Benjamin Constant, Destutt de Tracy, and Pierre Cabanis, as well as key members of the National Convention's Committee on Public Instruction (Marie Joseph Chénier, Emmanuel Joseph Sieyès, Joseph Garat, and Pierre Guinguené) formulated a legislative agenda to implement a secular program of moral reform.[14]

From at least the spring of 1794 the national government's Committees on Public Safety and Public Instruction had been receiving reports deploring the state of French intellectual culture.[15] In the view of these

[13]Staum, "*Volney et l'idée d'une science morale à l'Institut*," pp. 135–138.

[14]Picavet, *Les Idéologues*, pp. 27–31.

[15]BN: Nouv. acq. fr. 1836, feuilles 27–29, report from Jean-Baptiste Lefebvre de Villebrune to the Committee of Public Safety concerning the state of the book trade, 12 ventôse, an II (March 2, 1794), forwarded to the Committee of Public Instruction on 24 ventôse, an II (March 14, 1794); and AN: F17 1009C, doss. 2216, report from Villebrune to the Committee of Public Instruction, titled: "*Considérations sur le commerce de la librairie française*," n.d., received by the Committee on 29 ventôse, an II (March 19, 1794). This second report has been reproduced in M. J. Guillaume, ed., *Procès-verbaux du Comité d'instruction publique de la Convention Nationale*, 7 vols. (Paris: Imprimerie Nationale, 1891), vol. 3, pp. 612–618. For a more complete discussion of the perceived crisis in letters and con-

distressed officials, the collapse of the royal academies and other forms of official cultural patronage between 1789 and 1791 and the concomitant declaration of freedom of the press and freedom of commerce had left the fate of French literary culture exclusively in the hands of the uneducated consumer and the profit-oriented publisher. Far from unleashing the forces of reason, virtue, and public utility, reports suggested that the Revolution had led instead to an explosion of decadent literary publications, which preyed on the private passions and moral weaknesses of citizens. Of special concern to republican cultural elites was the public's seemingly insatiable appetite for prose fiction—books that encouraged sensuous obsessions and distracted citizens from more edifying pursuits.

By the fall of 1794, Henri Grégoire, a key cultural luminary of the thermidorian National Convention, had begun to address these concerns. In a major report to the deputies of the assembly, he asked for nothing short of a cultural Thermidor.[16] The government, he argued, must repudiate its Rousseauvian antipathy to intervention in the nation's cultural life. Just as representative government would eclipse direct revolutionary democracy with the promulgation of the new Constitution of the Year III, so too official representatives of a regenerated republican culture would have to be designated.

Specifically, active government patronage of selected authors and publishing ventures would replace the laissez-faire cultural policies that the government had implemented after 1789 in a misguided attempt to institute the Rousseauvian ideal of transparent and unmediated intellectual exchange among citizens themselves. The National Convention responded enthusiastically by voting to distribute huge sums to "encourage and reward" select writers, scholars, and artists to shape the cultural life of the postrevolutionary Republic.

And then, a year later, on August 22, 1795, the new Constitution moved further toward the consolidation of the intellectual world and announced the immediate foundation of a national institute "charged to gather together discoveries and to perfect the arts and sciences." By this act the cultural leadership of the secular materialists in the new regime

---

sequent reorientation of French government cultural policies after 1794, see Carla Hesse, *Publishing and Cultural Politics in Revolutionary Paris (1789–1810)* (Berkeley: University of California Press, 1991), chap. 4.

[16]Henri Grégoire, *Rapport sur les encouragements, récompenses et pensions à accorder aux savants, aux gens de lettres et aux artistes* (Paris: Imprimerie Nationale, an III [1794–95]). See also Guillaume, ed., *Procès-verbaux du Comité d'instruction publique de la Convention Nationale*, vol. 4, pp. 758, 766–767.

was assured. A further decree, on October 25, 1795, put all the elements of the new Institute into place. Most important, the new Institute, in contrast to the old royal academies, would create a "class of moral and political sciences" as one of the three research groups, alongside the exact sciences and literature and beaux arts.[17] The inauguration of the Institute thus represented a key turning point in the history of modern philosophy in France: For the first time, secular moral philosophy was institutionalized as a professional scientific pursuit.

Thus conceived at the highest levels, moral reform was to percolate downward from the new Institute through the new system of public schools established along with the Institute in the fall of 1795: separate primary schools for each sex, providing a basic education in mathematics, reading, writing, and morality tailored to the different social roles appropriate to future female homemakers on the one hand, and male breadwinners on the other. A series of secondary schools, called *Ecoles centrales*, were to develop more specialized educational curricula and teacher training at the secondary level.[18] Adopting Cabanis's physiological theory of the differential intellectual potentials of the two sexes—and, conversely, rejecting Condorcet's Cartesian egalitarianism —the republican government excluded women from all public institutions of higher learning.[19]

The organizing principle of the new research groups, the research methods adopted in the Institute, and the new pedagogical techniques derived from them all embodied the Enlightenment credo that progress in human understanding depends on the analysis of empirical data. The first section of the "class of moral and political sciences" at the Institute was devoted to "the analysis of sensations and ideas."[20] Courses in the analytic method were designed for the new Central Schools. Analysis was to be applied to every form of human knowledge from botany to grammar and foreign language instruction.[21] In moral philosophy this

[17]François Bibal, *L'Institut de France* (Paris: Bibal, 1988), p. 20. See also Picavet, *Les Idéologues*, pp. 69–71, and Martin Staum, "The Class of Moral and Political Sciences, 1795–1803," *French Historical Studies*, vol. 11 (1980): 371–397.

[18]Robert R. Palmer, *The Improvement of Humanity* (Princeton, NJ: Princeton University Press, 1985), pp. 230–236, 242–256.

[19]See Jaton, "*La Définition de la féminité*, p. 189. See also Palmer, *The Improvement of Humanity*, pp. 231, 316. On the Cartesian feminist tradition, see Erica Harth, *Cartesian Women: Versions and Subversions of Rational Discourse in the Old Regime* (Ithaca, NY: Cornell University Press, 1992).

[20]Picavet, *Les Idéologues*, pp. 70–71.

[21]Ibid., pp. 32–39.

meant that one worked from particular examples to discover the underlying general rules of conduct. Indeed, if moral duty was the order of the day, "analysis" became the method, *par excellence*, toward the fulfillment of this end.

Thermidorian cultural policy thus effected a dramatic reorientation in the Revolution's relationship to Enlightenment philosophy. First, it represented an attempt to reassert the power of an officially sponsored academic philosophy over whatever mechanisms of private patronage, the salon, or the commercial marketplace might produce. Equally significant, especially for women, the new philosophical practices encouraged by the government, in sharp contrast to the prerevolutionary philosophical movement, privileged analytic over narrative modes of philosophical inquiry and exposition. Serious philosophical reflection ceased to be an intellectual enterprise open to the literate classes at large, and was now to become the exclusive domain of an officially sanctioned and subsidized corporation of professional academics.

A key motive behind these developments was the desire to temper public passions inflamed by market-driven literary culture. Personal happiness and the public good might be possible to marry with relative ease at the level of theoretical exposition, but when it came to public policy, secular materialists acknowledged the need for pedagogy and policing to ensure their harmonious union. Official academic culture would inculcate the chaste virtues of reason and self-discipline in the service of public morality and discourage a misguided submission to immediate personal desire. In generic terms, cultural authorities endorsed the analytic philosophical essay or treatise as a pedagogical antidote to prose fiction and especially novels, the most potentially inflammatory of modern literary forms. Even good, pedagogical novels aimed only to recount particular moral examples rather than to disclose general ethical truths.

Significantly, novels were also the one genre of moral philosophizing in which women were known to excel. So thermidorian cultural and educational policies specifically excluded women from the new arenas where serious philosophical discourse was to take place. At the same time they devalued the genre in which women might find an alternative venue for philosophical reflection.

I have dwelled on the broader cultural context in which Isabelle de Charrière found herself in 1794–1795 at such great length because it is absolutely critical to understanding the motivations behind, and the significance of, the introduction of Immanuel Kant's ethical writings into the French language and Charrière's response to them. Indeed, the links between the cultural policies of the thermidorian government, Kant's publication in France, and Charrière's novel are quite direct.

Within weeks of his speech to the Convention outlining his policy recommendations for moral reform, Henri Grégoire began making inquiries among German-speaking republican intellectuals about Kant, hoping to find in his writings a secular moral philosophy powerful enough to counteract the post-thermidorian Christian revival on the one hand, and the spread of atheistic materialism on the other.[22] Among the members of the Committee on Public Instruction and the new "Class of Moral and Political Sciences" at the Institute, the former priest, Grégoire remained the most concerned about the inadequacies of the purely materialist account of moral development.[23] Like Immanuel Kant, he doubted that an easy reconciliation between "happiness" and "virtue" was possible. And like Kant, he saw the logic of consequentialist reasoning as a slippery slope toward immorality—a license, down the line, to lie, cheat, or steal. For Grégoire, and people like him, virtuous behavior could only result from a disciplined restraint of people's natural inclination to pursue selfish pleasure. Perhaps the Kantian idea of a "categorical imperative" to live by universal ethical rules could reconcile secular materialism with some theory of an *a priori* moral absolute. The former priest hoped so.

News of French government interest in Kant spread quickly. The German-born and -educated journalist-translator Louis-Ferdinand Huber (1764–1804) wrote to his former mentor, Friedrich Schiller, on January 31, 1795:

> I made a first attempt to introduce a selection of Kantian philosophy in France by translating and offering long excerpts of Kant's article in the *Berlinische Monatschrift* on *Theory and Practice* and I sent it to a friend in Paris. Grégoire of the Committee on Public Instruction seems to have taken great pleasure in it and I think that a more complete essay on Kantian philosophy would be well received in a place where the end to the oppression of Robespierre

---

[22]Letter from Müller to Grégoire, October 27, 1794, cited in François Azouvi and Dominique Bourel, *De Königsberg à Paris* (Paris: Vrin, 1991), p. 68; and in Boas, *French Philosophies*, p. 168.

[23]Staum, *"Volney et l'idée d'une science morale à l'Institut,"* pp. 133–134.

has provoked a lively movement toward more serious scientific learning.[24]

He was right. The government found in Kant's political writings a powerful idiom for legitimating its faith in a secular republicanism rooted in the fraternal discourse of universal reason. In March 1795, Huber reported that plans were under way for a French translation of Kant's *Perpetual Peace.*[25] Then in April an article on Kant, written by Huber, appeared in the *Moniteur,* which celebrated him as a German genius "capable of giving philosophy a new life" in France.[26] The next year, 1796, *Perpetual Peace* was published in Paris by Henri Jansen, with a government subsidy.[27] Kant thus became in the eyes of some French government officials the thermidorian philosopher *par excellence:* an academic who stood apart from worldly affairs and advocated conformity to philosophical principles rooted in abstract reason rather than in religious faith or historical materialism. He seemed to offer a promise for the sort of moral stability critical to the success of the secular republicanism of the French Directorate government.

Louis-Ferdinand Huber was not working alone in bringing Kant to the French.[28] He had installed himself in Neuchâtel in the summer of 1794, and there, in the continuous company of Isabelle de Charrière—already a noted novelist—and the soon-to-be-noted novelist-politician Benjamin Constant, he continued his studies of Kant and began his translation of the essay on *Theory and Practice.*[29] In these same months, as Huber strategically courted the patronage of the Committee on Public Instruction, Benjamin Constant returned to Paris in the late fall and there joined the circle of secular philosophers who were hammering out

[24]For Huber's correspondence with Schiller and Grégoire in the spring of 1795, see François Picavet, *"Philosophie de Kant en France de 1773 à 1814,"* preface to Immanuel Kant, *Critique de la raison pratique,* Picavet, trans. (Paris: Alcan, 1888), pp. i–xxxvii; B. Munteano, *"Episodes kantiens en Suisse et en France sous le Directoire," Revue de littérature comparée* vol. 4, no. 3 (July–September 1935): 420–237, esp. p. 410; and Azouvi and Bourel, *De Konigsberg à Paris,* p. 70.

[25]Azouvi and Bourel, *De Königsberg à Paris,* p. 71.

[26]See Azouvi and Bourel, *De Königsberg à Paris,* p. 68; and Boas, *French Philosophies,* p. 167.

[27]See Azouvi and Bourel, *De Königsberg à Paris,* p. 69; and Hesse, *Publishing and Cultural Politics,* p. 192.

[28]See Munteano, *"Episodes kantiens en Suisse,"* pp. 407–408.

[29]See Azouvi and Bourel, *De Königsberg à Paris,* pp. 69–70; and Charrière's letters of December 16–20, 1974, and December 18, 1794, in Isabelle de Charrière, *Oeuvres complètes,* vol. IV, pp. 670, 673.

a secular account of the origins of morality. Throughout the fall and winter, Constant functioned as a liaison between the little Kant reading group in Neuchâtel and Parisian intellectual debate.

During this same period, he remained in continuous correspondence with Charrière who was by this time both his mistress and his intellectual collaborator. Over the course of the fall, they hotly debated the differences between a materialist account of the foundation of morals in a physiology of sensation or correct training, on the one hand, and Kant's theory that categorical moral imperatives are derived from synthetic, *a priori* ideas on the other. On December 18, 1794, Charrière sent Constant in Paris an extraordinary diagram of the two competing genealogies of morals. She placed a question mark strategically between the two options (see Figure 5.1). Constant responded definitively on behalf of the materialists, and he would work out his consequentialist response to Charrière's diagrammatic query in a pamphlet titled, *On the Right to Lie*, the following year. Charrière's own response to the new materialist theories of morals that were shaping thermidorian cultural policies on the one hand and to Kant's theory on the other, was tellingly, not a philosophical tract, but a novel: *Trois Femmes* (*Three Women*).[30]

The novel first appeared under the pseudonym of the "Abbé de la Tour" in the fall of 1795, just as the new research group in "moral and political sciences" was being installed at the Institute in Paris. The frontispiece to the novel represented allegorically the two competing moral genealogies she had outlined in her letter to Constant (Figure 5.2)—absolute duty depicted as the light of the sun, and the consequentialist logic of the materialists as the everyday world of the human city. The book is divided into two parts: Part one is a tale recounted by its pseudonymous author/narrator, describing the moral dilemmas of three women of his acquaintance. Part two shifts into the epistolary mode and consists of a series of letters written principally by one of the three women to the Abbé/narrator. Taken together, the two parts of the novel are at every level a searing *cri de coeur* against the emerging cultural agenda of the Committee on Public Instruction in Paris.

In response to the postrevolutionary cult of the philosopher as

---

[30]Charrière began writing *Trois Femmes* in November or December 1794. It was completed by early April 1795. It first appeared in a German translation by Huber in Leipzig in the fall of 1795, under the pseudonym of the Abbé de la Tour, and then in a mutilated French edition, printed in London in 1796. See Philippe Godet, *Madame de Charrière et ses amis (1740–1805)*. 2 vols. (Geneva: Julien, 1906), vol. II, pp. 215, 217, 232. See also Charrière, *Oeuvres complètes*, vol. IX, pp. 26–30.

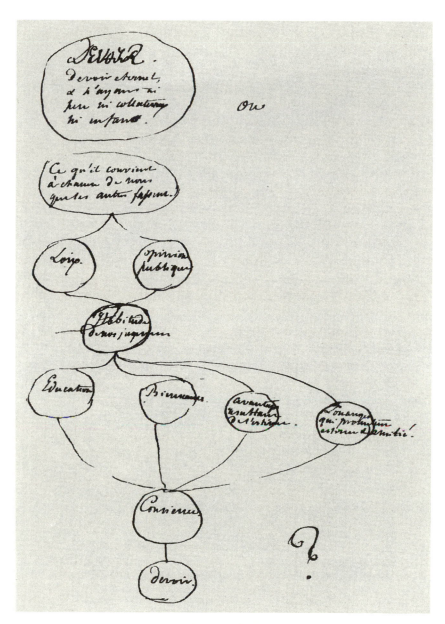

Figure 5.1 A sketch of two genealogies of the concept of moral duty, sent by Isabelle de Charrière to Benjamin Constant, December 18, 1794. Slatkine Reprints, Geneva.

Figure 5.2 An allegorical representation of the two genealogies of moral duty. Frontispiece of the first complete edition of Isabelle de Charrière's *Trois Femmes* (Leipzig [Zurich], 1798). Slatkine Reprints, Geneva.

an officially sanctioned public servant—be that philosopher Voltaire, Rousseau, or Kant—Charrière offered the pseudonymous and generic figure of the cosmopolitan, freethinking Abbé de la Tour, no doubt an ironic reference to the ex-*abbé*, Henri Grégoire. Indeed, the second part of the novel is an explicitly satirical critique of the educational and cultural reforms espoused by Grégoire and his sympathizers during the thermidorian regime. Here Charrière overtly expresses her misgivings about the sanitized literary culture to be proffered in the new republican textbooks, public libraries, and curriculum of the Central Schools. She denounces, even more adamantly, the professionalization of philosophy and the emergence of a state-sponsored author-cult: "The philosophical clergy," she writes, "is as much a clergy as any other, and it was not worth the trouble to drive the curé from Saint Sulpice in order to ordain the priests of the Pantheon."[31]

At a deeper level, she expressed her dissent from the thermidorian cultural regime through her very choice of genre. In response to official support for the analytic philosophical essay or treatise, Charrière revived the popular prerevolutionary genre of the *conte philosophique*, the philosophical tale. The opening of the novel is an explicit pastiche of Voltaire's *Candide*.[32] And by naming her principal female protagonist Emilie she adds yet another layer of allusion to the prerevolutionary tradition of the philosophical narrative, this time to Rousseau's *Emile*. Charrière's story, however, is decidedly postrevolutionary. Unlike her prerevolutionary predecessors, who provided their heroes with the guidance of a philosopher-preceptor, Charrière has her innocent heroine cast out into the world "with no other mentor than herself."

Finally, while the publication of Kant's essays in France was made possible through government subsidy, Charrière's novel was financed by raising private subscriptions, with any profits from its sale to go to a female friend in financial distress.[33] The composition and publication of

---

[31]Charrière, *Trois Femmes*, in *Oeuvres complètes*, vol. IX, p. 106. See also, ibid., vol. IX, pp. 100–105. She was to develop this criticism of the modern author-cult more fully in a later essay titled *"De l'Auteur,"* which unfortunately was inadvertently omitted from the recent edition of her complete works and consequently remains unpublished. See Jeroom Vercruysse, "The Publication of the *Oeuvres complètes:* Navigating the Risky Waters of the Unforeseeable," in *Isabelle de Charrière Belle van Zuylen*, Béatrice Fink, ed., a special issue of *Eighteenth-Century Life*, vol. 13, new series 1 (February 1989): 69–78.

[32]See the editor's introduction to *Trois Femmes* in Charrière, *Oeuvres complètes*, vol. IX, p. 23.

[33]See Godet, *Isabelle de Charrière et ses amis*, vol. II, pp. 216–218; and Charrière, *Oeuvres complètes*, vol. V, p. 44. On Charrière's complex relationship to the process of publica-

Charrière's novel were thus made possible by the persistence of the textual practices and modes of production characteristic of the oppositional enlightenment of the Old Regime, rather than the official enlightenment of the new one.

However rooted in certain prerevolutionary intellectual traditions Charrière's novels might have been, her objection to the thermidorian creation of a professional academic class of philosophers was not born of nostalgia for Old Regime culture. It was a decidedly postrevolutionary, and a decidedly feminist, response to the problem of modern ethical self-constitution as it was presented by Kant in the essay on *Theory and Practice*. It raised a question that Kant had too readily dismissed: What was the part played by sexual difference in the fabrication of a postrevolutionary conception of moral autonomy, which was purportedly the foundation of selfhood?

The preface to *Three Women* opens in a salon with a group of friends discussing the meaning of duty. There is a theologian, a Kantian, and a sensationalist. Each one stakes out his own theory. The good-natured Abbé de la Tour suggests to his hostess that the complexities of Kant's theory of the categorical moral imperative can perhaps be best illuminated by the stories of three women of his acquaintance. In Part one of the novel, the Abbé recounts their tales: Each woman finds herself caught in a moral compromise in which she sacrifices absolute virtue for the sake of happiness—both her own and that of those she loves.

Charrière's tale is at one level a witty exposition of the consequentialist critique of Kantian morality that was being elaborated at that very moment by numerous contemporaries, and, in particular, by her friend and lover Benjamin Constant.[34] But it is more than that. It offers a critique of the Kantian moral system not only from the perspective of contingent versus absolute values but on the basis of even a more fundamental problem—the nature of moral autonomy itself. *Three Women* is

tion, see Susan K. Jackson, "Publishing Without Perishing: Isabelle de Charrière a.k.a. *la mouche du coche*," in Elizabeth C. Goldsmith and Dena Goodman, eds., *Going Public: Women and Publishing in Early Modern France* (Ithaca, NY: Cornell University Press), pp. 195–209.

[34]Immanuel Kant, "On the Proverb: That May Be True in Theory But Is of No Practical Use (1793)," in *Perpetual Peace*, pp. 61–92. The two relevant consequentialist critics in this context are Charles Garves and Benjamin Constant. For Garves's critique, see Kant, "On the Proverb," in *Perpetual Peace*, pp. 63–71; and for Constant's critique, see Behler, "*Kant vu par le groupe de Coppet*," *Actes de Coppet*, pp. 137–140; Azouvi and Bourel, *De Königsberg à Paris*, pp. 95–101; and B. Munteano, "*Episodes kantiens*," pp. 407, 444–445.

in fact a systematic rewriting of Kant's essay *On the Proverb: That May Be True in Theory But Is of No Practical Use* from a woman's point of view. Read as a feminist, rather than a consequentialist, response, the novel makes clear that it is the question of autonomy, rather than contingency, that lies at the heart of her critique of the Kantian moral system. Indeed, it is actually a critique of the sexist assumptions of *both* Kantian and sensationalist moral theory.

Kant's essay was intended as a concise refutation, for a broad audience, of consequentialist reasoning. In it, he illustrates the three maxims of the categorical imperative in the form of a response to *three men:* "the man of affairs," represented by Charles Garves; "the statesman," represented by Thomas Hobbes; and the "man of the world," represented by Moses Mendelssohn.[35] His purpose is to demonstrate that the *a priori* categorical imperative can and should be sustained not only in theory, but also in practice by men in the real world.

The man of affairs must never lie because he must "act only on a maxim that [he] can at the same time will to be universal." This is because, as the statesman's case illustrates, he must "act so as to treat humanity in oneself and others only as an end in itself and never merely as a means." In other words, to assume your own moral autonomy, you must respect that of others—that is, you must posit their freedom and equality as well as your own. Finally, the condition of the "man of the world," he who seeks universal freedom, illustrates the third maxim, that you must "act so that your will can at the same time regard itself as giving in its maxims universal laws," good for all times and all places.[36] True to the analytic method of philosophical exposition, the stories of Kant's three men serve as examples whose purpose is simply to demonstrate the three universal axioms of the categorical imperative.

Kant's theory presupposes a universal freedom and equality among moral agents. Though their circumstances may be unequal (some rich, some poor, etc.) they must be able, at a minimum, to recognize their shared humanity with others in order to act as autonomous moral agents. In a critical passage of the essay, however, Kant explicitly excludes two categories of individuals from full participation in the "originating contract" among citizens, which is a precondition for the func-

---

[35]Immanuel Kant, "On the Proverb," in *Perpetual Peace*, pp. 61–92.

[36]See Warner Wick, "Introduction" to Immanuel Kant, *Ethical Philosophy: Grounding for the Metaphysics of Morals . . .* , James W. Ellington, trans. (Indianapolis: Hackett, 1982), pp. xvii–xx.

tioning of the three maxims of the categorical imperative: women and children.[37]

Women and children, Kant writes, *by nature*, do not have the mental capacity necessary to achieve maturity, that is, autonomous self-determination. Servants, though for more historically contingent reasons, are also dependent, and are thus excluded from active participation in legislative rule making. Women and servants—the one by reason of nature and the other by social standing—are therefore passive citizens who must obey the law even though they are only virtually represented —through the husband and master—in its enactment. More deeply, Kant viewed moral law as given rather than made; therefore, his views on women denied them the capacity, and the dignity, to be able to choose to obey moral law.

What Charrière discovered in her study of postrevolutionary ethical debates, then, was that both Kantian and sensationalist theories resulted in the same consequences for women. Whether, as Kant argued, women were by nature mentally incapable of apprehending and abiding by *a priori* laws, or, as the sensationalists believed, they were physiologically incapable of extrapolating general rules from particular experiences, it amounted to the same thing. Women were not capable of moral self-governance and, hence, should be juridically subordinated to men.

Charrière's "three women" take on a different significance in this light. They serve as three counterexamples of postrevolutionary women who, by the fact of sexual difference, are put in a different and unequal relationship to both moral and juridical law. Her examples thus pose a somewhat different question to the Kantian ethical model than the one raised by consequentialists: Can women act morally without recourse

[37]Kant, "On the Proverb," in *Perpetual Peace*, p. 76. There is now a great deal of feminist scholarship concerning Kant's attitudes toward women and gender. Much of this work has focused on his anthropological writings, where he offers his most fully developed reflections on these questions. For the current discussion of women and gender in the anthropological writings, see Olga Lucia Valbuena, "The Charming Distinction: *Urteil* as the En-gendering of Reason in Kant's Thought," *Genders*, no. 4 (March 1989): 87–102. The feminist discussion of Kant's ethical writings has, for the most part, followed in the path of other materialist critiques. For a very suggestive article that moves beyond this general trend, see Beverly Brown, "'I Read the Metaphysics of Morals and the Categorical Imperative and It Doesn't Help Me a Bit,' Maria von Herbert to Immanuel Kant, August 1791," *Oxford Literary Review*, vol. 8, nos. 1–2 (special issue on "Sexual Difference"): 155–163. See also Robin Schott, *Cognition and Eros: A Critique of the Kantian Paradigm* (Boston: Beacon Press, 1988); and Robin Schott, ed., *Feminist Interpretations of Immanuel Kant* (University Park: Pennsylvania State University Press, 1997).

to any general moral precepts, whatever their origin?[38] Rather than seeking to demonstrate that women are able to act like men, Charrière sets out to explore the deeper question of what it would mean to act ethically without general rules to guide our behavior.

Let us consider her three stories a bit more closely. Charrière's three women are all legally independent of both fathers or husbands: All are in their majority but are either unmarried or widowed. They have no male authorities to guide them or to answer to. And, like Kant's men, Charrière's women represent three juridically distinct spheres: the private sphere of the household, the civil sphere constituted through marriage, and the cosmopolitan sphere of multinational business.

The first story concerns Josephine, faithful servant to the young, orphaned Emilie. Josephine's understanding of her duty as a servant is to sacrifice everything—including her honor, if need be—for her mistress. Thus she succumbs to the seductions of the man-servant at the nearby chateau, in part because she likes him, and in part because she expects to derive benefits from the liaison for her mistress.

But Charrière is interested in Josephine not because of her calculation, but because of her status as a moral actor. She is, in fact, doubly excluded from participation in the Kantian self-regulating moral community on the basis of her sex and her social status. If, by nature, she is incapable of self-rule, how can she therefore be held accountable for her actions by whatever moral philosophy they are to be judged? Josephine points out that the blame for her lapse in virtue should lie with her mistress, because it was *she* who failed in her duty as mistress to regulate her servant's moral conduct effectively.[39]

But, of course, the *female* mistress herself did not have the ultimate capacity to lay down the law in the home, according to either Kant or the sensationalists. Nor did she even have the legal authority. In fact, the story of Josephine was taken from Charrière's personal experience. Her own chambermaid and companion, Henriette Monachon, had a second illegitimate child in 1795 and refused to marry the father. As a conse-

---

[38]Let me be clear here that I do not necessarily mean law in the juridical sense, but rather in the normative sense, referring to universal and equal application. Kant writes, "The notion of duty can only contain self-constraint (by the idea of the law itself)", cited in Immanuel Kant, *Ethical Philosophy: The Complete Texts of Grounding for the Metaphysics of Morals, and Metaphysical Principles of Virtue, part II of The Metaphysics of Morals* (James W. Ellington, trans., Introduction by Warner A. Wick (Indianapolis: Hackett Publishing Company, 1983).

[39]Charrière, *Trois Femmes*, in *Oeuvres complètes*, vol. IX, pp. 46.

quence, the Council of State of the Principality of Neuchâtel found her guilty of moral depravity and expelled her from the principality, *despite* the petitions and pleas of her mistress, Charrière.[40] Deprived, in both moral theory and historical reality, of the power to regulate the morals of her own household, Charrière, in her fictionalized version, imagined a recourse beyond both moral and juridical law: The young mistress, Emilie, permits herself to lie in order to manipulate the two servants into a marriage, thus preserving, legally at least, the honor and employment of the faithful and devoted servant girl. Charrière thus raises the following question: When both servant and mistress have no apparent capacity to embrace universal rules, and no say in making the civil laws, do they nonetheless have a duty to abide by them?

The second story is that of the young mistress Emilie herself. She is the orphan of a French noble émigré. It was not her choice to leave revolutionary France and thus renounce any legal claim to her family's fortune. She is deprived of both fortune and country by no act of her own will. Emilie falls in love with Théobald d'Altendorf, the heir to the local German manor. Lacking the social and financial resources to earn the approval of his socially conservative parents, does Emilie have a categorical duty to forgo her love? Or might she elope with the young man without dishonor?

Her moral situation is further complicated by the fact that if she marries the German baron she will by law lose her French citizenship. Is love of country a higher duty than private love? Here again it becomes clear than the line between moral virtue and civic duty cannot be drawn absolutely. Emilie's dilemma was not circumstantial; it was categorical: All French women who married foreigners by law lost their native citizenship and were literally assimilated into the husband's legal identity.[41] In other words, she was forced into making a decision on the basis of its consequences because as a woman she was unable to make it as either a morally or a juridically autonomous subject.

Unlike a man in her circumstances, the generic fact of Emilie's sexual status as a woman put her private desire for self-determination at moral odds with her civic identity and duty. Emilie chooses to follow

---

[40]Charrière, *Oeuvres complètes*, vol. V, p. 9.

[41]On the question of marriage and female citizenship status in the eighteenth century, see Isadore Alauzet, *De la Qualité de français et de la naturalisation* (Paris: Cosse-Marchel, 1867), pp. 17, 20; and Carla Hesse, "Reading Signatures: Female Authorship and Revolutionary Law in France, 1750–1850," *Eighteenth-Century Studies* vol. 22, no. 3 (Spring 1989): 469–487.

her desire, but at the loss of her legal citizenship and her autonomous legal identity as an unwed woman in her majority. The disgrace and disinheritance risked by the attempted elopement of the young couple is narrowly averted by the intervention of Emilie's friend and mentor Constance, who rallies the support of Théobald's parents for their marriage before the couple's flight becomes public. The moral disgrace of their attempt is thus concealed through a fictional sleight-of-hand, a white lie.

Charrière's third woman, her "woman of the world," is Emilie's friend from the previous story—Constance. A French-born widow, she is the sole heiress to a great fortune made unscrupulously in the French colonies and now secured in investments throughout Europe.[42] Though acquired by immoral means (the slave trade, one suspects), her claim to the fortune is, she reports, legally secure. Moreover, there are no retrievable traces of the private persons from whom the fortune had been extracted by her husband's ancestors. In the face of these circumstances, did she have a moral obligation to restore the fortune and, if so, to whom? Constance is literally a woman of the world in the sense that, through marriage, then widowhood, and then emigration, her lineage (both familial and national) has been obliterated. Perhaps, Emilie suggests, she has an obligation at least to restore the fortune to the various states in which it was made. But her fortune is now dispersed throughout the globe. Therefore, to which nation should it be restored? To what nation does she owe allegiance? That of her birth? Of her dead father? Or of her dead husband? What moral obligation does she have to atone for crimes she did not commit, or to benefit nations she did not choose? Finding herself beyond the laws of any nation, Constance decides that she is free to make use of her fortune as best she can for the good of those around her.[43] The legal obliteration of women's identity makes other

---

[42]Charrière, *Trois Femmes*, in *Oeuvres complètes*, vol. IX, pp. 63–65. At one level, Constance's story is an explicit rewriting of the example Kant employs in his response to Garves, but from the female point of view. Both stories examine the moral dilemmas of transmitting an inheritance under circumstances in which a lineage has been disrupted. See Kant, "On the Proverb," in *Perpetual Peace*, p. 69.

[43]While there are many important studies of the dramatic changes in European family law during the era of the French Revolution, to my knowledge there is as yet no substantial study of the complex legal question of female inheritance, and of the legal status of widowed women, in particular, that might offer a definitive resolution to the tangled legal question of the civil status of a women in Constance's circumstances with regard to either her citizenship or her inheritance rights. In France, these were matters of continuous debate and reform from 1789 until the promulgation of the Civil Code in 1804. For

than consequentialist acts impossible. She could not be a universal moral subject even if she wanted to be, because her moral parameters are simply not possible to determine in absolute terms.

As these stories make apparent, Charrière's central criticism of Kant's essay on *Theory and Practice* did not reside in the problem of contingency per se—that is, in the distinction between theory and practice. Rather, it resided in the question of autonomy—in the "natural" distinction Kant makes between man and woman. The Kantian model, Charrière revealed, left the problem of female moral autonomy *categorically* contingent on women's relationships to men and their laws. They had no moral standing on their own. Moral contingency was a symptom of their being categorically denied the right of autonomous self-constitution. Her critique of Kant's examples, then, was not simply based on the consequentialist perspective. It was written from the perspective of those who remained categorically outside both moral and juridical law.

Charrière's three women, like Kant's modern men, are postrevolutionary actors, who, freed from their lineages through political upheaval, confront the possibility of self-governance, but from a very different point of view. Each of the three women in fact inhabit a legal twilight zone. They are all adult women, between or beyond father and husband, and between or beyond nations. But that postrevolutionary world still did not offer them the Kantian possibility to reconstitute themselves as independent subjects of the law, capable of imagining their will as universal.

In the end, Charrière's story becomes a story of how these three women constitute their ethical life beyond the laws of men and without regard to absolutes. *Trois Femmes,* as scandalized readers recognized at the time, was the story of a band of outlaws; a story of the ethical life of women beyond the laws of propertied men.[44] Charrière's three women

---

current literature that most directly addresses the questions her situation raises, see J.-F. Chassaing, "*Les Successions et les donations à la fin de l'Ancien Régime et sous la Révolution,*" *Droits et Cultures* (1982): 85–111; André Dejace, *Les Règles de la dévolution successorale sous la Révolution (1789–1794)* (Bruyant: Bruxelles, 1957); M. Garaud et R. Szamkiewicz, *La Révolution française et la famille* (Paris: PUF, 1978); James Traer, *Marriage and the Family in Eighteenth-Century France* (Ithaca, NY: Cornell, 1980); and Elizabeth Darrow, *Revolution in the Household* (Princeton, NJ: Princeton University Press, 1989).

[44]Benjamin Constant warned Charrière that the novel would be considered scandalous. And, indeed, it generated considerable private and public controversy concerning its morality both during and after its publication. The first French edition was heavily censored on religious, political, and moral grounds by the London agent, the Catholic-

band together through self-election and form an outlaw community based on the ethical principle of total sacrifice to one another, and a reservation of the right to bend rules that they had no part in creating. This female outlaw bond is symbolically represented by the gift from Constance to Emilie of a ruby, bearing the interlocking first initials of the two women, on the eve of Emilie's marriage to Théobald. This scene—the gift of the jewel from one woman to the other—ends Part one of the book by sealing the outlaw bond between the women *before* the legal bond between man and wife.[45]

But perhaps the views of both Kant and the sensationalists regarding women's nature were simply wrong. Perhaps, given an opportunity, both women and servants could become morally autonomous actors, capable of self-critical maturity. The second part of the novel addresses these possibilities through a series of pedagogical experiments intended as a countermodel to the sex-specific curriculum being devised in republican France. Emilie's young husband Théobald decides to devote himself to the thermidorian pedagogical project of bringing talented men in the community to critical maturity through enlightened education. Like Grégoire and the Committee on Public Instruction in Paris, he builds a school and a library in the local village and supervises its progress. Simultaneously, Constance embarks on two parallel experiments. Two baby boys—one of noble, the other of plebeian origin—are accidentally switched at birth and Constance views this accident as an opportunity to see what happens if they are raised in absolute equality. It would then be possible to determine whether traits of nobility are biologically or socially transmitted.

A second opportunity presents itself when two twins, one male and one female, are born to a single woman who dies in childbirth. Constance decides to adopt them and then raise them with all the usual marks of gender inverted: the boy is to be named Charlotte, and the girl

royalist emigré Lally-Tollendal, before its publication (1796). Both the German edition (1795) and the first complete French edition (1798) met with harsh criticism in the press for immorality, particularly because of Charrière's indulgent view of Josephine's sexual appetites. For a more complete discussion of the reception of the novel in the French, Swiss, and German press, see the editor's introduction to *Trois Femmes*, in Charrière, *Oeuvres complètes*, vol. IX, pp. 30–33. For censorship of the first French edition, see Denise Hermann, "*La Première édition des* Trois Femmes *de Mme de Charrière*," *Etudes de Lettres*, no. 33 (1938): 76–89; and Jean-Daniel Candaux, "*Notes sur deux éditions mutilées de Mme de Charrière*," *Revue des Sciences Humaines*, vol. 137 (Janvier–Mars 1970): 87–92.

[45]Charrière, *Trois Femmes*, in, *Oeuvres complètes*, vol. IX, p. 85.

Charles; she is to learn tasks appropriate to boys, he is taught those normally assigned to girls. Constance writes:

> This ought to suffice, and it should prove to everyone that there is nothing in the nature of man and woman that determines anything whatsoever relating to our intellectual capabilities.[46]

Constance's experiments were manifestly directed against Pierre Cabanis's and Kant's categorical exceptions of women to the rights to higher education and citizenship because of the purported "facts of nature."[47] They seemed to promise the possibility under appropriate social circumstances of female assimilation into the male social compact.

But Charrière left the outcome of these pedagogical experiments in limbo. In fact, resistance to settling definitively the nature of sexual difference—and, consequently, the capacity of her three women as moral agents—emerges in the second part of novel as a central thematic preoccupation. Thus Constance's confident assertion that her pedagogical experiment with the twins will irrefutably determine the intellectual equality of the sexes is immediately followed by a long meditation on the limited efficacy of empirical evidence to prove absolute truths. She observes that even though the equal capacities of women have been demonstrated convincingly time and again, human beings need, and will always need to see things proved over and over again. She then offers what can only be read as a Humeian proverbial rejoinder to Kant's own proverbial point of departure for his essay. She writes to the Abbé, "The proverb that says: 'Two certainties are worth more than one,' has it not greater wisdom and does it not better suit the imperfections of human faculties?"[48] Moral truth, then, like the ontological truth about sexual difference upon which it stands, she suggests, is only probabilistic and only meaningful through its enactment—in every instance in which it is demonstrated. There can, in this sense, be no end to the story of sexual difference, nor of its consequence for moral conduct, it will always be in need of further determination. There is no *a priori* female self. What it is to be a woman cannot be answered, categorically, once and for all. It will have to be determined every day in the life of every woman.

This ultimate indeterminacy of sexual and moral identity is dramatically enacted through the narrative strategy of the second part of

---

[46]Charrière, *Trois Femmes*, in *Oeuvres complètes*, vol. IX, p. 115.
[47]Kant, "On the Proverb," in *Perpetual Peace*, p. 76.

the novel, which works in a riptide-like relationship to its thematic content. Thematically, the first part of the novel offers case studies of women at the moral crossroads between a traditional world bounded by lineage and a modern one rooted in self-determination. The second part turns to the efforts of women to construct a new, postrevolutionary order through a series of pedagogical experiments and reforms. But it immediately becomes apparent that the very textual basis for establishing this new order can never be firmly grounded. With Part two, the narrative form of the novel shifts from a stable third-person account of the stories of the three women, recounted in the past tense by the Abbé de la Tour, to a series of letters written in the first-person present tense, primarily by Constance, to the Abbé de la Tour in Paris, reporting on the pedagogical reforms that she, Théobald, and Emilie are undertaking in Altendorf. The shift to the epistolary form thus sets the pedagogical problem temporally into the open-ended present.

Moreover, though a certain degree of unity in the narrative voice is sustained in the second part through Constance's role as principal correspondent with the Abbé de la Tour, Constance's letters are never entirely her own: Frequently Théobald interrupts her as she writes, inserting his own, often conflicting, account of the subject at hand, or adding an ironic postscript. Thus, the differences of opinion between the reformers in Altendorf, and most notably between Théobald and Constance on the question of sexual equality, are not simply reported in the letters, but are enacted through their very composition. There is only one set of letters to the Abbé, but these letters are many-voiced and embody conflicting and constantly shifting viewpoints.[49] It is thus the recipient, rather than the sender(s) of the letters, the reader rather than the author(s), who comes to form the only stable point of reference for the narrative.

Ultimately, the letter-writing voice is not merely destabilized, but disrupted entirely by the appearance in Altendorf of British troops. Both Constance and Emilie fear that they will be identified as French women and, consequently, delivered by the English to their distant relatives in France. They thus determine to flee into further obscurity along the bor-

---

[48]Charrière, *Trois Femmes*, in *Oeuvres complètes*, vol. IX, p. 116. For Charrière's abiding enthusiasm for and interest in David Hume (whom she met in April of 1767), see her correspondence concerning Hume, in the *Oeuvres complètes*, vol. I, p. 200; vol. II, pp. 11, 39; vol. III, p. 425; vol. V, pp. 296, 336, 383; vol. VI, pp. 242, 248, 263, 276, 289, 294, 298, 323, 330, 336, 432, 438, 448, 450, 499.

[49]Ibid., vol. IX, pp. 94, 112, 116–117, 122–123.

ders of the Rhine. This disruption by the flight of two of its (female) authors is literalized in a final letter comprising of a series of disjointed and fragmentary passages, punctuated by long elisions, in which Constance informs the Abbé that in order to remain anonymous they will no longer be able to send or receive letters.[50] Thus the stories of the three women do not end with their coming into full moral personhood. Rather, the protagonists simply move on.

Instead of opting for either the idealist or the sensationalist solution of demanding entrance for women into the moral compact of universal law or general precept, Charrière held on to the separate and contingent relation of women to both moral and juridical law. Emilie may become *legally* German in marrying Théobald, but she reserves her right *to act* like a French woman. Charrière thus offered a reworking of postrevolutionary philosophical identity as the figure of the outlaw. She sought to expose the limits of both Kantian and sensationalist moral systems from the perspective of the categorically subordinate outsider. In so doing, she drew from the French prerevolutionary traditions of the underground Enlightenment its pseudonymous and contingent relationship to the law, and its use of ironic narrative to undermine and expose.

Her refusal to write an end to the story of gender identity was also a refusal to determine where women should ultimately stand in relation to moral rules. Moral autonomy remains as elusive as the ultimate meaning of womanhood. Through her resistance to closure, a gesture common to many of Charrière's works, she ended her novel by celebrating the power of narration itself.[51] Thus, in response to Théobald's impatience to institute a new order rooted in moral perfection, Constance retorts, "*Il faut se contenter de louvoyer*" (We must be content with tacking, improvising).[52]

Charrière constituted postrevolutionary female moral agency as contingent on, though not independent of, the law. Like the pseudonymous authorial identity, the Charrièrian moral actor has no *a priori* existence independent of a particular problem or task. Charrière's *Trois Femmes* thus enacted an alternative ethics to that advanced by the thermidorian regime. In response to the postrevolutionary ideal of the philosopher as an autonomous moral actor, devoted to the universal

---

[50]Ibid., vol. IX, p. 124.

[51]See Elizabeth J. MacArthur, "Devious Narratives: Refusal of Closure in Two Eighteenth-Century Epistolary Novels," *Eighteenth-Century Studies,* vol. 2, no. 1 (Fall 1987): 1–20.

[52]Charrière, *Trois Femmes,* in *Oeuvres complètes,* vol. IX, p. 110.

good of the public, Charrière offered an outlaw ethics of acting in the best interests of private individuals in particular circumstances, of contingent self-constitution in relation to both inlaws—husbands, parents —and the outlaw band. This conception of the self as ever-fleeting, moving always on the margins, marked a departure, not only from Kant but from Voltaire as well. Unlike her revolutionary predecessors, Charrière did not seek entry into the male legal compact but, rather, the freedom to move, like Constance and Emilie, always along and across its borders.

Charrière emerged from the revolutionary experience convinced that there existed no absolute moral autonomy or political certainty. Thus she wrote to her friend Mlle Henriette L'Hardy in the fall of 1794:

> My skepticism is ever-growing, and I cannot resolve to be very democratic, even in the bosom of a tyrannical monarchy, nor to be very aristocratic within even the most chaotic of republics. . . . I think about these great, irresolvable questions as infrequently as I can, and limit myself to little indignities and to lesser, individual, private sorrows.[53]

Contingent reasoning thus became for Charrière more than a weapon to criticize the sexual inequality of republican "moral science." It was also the shifting ground on which an ethics—at once skeptical and pragmatic—could be imagined for modern woman.

[53]Letter form Isabelle de Charrière to Mlle Hardy, September 26, 1794, cited in Philippe Godet, *Madame de Charrière et ses amis* (Geneva: Slatkine Reprints, 1973), 2 vols., vol. II, pp. 134–135.

CHAPTER SIX

Fiction as Philosophy

In order to destroy the empire that the miraculous enjoyed, reason alone was not sufficient. Something stronger, and of greater penetration was necessary. Cervantes created a new path and he has had a prodigious success.
—Mme Adélaïde de Souza (1794)[1]

[In a Republic,] literature, properly speaking, becomes women's domain and men consecrate themselves uniquely to higher philosophy.
—Mme Germaine de Staël (1800)[2]

L iterature, as Mme de Souza and Mme de Staël so eloquently testify, was to become the chosen arena for female self-constitution and philosophical reflection in modern France. This turn to literature can be explained, in part, by the formal exclusion of women from higher education, and hence from all institutional forms of higher intellectual pursuit, until the first decades of the twentieth century. But it was not simply by default that women took up fiction as a preferred space for inquiry into the nature of the modern self. In contrast to scientific forms of inquiry and description, literature held out the possibility for women to carve out spaces of cultural autonomy within the larger context of their social, juridical, and political subordination. More deeply, literature made it possible for them to assert the specificity of their experience as women without falling into the trap of biological essentialism.

In the wake of the French Revolution, scientists elaborated new biological theories of gender difference as a means of justifying the continued civil and political subordination of women.[3] Early in the Revo-

---

[1]Mme Adélaïde de Souza, Countess of Flahaut, *Adèle de Sénange ou lettres de Lord Sydenham* (London: Debrett, 1794), p. x.

[2]Mme Germaine de Staël, *De la Littérature* (orig. ed., Paris: Maradan, 1800) (Paris: Garnier-Flammarion, 1991), p. 335.

[3]Geneviève Fraisse has charted the trajectory of this discourse from Pierre Roussel, *Système physique et moral de la femme* (1775) to Pierre-Jean-Georges Cabanis, *Rapport du physique et du moral de l'homme* (1802) and Julien-Joseph Virey, *De la Femme sous ses rapports physiologique, moral et littéraire* (1823) and *De la Physiologie dans ses rapports avec la philosophie* (1844). See Geneviève Fraisse, *Muse de la raison. Démocratie et exclusion des femmes en France* (Paris: Gallimard, 1995). See also Lynn Hunt, *The Family Romance of the French Rev-*

lution, the Marquis de Condorcet and others had put the lie to the traditional biological argument that man was destined to rule woman in modern political affairs simply because of his superior physical strength.[4] Advocates of women's political rights argued, following John Locke, that the capacity for self-government resided not in physical force, but in the ability to reason—a capacity shared equally by both sexes. Mental equality between the sexes thus conjured up the specter of female self-governance.

The new biological science of the postrevolutionary period was aimed directly at this threat. In 1802, Pierre Cabanis, most notably, argued in his *Rapports du physique et du moral de l'homme* (*The Relation Between Physical and Moral Man*), that the capacity for independent reasoning was an attribute of the male sex alone.[5] According to Cabanis, the male sexual organ functioned independent of the brain, while female sexuality was not specific to an organ. Rather female sexuality permeated the entire body, including the brain, which it linked to the particular aims of reproduction. In this new biology, women were seen as unsuited to govern, not because of physical weakness, but rather because of mental incapacity.[6]

Based on these new theories, a full-blown assault was launched, not on women in general, but specifically on *women writers* after the French

---

olution (Berkeley: University of California Press, 1992), esp. chap. 6; Michel Feher, *"La Retraite des femmes aimables,"* *Critique* (Juin 1997): 1–25; and Anne C. Vila, *Enlightenment and Pathology: Sensibility in the Literature and Medicine of Eighteenth-Century France* (Baltimore: Johns Hopkins University Press, 1998). For sustained treatments of the subject of gender and science in the revolutionary era, see Thomas Laqueur, *Making Sex: Body and Gender from the Greeks to Freud* (Cambridge, MA: Harvard University Press, 1990); Londa Schiebinger, *The Mind Has no Sex?: Women in the Origins of Modern Science* (Cambridge, MA: Harvard University Press, 1989) and Londa Schiebinger, *Nature's Body: Gender and the Making of Modern Science* (Boston: Beacon Press, 1993).

[4]Marie-Jean-Antoine-Nicolas Caritat, marquis de Condorcet, "On the Admission of Women to the Rights of Citizenship" (1790), in *Selected Writings*, Keith Michael Baker, ed. (Indianapolis: Bobbs-Merrill, 1976), pp. 97–104.

[5]Pierre Cabanis, *Les Rapports du physique et du moral de l'homme* (Paris: Crapart, Caille et Ravier 1802); Anne-Marie Jaton, *"La Définition de la femininité dans 'Les Rapports du physique et du moral, de Cabanis et dans 'La Loi naturelle de Volney,"* in *Volney et les idéologues: Actes du colloque d'Angers, textes réunies par Jean Roussel* (Angers: Presses Universitaires d'Angers, 1988), pp. 183–191.

[6]See Geneviève Fraisse, *La Muse de la raison: Démocratie et exclusion des femmes en France*, and Michel Feher, *"La Retraite des femmes aimables,"* esp. p. 7. Feher quotes, for example, the following passage from Cabanis, *Rapports du physique et moral de l'homme* (1802): *"Les fibres charnues sont plus faible et le tissu plus abondant chez les femmes que chez les hommes. . . . On ne peut douter que ce soit la présence et l'influence de l'uterus et des ovaires qui produisent cette différence."*

Revolution. And this new mode of argumentation had consequences far beyond the debates about civil and political equality. It went right to the heart of cultural life itself, questioning the capacity of women for moral self-regulation and their suitability for the production of knowledge through reading and writing. Proponents of the new biology advocated a very limited education for women, tailored narrowly to their maternal role.

Drawing on the theories of Cabanis, certain men of letters at the turn of the century mounted a full-scale reaction to the increasing prominence of women in the world of print. They began to argue publicly that women were born to be objects rather than subjects of knowledge, to be represented by men because they were incapable of adequately representing themselves. And, thus, by extrapolation, women who wrote were to be deemed not only antisocial, but also unnatural.[7] Here are a few lines from Echouhard-Lebrun's verses dedicated "To the beauties who would be poets" published in 1796: "If you wish to be muses, Inspire, but don't write."[8] Sylvain Maréchal, went further still, arguing against female literacy, in his notorious *Projet d'une loi portant défense d'apprendre à lire aux femmes* (*Project for a Law Prohibiting Women from Learning to Read*) of 1801.[9] This proposal was clearly satirical in nature, but coming as it did on the heels of the new sex-specific curriculum for the primary schools and the denial of higher public education to women, the threats of further restrictions on the cultural skills and power deemed suitable for women seemed real enough.[10]

The question of woman's influence on literary life became a full-blown matter of public debate in 1809 when the Society of Sciences, Let-

---

[7]See Christine Planté, "*La Désignation des femmes écrivains,*" in *Langages de la révolution (1770–1815): Actes du 4ème colloque international de lexicologie politique* (Paris: Klincksieck, 1995), pp. 409–415. See also Simone Balayé, "*Comment peut-on être Mme de Staël? Une Femme dans l'institution littéraire,*" *Romantisme,* vol. 77 (1992): 15–23.

[8]Ponce Denis Ecouchard-Lebrun, "*Aux Belles qui veulent devenir poètes*" (1796), in *Oeuvres* (Paris: Berquet 1811), tome 1, livre VI, Ode III, pp. 368–369, cited in Fraisse, *La Muse de la raison,* p. 77.

[9]Sylvain Maréchal, *Project d'une loi portant défense d'apprendre à lire aux femmes* (Paris: Massé, 1801).

[10]For an account of the retrenchment of democratic educational policies in the primary schools after Thermidor, see Isser Woloch, *The New Regime: Transformations of the French Civic Order, 1789–1820s* (New York: Norton, 1994), pp. 208–239. For the gender differences in curriculum and the exclusion of women from higher education after Thermidor, see Robert R. Palmer, *The Improvement of Humanity: Education and the French Revolution* (Princeton, NJ: Princeton University Press, 1985), esp. p. 316. See also Françoise Mayeur, "The Secular Model of Girl's Education," in *A History of Women,* Georges Duby and Michelle Perrot, eds. (Cambridge, MA: Harvard Belknap, 1993), vol. IV, pp. 228–245.

ters and Arts of the city of Mâcon sponsored an essay competition on the question of "the influence of women on taste in literature and the beaux arts." The winner of the essay prize, Jean-Joseph Virey, deployed the full arsenal of the new biology to argue that the physiological predisposition of women was to be passive recipients, rather than producers, of culture. Thus he writes:

> Woman, because of her delicate constitution, and the fluidity of her feelings, is childlike by nature. Born to be subjugated, she is not capable of good self-governance. . . . The weakness and flexibility of her members, and her strong penchant for imitation, assigns her by nature to a second rank of being. Because of her impressionable imagination, susceptible to everything, she is better at understanding than creating. . . . She receives sentiments rather than ideas; she is guided more by feelings than by the light of reason.[11]

Moreover, Virey argued, there were real dangers in permitting women too much participation in public culture. Women soften and temper literary forms. History revealed to Virey that too much feminine influence on the arts and letters, or influence insufficiently subordinated to masculine discipline, inevitably leads to cultural decadence and political decline.

The scientific chauvinism of the postrevolutionary period laid the basis for theories of gender difference in the modern era. These theories were elaborated over the course of the nineteenth and twentieth centuries and have shaped not only scientific but also cultural assumptions about sexual difference down to our own times.[12] Thus, over a century after Virey, in 1929, the literary historian Jean Larnac could still query in the preface to his *Histoire de la littérature féminine en France*:

> Is it true that the physiological differences that distinguish woman from man create intellectual differences that time and will can never erase?[13]

Though he speculated that the physiological differences between the sexes might, ultimately, prove to be environmentally or socially deter-

---

[11]Jean-Joseph Virey, *De l'Influence des femmes sur le goût dans la littérature et les beaux-arts pendant le XVIIe et le XVIIIe siècle. Discours qui a remporté le prix sur cette question proposée par la Société des Sciences, Lettres et Arts de Mâcon, en 1809* (Paris: Deterville, 1810), p. 13.

[12]Laqueur, *Making Sex.*

[13]Jean Larnac, *Histoire de la littérature féminine en France*, 2nd ed. (Paris: Edition KRA, 1929), p. 5.

mined, Larnac answered his question in the affirmative: "No woman could have composed the *Discourse on Method*. But neither could any man have written the *Letters* of Mme de Sévigné or certain pages of Colette."[14] For Larnac, sexually distinctive intellectual traits were rooted in physiological differences. Sexual physiology might, in the future, be transformed by a revolution in socioeconomic life. Only then would the mental differences between the sexes disappear.

By the 1920s, this revolution had yet to occur. The postrevolutionary period thus marked a critical turning point in the history of theories of gender difference. The secular philosophers of Thermidor attempted to establish a scientific basis for a sexual organization of modern social, political, and cultural life that could legitimate the subordination of women to men.

The cultural conclusions drawn from the new biology met with immediate criticism from both men and women.[15] In the female responses to the new science of the postrevolutionary moment we can begin to see the crystallization of a set of modern female esthetic strategies—representational tactics, if you will—adopted in response to the assault on their intellectual abilities, their capacity for moral self-governance, and their right to literary self-representation.

The most prominent women writers of the revolutionary period responded vociferously to this assault on female cultural equality and moral autonomy, and they mobilized a formidable arsenal of historical and linguistic erudition to their cause. The republican poet Constance Pipelet launched a poetic counterassault on Echouhard-Lebrun's poetic insults in her *Epître aux Femmes* (*Epistle to Women*) (1797):

> But already thousands condemn our courage / They are shocked, they whisper, they are unnerved, they heckle / They want to take our pens and our paintbrushes away / Each has against us song or a *bon mot*.[16]

---

[14]Ibid., p. 279.

[15]Two of the most eloquent male defenders of female intellectual equality were Gabriel Legouvé, *Le Mérite des femmes* (Paris: Renouard, 1801), and Charles-Guillaume Thérémin, *De la Condition des femmes dans les républiques* (Paris: Laran, an VII [1799]).

[16]Constance Pipelet, the princess of Salm, *Epître aux Femmes* (1797), reedited in Geneviève Fraisse, ed., *Opinions des femmes de la vielle au lendemain de la Révolution française* (Paris: Côtés-femmes, 1989), p. 69. On Constance Pipelet's self-fashioning as a writer, see Elizabeth Colwill, "Laws of Nature / Rights of Genius: The *Drame* of Constance de Salm," in Elizabeth C. Goldsmith and Dena Goodman, eds., *Going Public: Women and Publishing in Early Modern France* (Ithaca, NY: Cornell University Press, 1995), pp. 224–242.

Isabelle de Charrière's novel *Trois Femmes* (1795), as we have seen, directly spoofed the sex-specific curriculum of the new French higher schools and, more generally, the assertion of female intellectual inferiority.[17] Mme de Staël devoted an entire chapter of her treatise *De la Littérature* (1800) to "Women who cultivate letters."[18] These three efforts were followed by Fanny Raoul's *Opinion d'une femme sur les femmes* (1801); Albertine Clément-Hémery's *Les Femmes vengées de la sotise d'un philosophe du jour, ou réponse au projet de loi de M. S**. M***, portant défense d'appendre à lire aux femmes* (1801), Mme Marguerite Ursule Fortunée Bernier Briquet's *Dictionnaire historique, littéraire et bibliographique des françaises et des étrangères naturalisées en France* (1804), Mme Marie-Armande-Jeanne d'Humières Gacon-Dufour's *De la necessité de l'instruction pour les femmes* (1805), Mme Adélaïde-Gillette Billet Dufrénoy's two-volume novel, *La Femme auteur ou les inconvénients de la célébrité* (1812), and, not least, Mme Stéphanie de Genlis's 1811 treatise, *De l'Influence des femmes sur la littérature française*, where, in an extraordinary opening passage, this Catholic and royalist scion of the Orleanist entourage openly acknowledged that in the face of recent attempts to prohibit women from writing and publishing she had decided to break her silence on these matters and come to the defense of literary women.[19]

None of these women asserted the physical equality of women and men, nor did most of them demand equal civil or political rights (indeed, they held an extraordinary range of views on these matters). All of them, however, from the royalist Genlis to the republican Pipelet, insisted on the intellectual equality of women and their right to moral autonomy, even from their husbands. All of them found the antifeminist argument—that woman's intellectual capacities were biologically determined—to be specious and degrading. Fortunée Briquet thus emblazoned the title page of her *Dictionnaire* with an epigram that she, not insignificantly, attributes to Jean-Jacques Rousseau: "The soul has no sex."[20] All of them insisted on the right of women to create through

---

[17]Isabelle de Charrière, *Trois Femmes* (1795), in *Oeuvres Complètes* (Geneva, Slatkine, 1981), vol. IX.

[18]Mme de Staël, *De la Littérature considérée dans ses rapports avec les institutions sociales* (Paris: Garnier-Flammarion, 1991 [1st edition, 1800]), Part 2, chap. 6, pp. 332–341.

[19]Genlis, *De l'Influence des femmes*, p. xxxiii.

[20]Fortunée Briquet, *Dictionnaire historique, littéraire et bibliographique des françaises et des étrangères naturalisées en France* (Paris: Gillé, 1804). For the passage in the *Nouvelle Héloïse*, see Jean-Jacques Rousseau, *La Nouvelle Héloïse* [1761] (Paris: Hachette, 1925), vol. 2, p. 269. Not insignificantly, Fortunée Briquet transforms a query of St. Preux (*"l'âme a-t-elle un sexe?"*) into an affirmative.

writing and the visual arts and to thereby constitute an independent moral and intellectual life. All of them defended, as Albertine Clément-Hémery put it, "the need that [women] have to depict their woes and their happiness."[21] And all would have concurred, no doubt, with Pipelet that "for us as for men, being forgotten is the greatest of ill fates, and it is the hope of escaping it that sends our thoughts to higher spheres."[22] In a fundamental sense then, the feminist politics that emerged in response to the new biology of the postrevolution was centrally preoccupied with the literary—the right of women to cultural self-representation.

THE WOMAN WRITER AS A DOUBLED SELF

Two of the greatest contributions to modern French literary theory made by women, Mme de Staël's *De la Littérature* (1800) and Mme de Genlis's *De l'Influence des femmes sur la littérature* (1811) were written in the context of, and in response to, this debate. Both were written to establish the achievements and the claims of women in literary life. These two texts departed from other works on women writers, like Louise de Kéralio's *Collection des meilleures ouvrages français composés par des femmes* (1786–1788) or Fortunée Briquet's *Dictionnaire historique, littéraire et biographique des françaises* (1804), in that they were not mere celebrations of women who wrote, but rather critical histories of literary creativity itself. As Genlis put it:

> There have been many voluminous works treating the history of women authors, but the greater part of these authors are mediocre. This work has a different goal: It will discuss only those women who have had some impact on French literature.[23]

Indeed, both Staël and Genlis attempted to recover the right to literary achievement for women in light of what appeared to them both as efforts by modern science to reduce women to their objective corporeal essence—to render them seen, but not heard.

---

[21]Albertine Clément-Hémery, *Les Femmes vengées de la sottise d'un philosophe du jour* (Paris: Benoist, 1801), p. 124.

[22]Constance Pipelet, the princess of Salm, *"Lettre CLXIII: Femmes auteurs,"* in *Ouvrages divers en prose, suivis de mes soixantes ans, par Mme la Princesse, Constance de Salm* (Paris: Didot, 1835), vol. 1, pp. 243–244.

[23]Genlis, *De l'Influence des femmes*, p. vii.

If one dimension of the biological objectification of women was their silencing, the other was their reduction to objects of male inquiry and observation. The central theme of Mme de Staël's chapter on women in *De la Littérature* is precisely the problem of the overexposure of women in modern society, and especially women who publish:

> It is worth remarking that as soon as a man realizes that you desire him, he almost always cools toward you. When a woman publishes a book she has put herself so much at the mercy of opinion that the dispensers of that opinion make her feel their power over her.[24]

In publishing, Staël suggests, one puts oneself up for public scrutiny, and women are especially vulnerable to this because they are always at greater risk of being read transparently, as though their words were transparent windows into their natures. The republican cultural politics of the revolutionary moment aggravated this tendency, because, even though it sought to encourage greater simplicity and openness in public discourse, the result was instead an unprecedented tolerance for crudeness in public expression:

> Since the Revolution, men have thought it politically and morally useful to reduce women to the most absurd mediocrity. . . . It wasn't possible to recover the simplicity of manners of earlier ages; rather, the result has been a coarsening of manners, less *délicatesse,* and less deference to public esteem.[25]

This loss of *délicatesse*—of respect for the distinction between private and public life, between person and author, in sum, between life and its representation—formed part of the same cultural tendency that sought to render women's nature transparently readable. In reaction to this, women who write under republics, she speculates, will likely find themselves turning from philosophy to literature. They will need to re-civilize public discourse to shield themselves from reductive representations by insisting on the opacity rather than the transparency of language—its power to create a gap between private and public life. Indeed, women may become, under republics, the sign of the literary itself:

[24]Staël, *De la Littérature,* p. 334
[25]Ibid.

> Perhaps it is natural that . . . literature, properly speaking, be-
> comes women's domain, and men consecrate themselves uniquely
> to higher philosophy.[26]

Fictional narrative could provide women with a means to engage in public discourse without overexposing their person to critical male scrutiny.
In response to the republican movement to naturalize woman's identity,
women would insist on their capacity to create identities through the artifice of literary fictions.

Two years after the publication of *On Literature,* Staël's novel *Delphine* appeared. Here she developed in fictional form a tragic account of
the risks of feminine self-revelation that she cautioned against in *On Literature.* Delphine's life story exemplifies the dilemmas of a woman who
openly reveals her true nature and who refuses to dissimulate in society:
She makes herself overly vulnerable to public scrutiny. The irony, Delphine discovers, is that in a society constituted by the art of dissimulation, transparent actions result only in misapprehensions. Purity of motives cannot protect virtuous women from the public assumption that
women dissimulate. The only hope for women is either to play the game
of social dissimulation—concealing one's true motives and willfully taking public opinion into consideration—or to renounce social life altogether. The revelation of one's true nature, for women, leads to tragedy.

Mme de Genlis took the themes of feminine refinement and self-
concealment even further in the preliminary discourse to *De l'Influence
des femmes sur la littérature.* She writes:

> It is claimed that women, by constitution, are gifted with a refine-
> ment that men are not capable of; this favorable judgment seems
> to me no better founded that the less flattering ones: Several
> works composed by men of letters are proof that this quality is not
> exclusive to women; but it is true that it is one of the distinctive
> characteristics of almost all of their writings.[27]

Genlis thus takes the trait of "refinement," attributed to female biology,
and reveals it to be, rather, merely an effect of literary artifice. Indeed,
she exposes the purported biological attributes of "feminine refinement" to be nothing more than a series of representational tactics chosen by women precisely because they produce a protective gap between
a woman's inner self and its public representation:

---

[26]Ibid.
[27]Genlis, *De l'Influence des femmes,* pp. xx–xxi.

This must be because education and proper comportment requires them to contain and to constrain practically all of their feelings and always to soften their expression: the result is those delicate turns of phrase, that acute refinement of making oneself understood without daring to explicate.[28]

The withholding of an explicit betrayal of one's inner feelings is not, she continues, a form of dissimulation, or an attempt to hide one's feelings; "to the contrary, when perfectly achieved it makes known without explaining, without employing words that could be quoted as a positive avowal."[29] Showing, rather than telling, is not simply the essence of women's art, she continues, but of all great art:

> What bad taste one must have to disclose all the mysteries of the soul, to extinguish all the traits of grace, by presenting—be it in a novel or a dramatic work—a heroine lacking modesty who expresses herself without reserve.[30]

The great effects of all fictional works, she writes, "are owed to reticence and to constrained sentiments."[31] All great works produce their dramatic effect by revealing the gap between inner feeling and its external representation.

These moments of constrained expression are not moments of self-concealment. To the contrary, they are examples of extraordinary self-possession, in which a self-willing individual can be seen to exist independently from, and in a determining relation to, its external representations. This doubling of the self, this gap between inner and outer, is precisely the essence and the sign of an individual's moral autonomy.

Genlis's 1811 treatise met with virulent criticism in the Parisian press, not least for her assertion that the greater literary achievement of men—including in that most masculine of forms, tragedy—was a result of their social and educational advantages rather than their sex. The noted critic Louis-Sébastien Auger wrote several articles and open letters to the author in the *Journal de l'Empire* between May and August of 1811 describing her has a "pathetic amazon who had nothing better to complain of than the troubles she has created for herself," in publishing

---

[28]Ibid.
[29]Ibid.
[30]Ibid., pp. xxiii–xiv.
[31]Ibid.

her book.[32] For Auger, to write, in and of itself, was unwomanly. Genlis replied that it was one thing to criticize a work, and another to stoop to personal attacks on the author. She could only respond that a woman who wrote did not cease to be a woman, and that it was ungentlemanly for Auger to resort to character assaults. Here, too, Genlis insisted on asserting the distinction between her writings and her person. The one could be publicly criticized, the privacy of the other should be respected.

One of the most striking features of women's writing of the revolutionary, and especially the post-thermidorian, era is the abundance of feminine figures of a doubled self—at once private and public. Early on in the Revolution, they emerge as embattled gestures of capitulation or resistance to misogynist attacks on politically active women: Olympe de Gouges, most notoriously, and most defiantly signed her *Prognostic sur Maximilien Robespierre*—the poster-pamphlet that precipitated her arrest and ultimate execution for treason—with the pseudonym of "an amphibious animal," an "animal without equal, neither male nor female, but bearing the traits of both."[33] This, to be sure, was a desperate rhetorical maneuver, an attempt to resurrect a separation between her private person and her public representations in a moment of extreme political conflict. But the problem of creating a public authorial persona that was powerful enough to resist biological and autobiographical reduction was shared by all women who wrote.

After Thermidor, the figuration of the woman writer as a doubled self was developed as a self-conscious and systematic motif in women's writing—both theoretical and fictional. Constance Pipelet, following the work of Charles-Guillaume Thérémin, responded to the new biology through a reprisal of the line of Enlightenment argumentation begun by John Locke and developed by the marquis de Condorcet. She writes:

> There are two beings in a woman, as there are in a man; the first is a moral being, free in essence, knowing no law except its own morality, and having no sex; the second, is a physical being, de-

[32]The entire set of exchanges is collected and reprinted in Louis-Sébastien Auger, *Ma Brochure en réponse aux deux brochures de Mme de Genlis* (Paris: Colnet et Delaunay, 1811). This quote is from p. 79.

[33]Olympe de Gouges, *Prognostic sur Maximilien Robespierre, par un animal amphibie* (n.p., n.d. [Paris: 1793]). She opens with a *"portrait exact de cet animal"* in the following terms: *"Je suis un animal sans pareil, je ne suis ni homme, ni femme. J'ai tout le courage de l'un, et quelquefois les faiblesses de l'autre."*

pendent on man in the same way that man is dependent upon woman. . . . This ingenious distinction throws a clear light upon perpetual contradictions.[34]

Unlike Condorcet, however, Pipelet did not view the existence of this independent moral self as the basis for equal female participation in civil and political society. Subscribing instead to the theory of virtual representation through the "head of the household," she argued that women were at once dependent on men in civil and political life, but nonetheless retain an independent moral voice. In short, Pipelet advanced the Kantian, as opposed to the Lockean, line of argumentation about women's rights: Women should be viewed at once as public individuals, that is, juridically subservient to the sovereign, and yet at the same time private individuals, that is, free moral participants in a critical public sphere.[35]

The motif of the woman writer as a doubled self, at once public and private, circulated in fictional forms as well at the opening of the new century. The most explicit example was Mme Adélaïde-Gillette Billet Dufrenoy's 1812 novel, *La Femme auteur, ou les inconvénients de la célébrité*. The novel is a thinly allegorized recounting of the struggles between Mme de Staël and Napoleon. But, in this fictionalized version, the young widowed woman writer, Mme Simiane, is able to triumph over the chauvinist prejudices of the military hero she adores by wooing him first under an assumed name, which permits him to see her virtues independent of her fame, and, ultimately, to overcome his avowed aversion to literary women.[36] It is only by producing a second self, as it were, that she can be seen for what she is. Dissimulation makes the recognition of feminine virtue possible.

The fear of objectification—the reductive interpretation of female narrators as no more than the voices of their authors ("Corinne is Staël," "Lélia is George Sand"); the insistence that esthetic choices made by women were not choices at all, but rather, biological defects of their sex—

[34]Constance Pipelet, the princess of Salm, "*Rapport sur un ouvrage intitulé 'De la Condition des femmes dans la republique'*" (1799), in *Constance de Salm, Ouvrage divers en prose, suivis de mes soixantes ans par Mme la Princesse Constance de Salm* (Paris: Firmin Didot, 1835), vol. 2, pp. 149–150.

[35]Immanuel Kant, "An Answer to the Question: What is Enlightenment?" (1784), in *Perpetual Peace and Other Essays*, Ted Humphrey, trans. (Indianapolis: Hackett Publishing, 1983), pp. 41–48.

[36]Adélaïde-Gillette Billet. Dufrenoy, *La Femme auteur, ou les inconvénients de la célebrite*, 2 vols. (Paris: Bechet, 1812).

haunted women writers throughout the nineteenth century. A typical expression of this anxiety is found in a 1835 letter from the poet Marceline Valmore Desbordes to M. Montferrand, the director of a new *Biographie des dames auteurs,* in which she conveys her pleasure at being included in the collection, but also her "terror of biography."[37] The very designation as a "woman writer" itself reduced the identity of these women to their sex, with all the negative stereotypes the term had come to acquire.[38]

The new biology of the postrevolutionary period had sought to naturalize and objectify female intellectual identity, fixing it on a second rung, beneath men's. In response to the objectifying empirical sciences, intellectual women identified themselves as writers of fiction as a means of insisting on their right to self-invention and public self-representation. Fiction made it possible to represent the self as constructed rather than given. It gave them the cultural means to produce a public, second self—one existing in an indeterminate relation to their biological being—that they could control. In literature, alone, modern woman could imagine herself in other circumstances than those determined by either her biological limits or her juridical subordination.

FICTION AND MORAL SELF-REALIZATION

In the wake of the Revolution, French women of letters became passionate advocates of sentimentalism and the sentimental novel.[39] Sophie de Condorcet translated Adam Smith's *Theory of Moral Sentiments* immediately after Thermidor.[40] Flahaut, Charrière, Cottin, Genlis, and Staël became the most celebrated practitioners of the genre. The sentimental novel permitted women to turn the new biology to their advan-

---

[37]BN: Nouv. Acq. Fr. 1308, Letter from Mme Valmore Desbordes to M. Montferrand, Lyon, December 15, 1835.

[38]On the stereotype of the woman author, see Christine Planté, "*La Désignation des femmes écrivains,*" in *Langages de la Révolution (1770–1815): Actes du 4ème colloque international de lexicologie politique* (Paris: Publications de l'INALF, collection "Saint Cloud," Klincksieck, 1995), pp. 409–416; see also Christine Planté, *La petite Soeur de Balzac* (Paris: Seuil, 1989).

[39]The best work on the politics of the sentimental genre is Margaret Cohen, *The Sentimental Education of the Novel* (Princeton, NJ: Princeton University Press, 1999), and "Women and Fiction in the Nineteenth Century," in *The Cambridge Companion to the Modern French Novel* (Cambridge, UK: Cambridge University Press, 1997).

[40]Marie Louise Sophie de Grochy, marquise de Condorcet, *Théorie des sentiments moraux, ou essai analytique sur les principes des jugements moraux qui portent naturellement les hommes* (Paris: Buisson, 1798).

tage by appropriating the idea that theirs was the sex of greater feeling as a literary strength, rather than a weakness. It also made it possible to assert that the truth of one's character resides in internal feelings, as opposed to purportedly "objective" external appearances—women could thus employ the sentimental genre to expose how they became victims of moral misperception in an unjust social world, still governed by patriarchal prejudice.

Probably the most successful novel of the revolutionary era, the Countess Flahaut's *Adèle de Senange* (1794), exemplified the genre in its recounting of the dilemmas of two virtuous individuals caught in the dilemmas of a society still governed by unjust aristocratic values. The novel is an exposé of the moral anguish created when a tyrannical mother forces her dutiful daughter to marry a man old enough to be her father, rather than the young man who loves her. The young man, virtuous yet faithful, expresses his moral dilemma in a turn of phrase that swept away the hearts of French readers of the period: "I cannot live with or without her!"

Adèle de Senange instantly became the exemplary novel in the sentimental genre for other women writers. Sophie Cottin's best-selling *Claire d'Albe* (1796)—another tale of misguided parental authority and marital mismatch—was essentially a rewriting of the earlier novel's plot in a tragic form. Isabelle de Charrière wrote to a friend that Flahaut's novel was one of her literary models for *Three Women*.[41] Charrière was so enamoured of the book that reading *Adèle de Senange* aloud figured as the exemplary moral exercise for the characters in her novel.[42] The young hero of *Three Women*, upon reading of the fate of Flahaut's hero, determines than he will elope rather than submit to the ill-fated marriage that his father intends for him. The moral dilemmas of children seeking to determine their own fate in love became a central preoccupation for the postrevolutionary generation: how to reconcile the pursuit of individual desire with the social demands of a world that—albeit republican—was still starkly patriarchal.

In her preface to the novel, Flahaut explicitly asserted that fiction, in her eyes, was moral philosophy by other means. Thus, she wrote:

> In order to destroy the empire that the miraculous enjoyed, reason alone was not sufficient. Something stronger and of greater pene-

---

[41]Isabelle de Charrière, letter to J. P. de Chambrier d'Oleyres, January 23, 1797, in *Oeuvres complètes*, Jean-Daniel Candaux et al., eds. (Geneva: Slatkine, 1981), vol. V, p. 285.

[42]Isabelle de Charrière, *Trois Femmes*, in *Oeuvres complètes*, vol. IX, p. 77.

tration was necessary. Cervantes created a new path and he has had a prodigious success.[43]

Fictional narrative, by creating an empathetic response in the reader, heightens the power of the moral message it is intended to convey. We experience virtue, rather than merely understanding it.

The following year, in her *Essay on Fictions* (1795), Mme de Staël further developed the theory of the sentimental novel as a form of philosophical reflection: "People usually make a separate case for what they call philosophical novels; all novels should be philosophical as they should all have a moral goal."[44] The novel presents general moral principles through particular stories, but that doesn't mean that they do not contribute to the general good. True to her liberal creed, Staël saw the cultivation of individual morality as the essence of public morality: "The novel . . . is one of the most beautiful creations of the human mind, and one of the most influential on individual morality, which is what ultimately determines the morality of the public."[45]

Staël went on to imagine a more expanded role for the novel in advancing human knowledge in the modern world. To date, she lamented, the novel had limited its scope to only one human passion, love. But imagine if it widened its embrace to explore ambition, greed, and vanity. The novel would distinguish itself from history in exploring these great themes in their private, individual, aspects. The novel would be, in effect, a history written from the register of the private. As such, novels could impart their moral messages with greater intensity and emotional penetration. "Some severe philosophers," she wrote, "condemn all emotions, wanting moral authority to rule by a simple statement of moral duty. Nothing is less suited to human nature."[46] Staël saw greater possibilities in fictional narrative: "What philosophical developments we would see, if we were eager to explain and analyze all passions, as novels have already done for love!"[47]

Novels used particular examples in a decidedly different way from the *exempla* of deductive, philosophical analysis. In deductive forms of

---

[43]Mme de Souza, Countess of Flahaut, *Adèle de Sénange ou lettres de Lord Sydenham* (London: Debrett, 1794), p. x.

[44]Germaine de Staël, *Essay on Fictions* (1795), in *An Extraordinary Woman: Selected Writings of Germaine de Staël*, Vivian Folkenflick, trans. and ed. (New York: Columbia University Press, 1987), p. 70.

[45]Ibid., p. 71.

[46]Ibid., p. 74.

[47]Ibid., p. 75.

philosophical argumentation that work from *a priori* statements of a general rule, the particular example is used simply as an illustration of that general rule. It has, as it were, no life of its own. Its meaning is pre-determined. *A posteriori* arguments, by contrast, proceed probabilistically, and they imply different narrative strategies, as their meaning evolves in light of each new event.[48] It is always possible, in a novel, for one further episode to change the entire picture.

In this sense, all knowledge—even moral knowledge—achieved through the reading of the novel is probabilistically contingent on what may or may not happen next. This formal indeterminacy of the novel made it possible for women to constitute moral identities that were in some fundamental sense always unfinished and always open to the possibility of radical change. As Mme de Staël wrote: "Everything is so true to life in such novels that we have no trouble persuading ourselves that everything could happen just this way—not as past history, but often, it seems, as the history of the future."[49] The pursuit of literature by modern women was not so much a turning away from philosophical reflection as it was the reprisal of the project of modern self-realization by other, antimimetic, and antideductive means. Fictional language could be used to invent rather than to describe the world; inductive narratives could leave moral possibilities open to further interpretation and revision.

THE ART OF SELF-MAKING

Over the course of the nineteenth and twentieth centuries—in the hands of the greatest women writers—Germaine de Staël, George Sand, Colette, and Simone de Beauvoir—new heroines would be fabricated from the antimimetic representational strategies of women set on finding a means to recover the possibility of self-making through a celebration of the opacity of language. Staël, Sand, Colette, and Beauvoir all succeeded in playing on the essentializing assumptions of both literary critics and the public-at-large that led them to read women's novels as autobiography. They succeeded in transforming this social liability into a powerful aesthetic weapon. Each used her work as a form of self-

[48]See, Ian Hacking, *The Emergence of Probability: A Philosophical Study of Early Ideas About Probability, Induction and Statistical Inference* (London: Cambridge University Press, 1975).

[49]Germaine de Staël, *Essay on Fictions*, p. 73.

exploration. They incessantly interwove material from their own lives into their work, constantly playing with the boundaries between auto-biography and fiction—inviting their readers to speculate endlessly on where truth ended and fiction began. They made art from their lives, and, in so doing, transformed their lives into works of art.

Delphine, Corinne, Lélia, Renée "the vagabond," and, not least, Françoise, the heroine of Beauvoir's greatest novel, *L'Invitée*—these fictional figures of modern self-inventing women have each, in turn, been readily recognized as figures of philosophical reflection. The most favored literary critic of the Napoleonic regime, Joseph Fievée, wrote in the *Mercure de France* that Mme de Staël's heroine, "Delphine . . . is an exalted mind. . . . She is a philosopher and a deist."[50] Mme de Genlis gave even more concrete characterization to the figure of the modern female writer as a philosopher in an 1803 novella. Titled *La Femme philosophe*, the novella was written as a moralizing warning to young women on the dangers in following the secular, philosophical path blazed by Mme de Staël.[51] In Genlis's eyes, secular morality—because she thought it opened an unbounded field for the play of egoistical desire—could lead to only two alternatives for women, suicidal despair or Christian repentance. Despite her negative judgment, Genlis nonetheless recognized Staël for what she was—a secular philosopher who pursued self-realization through fiction.

Staël immortalized the tragic figure of the self-determining female genius in her 1807 novel *Corinne*. The love between the Englishman Oswald and the Italian poetess Corinne is doomed to failure because Oswald cannot reconcile his passion for genius with the social requirements of an appropriately domestic and subservient wife. The independent woman, as depicted by Staël, is irreconcilable with patriarchal social order. For Staël, the modern female philosopher is a figure of tragedy, not (as Genlis would have it) because she is a victim of unbridled passions, but rather because of her alienation in an unjust social world.

---

[50]Joseph Fievée, review of *Delphine* in the *Mercure de France*, October 1802, cited by Simone Balayé, "*Comment peut-on être Madame de Staël?*" *Romantisme*, vol. 77 (1992): 18.

[51]Stéphanie Ducrest de Genlis, *La Femme philosophe*, in *Nouvelle Bibliothèque des Romans, dans laquelle on donne l'analyse raisonné des romans anciens et modernes, français, et traduits dans notre langue, avec des anecdotes, des notices historiques et critiques concernant leurs auteurs ou leurs ouvrages, ainsi que les moeurs, les usages du temps, les circonstances particulières et relatives; enfin, les personnages connus, déguisés et emblématiques. Par une société de gens de lettres, 5e année, Tome 6eme* (Paris: Maradan, an XI [1803]).

George Sand's heroine, the poet Lélia, in the 1833 novel that bore her name, offers us, as Dostoevsky recognized, the spectacle of "an immense ethical quest."[52] Lélia is the modern philosophical figure in its most tragic form. In the very first sentence of the novel, the young male suitor, Sténio, asks, "Who are you?" And, in her very first words, Lélia resists a determinate response, "Why do you want to know who I am and where I come from?" Further on, he attempts to reassure her that he doesn't view her as a "remarkable subject offered to the observations of a physiologist." But Lélia remains "evasive." She refuses to be possessed by him. Like the heroine of Charrière's *Three Women*, Lélia suffers from what Sténio describes as "an odious skepticism." Her commitment, even to God, is contingent. This is a woman who "hid herself." The withholding of an inner self, her insistence on inner self-possession, becomes both the source of her power and of her ultimate downfall at the hands of a man who cannot possess her.[53] Lélia dies for her independence.

Not a wife, nor a courtesan, nor a nun, Lélia finds her philosophical freedom in her ability to remain undetermined by men. This space of indeterminacy is created for Lélia, as it was for her literary predecessors, through a doubling of the figure of the self, producing an opacity that guards her inner sanctum. Like Charrière's "Three Women," Lélia's "true self," can never be fully disclosed without losing its autonomy. In the end, Sand, as she herself realized at the time, was unable to give the transcendent ideal of female poetic freedom stable aesthetic embodiment: Neither realist heroine nor timeless allegorical figure, Lélia testified to a dream as yet impossible to fulfill.[54]

"Is anyone imagining as he reads me, that I am portraying myself? Have patience: This is merely my model."[55] Colette thus deftly toyed with the readers of her *Naissance du jour* (*Break of Day*), undermining any hope they might have to sort out the real from the unreal. She, above all

---

[52]Feodor Dostoevsky, *The Diary of a Writer*, Boris Brasol, trans. (New York: Scribner's, 1949), vol. 2, pp. 343–349, cited by Maria Espinosa in her introduction to George Sand, *Lélia*, Maria Espinosa, trans. (Bloomington: Indiana University Press, 1978; original French edition, 1833), p. xix.

[53]George Sand, *Lélia*, Maria Espinosa, trans. (Bloomington: Indiana University Press, 1978; original French edition, 1833), pp. 3, 7, 8, 10, 31.

[54]On the problem of Sand's troubled relationship to realism and the aesthetic challenges of *Lélia*, see Naomi Schor, *George Sand and Idealism* (New York: Columbia University Press, 1993), esp. pp. 13–20, 55–67.

[55]Colette, *The Break of Day*, Enid McLeod, trans. (New York: Farrar, Straus and Cudahy, 1961) p. 35.

the others, made art from life: Claudine, Renée, and narrators of the memoir novels of her later years all served as examples of how women doubled their identities through fiction in order to escape the determinacy of circumstances. Take Renée, who appeared in 1911, as Colette's *Vagabonde*. Divorce, once again possible after 1884, brings with it a second chance for her heroine's self-realization. Having freed herself from an abusive husband and embarked on an independent career as a writer and actress, Renée must now, once again, choose between her independence and the love of a man who seeks to make her, again, a wife. Colette, like Staël and Sand, presents Renée's dilemma as a choice between love and freedom, between submission to a man (and perhaps a second disappointment) and the loneliness of artistic freedom. Is Renée too cowardly to risk love once again? Or does she, rather, muster the philosophical courage to embrace her freedom in lieu of happiness? Colette leaves us hanging:

> Happiness? Are you sure happiness is enough for me hencefor-ward? It is not only happiness that gives value to life. You wanted to brighten me with that commonplace dawn, for you pitied me in my obscurity. Call it obscurity, if you will: the obscurity of a room seen from without. I would rather call it dark, not obscure. Dark, but made beautiful by an unwearying sadness: silvery and twilit like the white owl, the silky mouse, the wings of a clothes-moth. Dark, with the red gleams of an agonizing memory.[56]

Here, again, in the life story of the "vagabond," a gap emerges between the inner and outer worlds, between the future social obscurity that Renée predicts for herself as "an old maid," and the richly animated inner life that she seeks to protect—the preserve of a free mental existence.

This luminous space of female independence left a deep impression on Simone de Beauvoir, one of Colette's most passionate young readers. Yet it has been little noted how deeply steeped Simone de Beauvoir was in the French female literary tradition. One would hardly know this from reading the most definitive intellectual biography of Beauvoir.[57] There, in the reconstruction of Beauvoir's mental formation, a scant five French women predecessors appear, engulfed in a sea of

---

[56]Colette, *The Vagabond*, Enid McLeod, trans. (London: Penguin Books, 1954; original French edition, Paris: Librarie Ollendorff, 1911), p. 191.

[57]Toril Moi, *Simone de Beauvoir: The Making of a Modern Intellectual* (Oxford, UK: Basil Blackwell, 1994).

canonical male philosophers.[58] The emphasis in most biographies of Beauvoir has been on her singularity as a modern woman philosopher. She would appear to be without precedent: The first to be professionally licensed, she had exceptional success on the notoriously difficult *aggrégation* exam in philosophy—her performance second only to that of Jean-Paul Sartre.[59]

If Beauvoir is most typically remembered as a singular woman, alone the equal among men, it is only because we have now forgotten the deep cultural influences she derived from her avid reading of earlier women writers. Beauvoir came of age at the threshold of a revolutionary change for French women. This is certainly how she saw herself: "The free woman is just being born," she wrote in 1949.[60] In the course of Simone de Beauvoir's lifetime, the ground shifted dramatically beneath the feet of female intellectuals. They gained, at least in principle, equal access to education and the professions—including the academic profession of philosophy—by the late 1920s. They gained the right to vote (1946). And by 1965 they achieved civil equality in marriage. It would not be an exaggeration to suggest that something like a revolution occurred for women in this single generation—a revolution that put them on an entirely new intellectual footing.

Though she was not in fact the first female *agrégée* in philosophy— that honor went to Mlle Baudry in 1905—Beauvoir was among the first generation to have access to formal training in the 120-odd years since philosophy had been professionalized as an academic discipline in 1795, and among the first to pass the examination on equal terms with her male cohorts. In this sense, she was the first woman since the generation of Mme de Staël and Isabelle de Charrière to approach the subject of philosophy on the same institutional terms as her male contemporaries. A chapter in the modern intellectual history of French women was, indeed, coming to a close in 1929 when Beauvoir passed the notoriously difficult exam.

But we miss something profoundly important for modern feminism by focusing exclusively on Simone de Beauvoir's competition with her male contemporaries and her engagement in the intellectual inheritance of Hegelian phenomenology: her obvious fascination with the fictional

---

[58]Mme de Lafayette, Mme de Staël, George Sand, Rachilde, and Colette.

[59]For her educational formation, see Moi, *Simone de Beauvoir*, pp. 37–72, esp. pp. 50–51.

[60]Simone de Beauvoir, *The Second Sex*, H. M. Parshley, trans. (New York: Vintage, 1989), p. 715.

legacy of her female predecessors.[61] Beauvoir's first published work, *L'Invitée* (*She Came to Stay*) (1943) was a novel rather than a philosophical tract. Moreover, despite her academic accomplishments, throughout her life Beauvoir insisted that she was "a writer" not "a philosopher." And fictional writing techniques deeply inform her one great philosophical treatise, *The Second Sex* (1949).

In *The Second Sex*, Beauvoir draws broadly on her reading of French women from the Middle Ages into the twentieth century. These women's writings form the core material, the empirical sources, from which Beauvoir generates her picture of the situation of woman. She cites over fifty French women writers who preceded her, and none more frequently than Staël and Colette.[62] Beauvoir saw herself as a bridge between these women and a new future for her sex. Beauvoir was both the last woman writer of the Old Regime for women of letters, and the first woman writer of the new.

Significantly, the fictional inheritance of French women becomes most central to the last section of *The Second Sex*, "Toward Liberation," where Beauvoir turns from her diagnosis of the condition of women to speculations on the possibilities for female emancipation—what Mme de Staël would have called "the history of the future." Almost every citation in this section of the work is to a fictional work and, with a very few notable exceptions, they are all writings by women. In turning to the future, Beauvoir turned to the space of female fiction making. It was in fiction that she first glimpsed the possibility of female emancipation: For Beauvoir, Colette's vagabond was a figure who opted for transcendence over immanence, in her refusal to give up her independent life as an artist for the security and "vassalage" of domestic love.[63]

Renée, the vagabond, was the beginning of an answer to the fundamental question of *The Second Sex*: "How can independence be recovered in a state of dependency?"[64] The more general answer lay in Beauvoir's understanding of transcendental freedom. She writes:

> Art, literature, philosophy are attempts to found the world anew on a human liberty: that of the individual creator; to entertain

---

[61]See, for example, Judith Butler, "Sex and Gender in Simone de Beauvoir's Second Sex," *Yale French Studies* (1986): 35–49.

[62]There are over twenty references to Colette in the English edition of *The Second Sex*, H. M. Parshley, ed. and trans. (New York: Vintage, 1989). Unfortunately, French editions of *The Second Sex* are not indexed.

[63]Beauvoir, *The Second Sex*, p. 694.

[64]Ibid., p. xxxv.

such a pretension, one must unequivocally assume the status of a
being who had liberty.[65]

All art, however, is not transcendental art. Beauvoir was deeply aware
that writing, for women, could become nothing more than a gilded cage,
a space of negation into which women escaped without freeing themselves:

> Woman's situation inclines her to seek salvation in literature and
> art. Living marginally in the masculine world, she sees it not in its
> universal form, but from her own special point of view. . . . Taking
> the attitude of negation and denial, she is not absorbed in the real:
> She protests against it, with words. . . . [S]he wishes to attain her
> being—but she is doomed to frustration; she can only recover it in
> the region of the imaginary.[66]

Beauvoir wanted to find a form of writing that would engage the real
world in positive terms. She felt that she must be able to define what
counts as truth, not only for herself, but for the world as well. And for
Beauvoir this meant rewriting literature as philosophy.

In 1795 Isabelle de Charrière rewrote one of Kant's philosophical essays as a novel. In 1949, Simone de Beauvoir performed the reverse gesture. *The Second Sex* was, in fact, a rewriting of the plot of Beauvoir's first
novel, *L'Invitée* (*She Came to Stay*), in universalizing terms.[67] The heroine of *L'Invitée*, Françoise, must learn to act entirely alone in order to free
herself from her dependence on the regard of others. She becomes herself by making the decision by herself to kill her rival:

> Alone. She had acted alone. As alone as in death. One day Pierre
> would know. But even he would only know her act from the out-
> side. No one could condemn or absolve her. Her act was her very
> own. *I have done it of my own free will.* It was her own will that was
> being fulfilled; now nothing separated her from herself. She had
> chosen at last. She had chosen herself.[68]

From *L'Invitée* to *The Second Sex*, the melodramatic story of a woman's
quest for autonomy from her lover's regard was rewritten as a formal,
existentialist treatise on woman's liberation from her position as the

---

[65]Ibid., p. 711.
[66]Ibid., p. 704.
[67]Toril Moi makes this excellent insight in *Simone de Beauvoir*, Part II, pp. 95–213.
[68]Simone de Beauvoir, *She Came to Stay* (New York: Norton, 1954), p. 404.

eternal "other." What Beauvoir's heroine achieved, that none before her had, was the possibility for moral autonomy *within* a relationship with a man.

As Toril Moi has acutely observed, in *The Second Sex,* Beauvoir's existentialist analysis of woman's situation operates on three levels: the ontological, the social-psychological, and the biological. On an ontological level, Beauvoir posits that men and women are caught equally in the tension between their desire for being (transcendence) and the temptations of mere existence (immanence). At the social-psychological level, women are singularly oppressed by a patriarchal order they must struggle against. At the biological level, anatomical sexual difference indelibly marks female consciousness.[69]

Female consciousness within patriarchal society imposes contradictions on women seeking independence. These contradictions inevitably divide their psyches in two: "She wants to live at once like a man and like a woman, and in that way she multiplies her tasks and adds to her fatigue," Beauvoir writes. And a few pages further on: "She will be a double for her husband and at the same time she will be herself. . . . she is torn and divided."[70] As long as women are dependent on men, economically, socially, or psychosexually, they will remain in a condition of alienation.

Women's liberation, by Beauvoir's lights, is above all a cultural rather than a political project—a transformation of female consciousness made possible by achieving moral independence at the social-psychological level. Transcendental creativity was made possible for women not by the claims to political or juridical equality demanded by the feminist movement of her day, but by financial and bodily independence—liberation from the coercion of the marital regime. Once freed from her dependence on men, she had the chance to integrate her distinctive sexual consciousness with her ontological quest for being (transcendence). The great modern women writers had all achieved this: Charrière, Staël, Sand, Colette. Staël and Colette, Beauvoir thought, especially, had succeeded in, at once, retaining their independence and commanding the desire of men.[71]

Transcendental freedom entailed embracing a life of perpetual self-overcoming, the creation of an indeterminate self. But however inde-

[69]I am relying here on Toril Moi's concise exposé of the structure of the work; see Moi *Simone de Beauvoir,* pp. 174–178.

[70]Beauvoir, *The Second Sex,* pp. 684, 695.

[71]Ibid., p. 685.

terminate this female self was, it could not, finally, escape either its sexed consciousness or its sexed representation. Thus, even for Beauvoir, the positing of a female philosophical subject entailed the deployment of a figure of doubled identity in order to recover the cultural ground from which transcendence could be attainable: "One is not born, but rather, becomes, a woman."[72] The essential rhetorical move in the dereification of female identity is the supplementation of a given with a fabricated identity—the recovery of the self's opacity and its performative potential.[73]

For Beauvoir, as for her female predecessors since the beginnings of the Enlightenment, the cultural project of becoming modern was a project of denaturalizing the concept of woman. Denaturalization would not result in a disappearance or transcendence of the two sexes or in the unification of their identities. Rather, it entailed a shared set of aesthetic strategies that, I hope I have shown, had their roots deep in the era of the French Revolution: philosophical skepticism, the indeterminacy of probabilistic narrative, and antimimetic modes of representation. Fiction, in this sense, was not an escape from the real but, rather, the positive act of creating new terms of existence. It may seem odd to trace a genealogy for modern female philosophical identity that runs from Mme de Genlis to Simone de Beauvoir, but our very failure to be able to identify the one woman with the other speaks to the success of their representational tactics in establishing the incommensurability of modern women. Nothing less was at stake in the cultural work of asserting that incommensurablity than the ontological possibility of female moral self-determination. Fiction made it possible to recover that philosophical ground.

[72]Ibid., p. 267.

[73]In this sense, the theoretical work of Judith Butler and Rosi Braidotti can be seen as descending from the philosophical legacy of Beauvoir. See Judith Butler, *Gender Trouble* (New York: Routledge, 1989); and Rosi Braidotti, *Nomadic Subjects: Embodiment and Sexual Difference in Contemporary Feminist Theory* (New York: Columbia University Press, 1994).

Conclusion

The French Revolution was an era of philosophical awakening for women. It freed them to begin to re-imagine the world in their own terms. Those turbulent years thus set the cultural project of modernity into motion. But the Revolution did not end for women in 1799, 1848, or even 1881. Rather, it came gradually to a close in the fifty years between 1920 and 1970. As educational, political, and, finally, civic equality became a reality for the generation of women born just before World War I, the circumstances of female intellectual life in France have steadily come into step with those of their male counterparts.

Women thus entered professional philosophical circles at the very moment when French academic philosophy was turning away from Kant and toward Hegelian phenomenology. The phenomenological school, fascinated as it has been with temporality and history, brought with it a renewal of interest in fictional forms of philosophical exposition. Simone de Beauvoir's *oeuvre* is the fruit of this historical convergence. In her hands, the aesthetic tactics of her female predecessors converged with the phenomenological revolution in French philosophy.

The future for women and for philosophy, in the wake of this feminist revolution, is still up for grabs. But writing as I do now, on the other side of that historical threshold, I am profoundly aware of the distance that separates me from the world in which the women in this book forged their lives. They wrote fiction in order to write philosophy, to create themselves as morally autonomous subjects. They worked outside the institutional structures of the professions and the academy from which they were excluded. I can now write their history as an engagement with what Simone de Beauvoir would have called "the real world"—the world of historical truth—based on a public record and in a genre open to all.

The story that emerges from this book is the story of the making of moral autonomy through writing, a tale not without its impediments and contradictions. First among these, and most fundamental, is that the supposedly liberatory movement of the bourgeois republics that came into being in the wake of the French Revolution insisted on the sexual subordination of women to men through both constitutional law and the regulatory mechanisms of civil society.[1] However, at the same time, the liberal commercial policies of the revolutionary era freed print culture from the corporate regulations of the Old Regime. The advent of a market economy in print made possible public debate in all arenas of intellectual and political life and, in so doing, it also made possible an unprecedented entry of women into the public life of letters. Thus, at the very moment when male legislators determined that the new French Republic was to be governed by male heads of household alone, women were rushing into the cultural space opened up by liberal economic policies. Capitalism and republicanism were thus pitted against one another with respect to the public role of women. And modern political feminism emerged precisely from this revolutionary conjuncture.

Excluded from higher education and the professions in the wake of the Revolution, it was in the realm of literature alone that women were able to command cultural authority and to carve out a space for their public self-constitution. At the heart of the impulse to write lay the problem of moral self-governance. While few women sought political equality, women across the entire political spectrum, from nascent republican socialists to royalists, insisted on women's right to moral autonomy: Like postrevolutionary men, they demanded not only independence from parental control in marital choice, but, more fundamentally, the

[1]For France, see Joan Landes, *Women and the Public Sphere in the Age of the French Revolution* (Ithaca, NY: Cornell University Press, 1988); Lynn Hunt, *The Family Romance of the French Revolution* (Berkeley: University of California Press, 1992); Geneviève Fraisse, *Reason's Muse: Sexual Difference and the Birth of Democracy* (Chicago: University of Chicago Press, 1994; original French edition, 1989); and Joan Wallach Scott, *Only Paradoxes to Offer: French Feminists and the Rights of Man* (Cambridge, MA: Harvard University Press, 1997). For the German case, see Isabel V. Hull, *Sexuality, State and Civil Society in Germany, 1700–1815* (Ithaca, NY: Cornell University Press, 1996). For the Russian case, see Laura Engelstein, *The Keys to Happiness: Sex and the Search for Modernity in Fin-de-Siècle Russia* (Ithaca, NY: Cornell University Press, 1993).

freedom to shape their own personalities and spiritual lives (sacred or secular), even within the marital regime.

In reaction to the specter of female independence, postrevolutionary biology put women's capacity for moral self-governance into question; it viewed them as physically less capable of intellectual and moral development than men because of their reproductive roles. The women whose work I study responded to this reduction of their personhood to their bodies by stressing the contingent relationship of their moral being to the biological. Fictional narrative became the means to denaturalize public identities, to show that women could be creators rather than mere creations of their circumstances, and to demonstrate that those circumstances were always open to further change. It made it possible for them to pursue a life of self-reflexive moral development within a regime of juridical subordination. The moral and the aesthetic thus came to be bound up with one another—not in the sense that the good implied the beautiful, but in that the capacity to create became a sign of the capacity to judge, and, hence, to govern. Whether reflecting on the nature of political authority, the suitability of a spouse, the pursuit of a life independent of the familial regime, or the existential quest for self-transcendence, French women intellectuals of the modern period gave shape to a distinctive poetics of self-making—one that was skeptical not idealist, fictional not scientific, situationalist not universalist. This dissident trajectory of the Enlightenment—from philosophical fiction to the phenomenological revolution—is a story of perpetual self-overcoming, and it is, categorically, one without end.

Bibliography of French Women, 1789–1800

Aelders, Etta Palm d'. *Appel aux françaises sur la régénération des moeurs et nécessité de l'influence des femmes dans un gouvernement libre.* Paris: imp. du Cercle social, 1791. in-8; IV–46p.
[MW]; [CHF], x, 654; BN: 8 Lb(39). 9980.
politics.

———. *Discours . . . lu à la Confédération des Amis de la Vérité.* Caen: Chalopin, n.d. in-8; 8p.
[MW]; BN: 8 Lb(40). 2610.
politics.

Allain-Labertinière, citoyenne et citoyen. *Chanson de la citoyenne Allain, femme Labertinière, aux défenseurs de la patrie, au nom des femmes. Chanson du citoyen Allain-Labertinière.* Paris: imp. de Boulard, n.d. in-8; 8p.
[MW]; BN: Velins. 2323 (7).
song.

Allart, madame Mary née Gay c. 1750–1821. *Discours . . . aux volontaires du Mont-Blanc.* N.l.: n.d.[1793].
in-8; 11p; CHF title: *Extrait du procès-verbal de la séance des Amis de la liberté de l'égalité de Chambéry, du 18 mars 1793. . . . Discours prononcé par la citoyenne Gay aux volontaires du Mont-Blanc.*
[MW]; [CHF], x, 750; BN: 8 Lb(40).2632.
politics.

———. *Elénore de Rosalba ou le confessionnal des pénitens noirs, traduit de l'anglais d'Anne Radcliffe, auteur de 'La Forêt ou l'abbaye de Saint-Clair,' par Mary Gay, avec figures de Queverdo.* Paris: Lepetit & Genève, J. J. Paschoud, 1797.
7t. in-18; translation of *The Italian or the Confessional of the Black Penitents*, by Mrs. Anne Ward Radcliffe (1797); other editions: 1) *nouvelle édition*, Lausanne, Hignou, 1797, 4t., t.I:292p, t.II:275p, t.III:272p, t.III:305p.; 2) JT 30 germ. VI lists another title that appears to be the same translation but under a slightly different name, *Paris, au magasin des romans nouveaux, chez Leprieur*, 7t. in-18; a different translation of this work was published by l'abbé André Morellet, under the title *L'Italien ou le confessional des pénitens noirs.* Paris: Denné jeune, Maradan,

Allart (*continued*)
    1797, 3t. in-12, t.I:390p, t.II:384p,
    t.III:460p.; ABF: 12, 395–399.
    [BGR]; JT 16.xii.97; Mag. enc. III
    1797 iii 105; Monglond.
    novel / translation.
    ———. *Les Secrets de famille, traduit de*
    l'anglais de M. Pratt sur la troisième
    édition par Mary-Gay Allart, traduc-
    trice d'Eléonore de Rosalba, orné des
    figures. Paris: Au Magasin des ro-
    mans nouveau, chez Lepetit, 1800.
    5t. in-12; t.I:702p (for 207, accord-
    ing to the entry), t.II:193p,
    t.III:183p, t.IV:167p, t.V:172p;
    translation of *Family Secrets, Liter-*
    ary and Domestic, by Samuel Jack-
    son Pratt (1797); other editions:
    1802, 5t. in-18.
    [BGR]; JT 20 therm. VI ('*sous*
    presse'), 1, 25 vend. VIII; Mon-
    glond.
    novel / translation.
Allemand de Montmartin, mademoi-
    selle fl. 1724. *Griselidis ou la mar-*
    quise de Salusses. 1789.
    new edition; previous editions: (1)
    1724, (2) 1789. ABF: 13, 152–153.
    [BGR].
    novel.
Amiard, veuve. *Petit Saint-Cyr Na-*
    tional, fondé par la société de bienfai-
    sance pour l'éducation des pauvres
    demoiselles, sans distinction de nais-
    sance. Paris: imp. de Pougin, n.d.
    in-8; 42p; signed by author.
    [MW]; BN: 8 R. Pièce. 7114 et 7229.
    education / pedagogy.
    ———. *Plan d'un hospice d'éducation,*
    pour les jeunes demoiselles dénuées de
    fortune, sous la protection de la na-
    tion, et approuvé par l'assemblée na-
    tionale . . . N.l.: n.d.
    in-4; 42p.
    [MW]; BN: Rp. 13439 et 4 R. Pièce.
    1090.
    education / pedagogy.

Antoine, Marguerite Henriette
    Garcinde Sabran veuve. *Pétition*
    adressée au Conseil des Cinq-Cents
    pour obtenir l'autorisation de com-
    penser le prix des biens nationaux
    soumissionnés par elle avec le mon-
    tant de ses créances sur l'état. Brig-
    noles: imp. de J. Guichard fils, n.d.
    [c. 1796].
    in-4; 7p; date from BLC.
    [MW];[CHF]; BN: 4 Ln(27). 488;
    BLC.
    petition / politics.
Antraigues, madame d' fl. 1795.
    Ernesta, nouvelle allemande, par la ce
    d'Antraigues. Paris: Moutardier,
    1799.
    in-12; 152p. ABF: 23, 398.
    [BGR]; Monglond.
    novel.
Audu, Louise Reine madame fl. 1789.
    Pétition pour Reine-Louise Audu lue
    à l'Assemblée Nationale, le . . . *24*
    janvier 1792, au nom de plus de 300
    citoyens actifs. [Paris]: 1792.
    in-8; 7p; signed R.L. Audu and
    Chenaux. ABF: 36, 433.
    BLC.
    politics.
    ———. *Requête présentée à l'Assemblée*
    Nationale par Reine-Louise Audu,
    accusée dans l'affaire des 5 et 6
    octobre, détenue au prison du
    Châtelet. Lue à la Société des Amis
    de la Constitution, le 24 octobre
    1790. Paris: imp. de Roland, n.d.
    [1790].
    in-4; 7p.
    [CHF], ii, 742; BLC; BNA: Lb(40).
    557.
    politics.
Aulnoy, Marie Catherine madame d'.
    1650 or 1651–1705. *Collection des*
    contes des fées. 1797.
    8 vol. in-8.
    [NL].
    short stories.

———. *Contes de fées, contenant la grenouille bienfaisante, le mouton et le nain jaune* . . . Paris: Bourdet, n.d. [1793].
in-12; reprint.
[Monglond].
short stories.

Bacqueville, veuve Ansart. *Mémoire justificatif pour le citoyen Ansart, habitant de Saint-Pol, condamné à la peine de mort, par jugement du tribunal révolutionnaire d'Arras du 18 floréal an II* . . . Paris: imp. de Guffroy, n.d.
in-4; 8p; [Du 4 germ. an III]; signed by author.
[MW][CHF]; BN: 4ø Ln(27). 457.
politics.

Bacquié, Sophie fl. 1790. *Élégie d'une fille adoptive de Marat, sur la Mort de l'ami du peuple, lue au temple de la raison, le 10 floréal an II.* Toulouse: Vialanes, 1794.
in-4. ABF: 44, 349–350.
[Monglond].
poetry.

———. *Hymne d'une religieuse à la vierge, sur l'assurance donnée au corps religieux que la communauté ne sera point rompue; ouvrage couronné en 1790 par l'académie des jeux floraux.* Toulouse: 1790.
in-8.
[Monglond].
religion.

Bagneris, Victoire. *La citoyenne Bagneris à la Convention Nationale.* Paris: imp. *de la 'Feuille des spectacles',* n.d.
in-4; 4p.
[MW]; [CHF]; BN: 4ø Lb(41).3722.
politics.

———. *Couplets adressés à mon époux pour le jour de sa fête.* Paris: imp. *de la 'Feuille des spectacles',* n.d.
in-8; 4p.
[MW]; BN: 8 Ye.Pièce.5135 et 5409

(2 ex.).
poetry.

Barthelemy-Hadot, Marie Adele called Armand 1763–1821. *Cange.* 1794.
Pour le Théâtre de la Cité, 18th brumaire an III; J. T. lists 15 brumaire an III, p. 643.
[Monglond].
theater.

Baudin, citoyenne. *La Rose, opéra en un acte.*
performed at the *Théâtre de l'Ambigu-Comique,* 14 ventôse an III (J. T. gives 19 ventôse an III, 93–94).
[Monglond].
theater.

Beaufort d'Hautpoul, Anne Marie de Montgeroult de Coutances comtesse de c. 1760–1837. *Achille et Déidamie.* Toulouse: Bénichet frères, 1799.
in-8.
[Monglond].
poetry.

———. *La Mort de Lucrèce, Héroïde.* Toulouse: 1800.
in-8.
Biographie Universelle.
poetry.

———. *Sapho à Phaon, héroïde couronnée par l'académie des jeux floraux, en 1790.* Toulouse: 1790.
in-8.
[Monglond].
poetry.

———. *La Violette.* Toulouse: Bénichet frères, 1797.
in-8.
[Monglond].
poetry.

———. *Zilia, roman pastoral.* Toulouse: Desclassans, 1789.
in-12; other editions: (1) Paris, 1796, in-12, (2) London, Baylis and Dulau and Co. printing house, Deboffe and Bossey, 1797,

Beaufort d'Hautpoul (*continued*)
in-24, pp:
xvi + 116.
[BGR]; BN has an edition listed as
in-16, 113p, title page missing;
BLC.
novel.

Beauharnais, Fanny comtesse de (real
name Marie Anne Françoise née
Mouchard, 1738–1813). *L'Abailard*
supposé ou le sentiment à l'épreuve.
Lyon: A. de la Roche, 1791.
in-8, 189 p; other editions: (1)
Neuchâtel: Société typographique,
1780, in-8; (2) Paris & Liège:
Lemarie, 1781; (3) Amsterdam &
Paris: 1781; (4) Paris & Liège:
Lemarie, 1782, in-12, 242p.; (5)
Lyon: A. de la Roche, 1791; (6)
Paris: 1796 an IV, in-8, 162p.
[BGR]; BLC.
novel.

———. *L'Aveugle par amour, par l'au-*
teur de 'Stéphanie' & de 'L'Abailard
supposé.' Lyon: 1791.
in-12, viii + 259p; other editions:
(1) Liège: Lemarie, 1781 (2) Paris
& Liège: Lemarie, 1782, in-12,
343p, (3) Lyon: 1791, in-12, (4)
Paris, 1798.
[BGR].
novel.

———. *Constance ou le triomphe de*
l'infortune, roman sentimental par
madame la comtesse de Beauharnois,
troisième édition, revue, corrigée et
augmentée. London & Paris:
Maradan, 1789.
4 part. in-12, Ier part:91p, 2e
part:92–206p, 3e part:123p, 4e
part:124–242p.
[BGR].
novel.

———. *Les Noeuds enchantés ou la*
bizarrerie des destinées. Rome: de
l'imprimerie papale, 1789.
2t. in-12; t.I:114p, t.II:116p.

[BGR].
novel.

———. *Pièces fugitives en vers.* Paris:
1800.
in-8.
poetry.

———. *Roseide et Valmor ou les vic-*
times de l'orgueil, traduit de
l'Anglais de Sir Horace Walpole,
par F. Beauharnay. Paris: Ancelle,
1800.
2t. in-18.
[BGR]; JT 20 pluv. VIII.
novel / translation.

Beaulieu, madame de. *La Sylphide ou*
l'ange gardien. Paris: Chez Dufart,
1796.
in-18.
[NL].
novel.

Beaumarchais, Amelie Eugenie
madame Caron de b. 1778. *Obser-*
vations soumises à l'examen des
citoyens députés à la Convention Na-
tionale. par la citoyenne-épouse de
Pierre-Augustin-Caron
Beaumarchais. N.l. [Paris]: n.d.
[1793].
in-8; 4p.
[Monglond];[CHF]; [MW]; 8
Ln(27). 1331; BLC.
politics.

Beaumont, madame de. *Le Bulletin et*
journal des journaux, réviseur impar-
tial du pour et du contre.
3 vols.; changes title: *Le Réviseur*
universel et impartial de tous les jour-
naux pour et contre, et bulletin de
mme de Beaumont (à partir du 3 oct.
1791); Le Réviseur universel et im-
partial, et bulletin de Madame de
Beaumont (à partir du Ier février
1792); Dir: Mme de Beaumont;
Paris, *trois fois par semaine, en*
livraisons de 4 p. in-4.
[MW]; BN: 4 Lc2.629–630.
journal.

Belle, veuve. *Les Imprimeurs employés par les corps administratifs du Gard à leurs confrères.* N.l.: n.d. [1797].
in-4; 3p.
[MW]; 8 Ln(27). 43165.
commercial.

Benjamin, femme de Jacob. *La Femme de Jacob Benjamin à la Convention Nationale.* Paris: imp. de Vve Hérissant, n.d. [1792].
in-8; 32p; Pièce.
[CHF], ix, 300; BLC; BN: Ln(27). 1536.
politics.

Bergeron, madame. *Justification d'un condamné, adressé au public et à ses juges par sa mère, curatrice à sa mémoire.* Angoulême: imp. de Texier Tremeau, n.d.
in-4; 29p; Pièce.
[CHF], ix, 304; BN: Ln(27). 1625.
politics.

Bertin-Cuvelier, Marie Thérèse. *Pétition à la Convention Nationale par la citoyenne Marie-Thérèse Bertin-Cuvelier . . . sur la fausse application, à son égard, de la loi du huit avril 1792, concernant les émigrés.* Paris: Imp. nationale, n.d. [1792].
in-8; Pièce; 4p.
[CHF]; BLC.
politics.

Bethomas, mademoiselle de. *Lettre à M. de Frondeville, président au Parlement de Normandie . . .* N.l.: n.d. [1789].
in-8; 15p.
[MW]; [CHF], x, 557; 8ø Lb(39). 7168; BLC.
letter.

Billet, Anne Louise Françoise Delorme (called Stéphanie-Louise de Bourbon-Conti) 1756–1825. *Détails sur les principes d'éducation enseignés et mis en pratique par J. J. Rousseau. Tirés des 'Mémoires his-toriques' de Stéphanie-Louise De Bourbon-Conti.* N.l.: 1798.
[Monglond].
pedagogy.

———. *Mémoire . . . à la Convention Nationale . . .* Paris: imp. de Poignée, 1796.
in-8; 16p.
[MW]; BN: 8 Ln(27). 4831; BLC.
politics.

———. *Mémoire présenté au roi . . .* Paris: imp. de Brasseur aîné, n.d.
in-4; 24p.
[MW]; BN: 4 Ln(27). 4834.
politics.

———. *Mémoires historiques de Stéphanie-Louise de Bourbon-Conti, écrits par elle-même.* Paris: chez l'auteur, 1797.
2 vols. in-8.
[Monglond]; [MW]; BN: Ln(27) 4832; BLC.
memoir / correspondence.

Blin, Marie Dorothée Isabelle Calonne dame Antoine-Vindicien. *Aux Membres composant la Convention Nationale.* Paris: imp. de Guffroy, 1795.
in-8; 14p.
[MW]; [CHF], iii, 113; 8 Lb(41). 1556 et 5246; BLC.
politics.

———. *Pétition en réclamation de biens, adressée par la Vve Blin à la Convention Nationale . . .* Paris: imp. de Guffroy, n.d.
in-8; Pièce.
[CHF], ix, 325; BLC.
politics.

Bogé, madame Sophie. *Les Crimes de la noblesse, ou le régime féodal, pièce en 5 actes en prose, . . . grand spectacle . . . représentée sur divers théâtres de la commune de Paris.* Paris: Barba, 1794.
in-8; 66p.
[MW]; BN: 8 Yth. 4233, 20944 et

Bogé (*continued*)
23244; BLC.
theater.
————. *La Folie de Jérôme Pointu, ou le procureur devenu fou, comédie en deux actes, en prose, etc.* Paris: n.p., 1795.
in-8.
BLC.
theater.
————. *Le Mari coupable, comédie en 3 actes . . .* Paris: Barba, 1795.
in-8; 51p; performed in Paris at the *Théâtre de la Cité*, 4e j.c. an II.
[MW]; BN: 8 Yth. 10963; BLC.
theater.
————. *Plus de Bâtards en France, comédie en trois actes en prose, par la citoyenne Villeneuve.* Paris: Barba, 1795.
in-8; 69p; performed at the *Théâtre de la Cité*, 4 floréal an III, 23 avril 1795.
[Monglond]; [MW]; BN: 8 Yth. 14355; BLC.
theater.
————. *Le Véritable ami des lois, ou le républicain à l'épreuve, comédie en 4 actes, en prose, à grand spectacle . . .* Paris: Barba, 1795.
in-8; 59p; performed at the *Théâtre des sans-culottes.*
[MW]; BN: 8 Yth. 18880; BLC.
theater.
Bontemps, madame. *Paris, ce 12 janvier 1793 . . . au citoyen président de la Convention Nationale et aux membres d'icelle.* Paris: imp. de Knapen, n.d. (1793).
in-8; Pièce.
[CHF], ix, 733; BN: Ln(27). 11707.
politics.
Boosere, madame. *Triomphe de la saine philosophie ou la vraie politique des femmes, par la C. B***.* Paris: se vend chez Debray, libraire, et à

l'imprimerie des femmes, 1795.
in-8; 117p; other edition: Paris, Debray, 1797, in-8, 117p.
[BGR].
novel.
Bossu, citoyenne Rosalie Delphine Josephe. *Accusateur public, juges et jurés du tribunal révolutionnaire d'Arras, imposteurs et prévaricateurs. La citoyenne Dubois, veuve, avec enfants, de Jean-Baptiste Brazier, . . . la citoyenne Rosalie-Delphine-Josephe Bossu, . . . et Victoire Hidou, veuve de Jean-Baptiste Bossu, . . . à la Convention Nationale.* Paris: imp. de Guffroy, n.d. [1794].
in-4; 7p.
[CHF], ix, 91; BN: Lb (41) 4158.
politics.
Boufflers-Rouverel, Marie Charlotte Hippolyte née de Campet de Saujon comtesse Edouard de 1725–c. 1800. *Pétition à la Convention Nationale pour demander à n'être point comprise parmi les parents d'émigrés dont les biens sont séquestrés.* N.l.: n.d.[1795]; [1794?], BLC.
in-4; 2p; ABF: 134, 236–241.
[MW]; [CHF], iii, 121; BN: 4 Lb(41). 1716.
politics.
Bouillon, Lucie Elisabeth b. 1747. *A la Mère patrie, prologue exécuté par des jeunes demoiselles à la fête donnée en famille.* Berlin: n.p. 1790.
in-8; ABF: 135, 403–404.
[Monglond].
theater.
————. *Nouvelle Géographie, à l'usage des instituts et des gouvernantes françaises . . .* Berlin: Decker, 1786–1790.
3 vol. in-8.
[Monglond].
pedagogy / natural science.
Bourdic-Viot, Marie Anne Henriette née Pavan de l'Estang later

Bourdic-Viot (*continued*)
   d'Autremont 1746–1802. *Éloge de
   Montaigne, par Henriette Bourdic-
   Biot*. Paris: C. Pougens, 1799.
   BLC records pub info: 1800, in-12,
   105p; ABF: 140, 227–233; 1054, 45–
   47; 1033, 278–279.
   [CHF]; x, 64; BLC; BN: Ln(27).
   14506 and 6 more ex.
   literature.
   ———. *L'Emigration du plaisir, et son
   retour en France*. N.l.: [1794].
   in-4.
   BLC.
   song.
   ———. *Six Romances avec accompagnement de clavecin & de violon obligé*.
   1791.
   music by M. Piccini.
   [FC].
   music.
   ———. *Vers à la comtesse de V . . . le
   jour de Sainte Catherine*. 1790.
   [BLC].
   poetry.
Brayer Saint-Léon, Louise Marguerite
   Jeanne Madeleine b. 1765. *Eugénio
   et Virginia, orné de figures dessinées
   par Lebarbier aîné et gravées par
   Baquoy et Patas*. Paris: Charles
   Pougens et Lefort, 1800.
   2t. in-12; t.I:xxviii + 197p,
   t.II:210p; BLC gives date 1799–
   1800; other edition: Paris, C.
   Pougens, Lefort, 1801, 2t. in-18,
   t.I:xlii + 211p, t.II:215p.; ABF: 150,
   144.
   [BGR]; BN: Y2. 23120–23122; Mag.
   enc. V 1799 iv 277; Monglond;
   BLC.
   novel.
   ———. *Rosa ou la fille mendiante et ses
   bienfaiteurs, traduit de l'anglais de
   Mistress Bennett, auteur d'Anna ou
   l'héritière galloise,' par Louise
   Brayer-St.-Léon*. Paris: Charles
   Pougens, 1798.

   7t. in-12; t.I:405p, t.II:477p,
   t.III:393p, t.IV:474p, t.V:473p,
   t.VI:421p, t.VII:544p; translation of
   The Beggar Girl and her Benefactors,
   by Agnes Maria Bennett (1797);
   other edition, Paris: Lepetit et
   Pougens, 1798, 10t. in-18.
   [BGR]; BN: Y2 17175–17181; JT
   23.x.97, 8 prair. VI; Mag. enc. IV
   1798 II 144, 348; Monglond.
   novel / translation.
Brissot de Warville, madame. *Lettres
   philosophiques et politiques sur l'histoire d'Angleterre depuis son origine
   jusqu'à nos jours, trad. de l'anglais et
   enrichies de notes sur l'original par
   Mme Brissot de Warville. 2me Édition*. 1789.
   2 vol. in-8; first edition, London &
   Paris: Regnault, 1785.
   [Monglond].
   philosophy / translation.
Brohon, Jacqueline Aimée mademoiselle 1731–1778. *Instructions édifiantes de Mademoiselle Brohoon [Bro-
   hon], morte en odeur de sainteté il y a
   douze ans*. Paris: Mme Lesclapart,
   1791.
   in-12.
   [Monglond].
   religion / pedagogy.
   ———. *Instructions édifiantes sur le
   jeûne de Jésus-Christ au désert*.
   Paris: imp. de Didot l'aîné, 1791.
   in-12.
   [Monglond].
   religion / pedagogy.
   ———. *Manuel des victimes de Jésus,
   ou extrait des instructions que le
   seigneur a données à sa première victime [Extrait des ouvrages de Mlle
   Brohon]*. N.l.: 1799.
   in-8.
   [Monglond].
   religion / pedagogy.
   ———. *Reflexions édifiantes, par l'auteur des instructions édifiantes sur le*

Brohon (continued)
  jeûne de Jésus-Christ au désert.
  Paris: imp. de Didot l'aîné, 1791.
  2 vol. in-12.
  [Monglond].
  religion / pedagogy.
Buzot, Marie Anne Victoire née
  Baudry. Au Conseil des Cinq-Cents,
  les héritiers Buzot. N.l.: n.d.[1797?].
  in-8.
  BLC.
  politics.
———. La Citoyenne veuve Buzot aux
  habitans du Calvados. N.l.:
  n.d.[1794].
  in-8; 3p.
  [MW]; [CHF], iii, 111; BN: 8
  Lb(41). 1508.
  letter.
———. Lettre . . . aux républicains du
  Département de l'Eure. Paris, le 20
  frim. an III . . . N.l.: n.d.
  in-8; 7p.
  [MW]; BN: 8 Lb(41). 1507.
  letter.
Cambis, madame de. Du Sort actuel
  des femmes. Paris: imp. du Cercle
  Social, 1791.
  in-8; 16p.
  [Monglond]; BN: 2 ex. Rp. 1482 et
  Rz. 3493.
  politics.
Candeille, Amélie Julie (later la Roche,
  later Simons, and later Périe de
  Senovert) (1767–1834). Catherine, ou
  la belle fermière, comédie en trois actes
  et en prose, mêlée de chant, etc. (Paris,
  Théâtre de la République, 27 novembre
  1792). Paris: Maradan, 1793.
  in-8; iv-108p; BN and BLC list
  another edition, Paris: Barba, an
  VI-1797, in-8, 67p; BN: 3 ex. Yf.
  11186, 8 Yth. 2787–2788.
  [BLC]; BN: 8 Yth. 2783–2786.
  theater.
———. Le Commissionnaire, comédie en
  deux actes, en prose . . . (Paris,

Théâtre de l'Égalité, ci-devant
  français, le 7 frimaire l'an III). Paris:
  Maradan, An 3[1794].
  in-8; 50p.
  BLC; BN: 8 Yth. 3766.
  theater.
———. Sonates (2 grandes) pour
  clavecin. Naderman.
  in-4; ABF: 179, 275–297; 890, 282–
  283; 1055, 60–64.
  [BN].
  arts / music.
Carault, Marie Anne Thérèse Lallier
  veuve. Condamnation à mort
  prononcé par le tribunal révolutionnaire d'Arras, contre un militaire in-
  culpé d'un délit qui n'emportait pas
  cette peine. Paris: imp. de Guffroy,
  n.d. [1793–1794].
  in-4; 40; BLC lists date [1795].
  [CHF], ix, 385 and xi, 91a; BLC;
  BN: 2 ex. Lb(41). 4159 et Ln(27).
  3536.
  politics.
Carcan, veuve A. et Brachoud. La
  Blanchisseuse de mousseux, ou
  les amours de M. Coco, pièce grivoise
  en I acte, mêlée de chants, dédiée à
  M. Bengala, Jourdan-Coupe-Tête,
  Saint-Huruge . . . , tous ci-devant
  compagnons et amis du ci-devant
  très haut, très puissant . . . , très
  illustre Prince S. A. S. Monseigneur
  le duc d'Orléans, actuellement
  Philippe Capet, gentilhomme
  malgré lui. Paris: chez les
  marchands de nouveautés,
  1791.
  in-8.
  [Monglond].
  theater.
Carteaux, madame Jean François.
  Liberté, égalité. A mes concitoyens.
  Paris: imp. de Grand, n.d.[1794].
  in-4.
  [CHF], ix, 74; BLC.
  politics.

————. *Reproduction, en réponse aux accusations portées contre son mari, d'une lettre adressée celui-ci, le 27 vent. an II, par le général Dommartin.* Paris: imp. de Grand, n.d.
in-4; 2p.
[MW]; BN: 4 Ln(27). 3762 et 4 Ln(27). 3601.
politics.

Cazenove D'Arlens, Constance de Constant-Rebecque de 1755–1825. *Alfrede ou le manoir de Warwick.* Lausanne: Louis Luquiens, 1794.
in-12; t.I:251p, t.II:252p.
[BGR]; Monglond; BLC.
novel.

————. *Henriette et Emma ou l'éducation de l'amitié.* Paris: Imprimerie des sciences et des arts, 1796.
in-12; 259 p.; also published in Leipzig, by Pierre Philippe Wolf.
[BGR]; Mag. enc. I 1795 vi 284; Monglond.
novel.

————. *Les Orphelines de flowergarden, orné de figures gravées par Mariage.* Paris: Lepetit, 1799.
in-12.
[BGR]; JT 30 pluv. VII; Monglond.
novel.

Cépoy-Buffon, madame de. *Copie de l'expédition du procès-verbal fait chez la citoyenne Cépoy, ci-devant Buffon, après la recherche ordonnée et faite par le tribunal révolutionnaire de sa section . . . —Déclaration de la citoyenne Cépoy-Buffon sur les faits à sa connaissance concernant le citoyen Égalité et ses enfants. (18 avril).* N.l.: n.d. [1793].
in-8; 4p.
[CHF], ix, 39; BN: LB(41). 2914.
politics.

————. *Déclaration . . . sur les faits . . . concernant le citoyen Égalité et ses enfants.* N.l.: n.d.
in-8; 4p.

[MW]; BN: 8 Lb(41). 2914.
politics.

Cerenville, Jeanne Elenore madame de 1738–1807. *Walter de Monbary, grand-maître des templiers, roman historique, traduit de l'allemande de l'auteur d'Herman d'Unna.'* Paris: Maradan, 1799.
4t. in-12; t.I:294p, t.II:302p, t.III:321p, t.IV:314p; translation of *Walther von Montbarry, Grossmeister des Tempelordens* by Christiane-Bénédicte-Eugénie Naubert.
[BGR]; JT 15 flor. VII; Monglond.
novel / translation.

Chabeuf, veuve Noirot. *Mémoire et pièces justificatives pour M. Noirot, co-accusé de M. Varnier.* Dijon: L. N. Frantin, 1791.
in-4; 15p.
[CHF], x, 96; BLC.
politics.

————. *Notice des pièces justicatives pour M. Noirot, co-accusé de M. Varnier.* Dijon: L. N. Frantin, 1791.
in-4.
BLC.
politics.

Champion, citoyenne. *Pétition des Citoyennes Républicaines Révolutionnaires, lue à la barre de la Convention Nationale.* Paris: imp. de l'égalité, n.d.
in-8; 4p.
[MW]; BN: 8 Lb(40). 2412.
politics.

Charrière, Isabelle Agnès Elisabeth van Tuyll van Scrooskerken van Zuylen dame de 1740–1805. *Éclaircissements relatifs à la publications des 'Confessions' de Rousseau, avec des réflexions sur la réputation, les apologies de MM. Cérutti et d'Holback, sur le moment présent, etc. . . .* N.l.: Imprimé chez Fauche-Borel, n.d. [1790].

Charrière (*continued*)
in-12; 31p; BLC gives [1789], in-8,
31p.
[Monglond]; BLC.
philosophy.

————. *Éloge de Jean-Jacques Rousseau,
qui a concouru pour le prix de l'Académie Française.* Paris: Grégoire,
1790.
in-8; 60p.
BN: Ln(27). 17984.
literature.

————. *L'Émigré, comédie en trois actes.*
N.l.: 1793.
in-12; 66p.
[Monglond]; Godet.
theater.

————. *L'Abbé de la Tour ou recueil de
nouvelles et autres écrits divers.*
Leipzig: Pierre Philippe Wolf,
1798–1799.
1798 (t. I-II)–1799 (t. III); 3t. pet.
t.I:323p, t.II:x + 289p, t.III:197 +
131p; other editions: (1) Paris: A.
Nepfeu, 1808, 2t., t.I:197 + 131p,
t.II:289p; (2) London: Colburn,
1808, 3t. in-12.
[BGR]; [Monglond]; BN (t. I-II).
novel.

————. *Aiglonette et insinuante. Conte
par l'auteur de 'Bien-Né.'* N.l.: 1791.
in-8.
[Monglond].
short story.

————. *Les Deux familles, conte.*
Zuylen: Fondation Château de
Zuylen, 1789.
in-12; 15p.
[BGR]; [Monglond].
novel.

————. *Lettres d'un évêque français à la
nation.* 1789.
in-12.
[Monglond].
politics.

————. *Lettres trouvées dans des porte-
feuilles d'émigrés.* Paris: n.p. 1793.

in-12; 140p.
[BGR]; [Mongond].
novel.

————. *Lettres trouvées dans la neige.*
1793.
[Monglond].
politics.

————. *La Nature et l'art, par Mistriss
Inchbald, auteur de 'Simple Histoire,'
nouvelle traduction par Mlle de G. et
Mme de C.* Paris: imprimé chez
Fauche-Borel, 1797.
in-8, 240p; collaborative translation, with madame de Gelieu;
other editions: (1) Geneva: J. J.
Paschould & Paris, Buisson, Tavernier, Petit, Huet, 1797, 2t. in-18;
(2) Paris: Tavernier, an VI, 2t.
in-18.
[BGR].
novel/translation.

————. *Plainte et défense de Thérèse
Levasseur.* N.l.: Imprimé chez
Fauche-Borel, n.d. [1789].
in-12; 12p.
[Monglond].
society.

————. *Réponse à l'écrit du Colonel de
La Harpe, intitulé: 'De la Neutralité
des gouvernants de la Suisse depuis
l'année 1789.'* N.l.: 1797.
in-8; 26p.
[Monglond].
politics.

————. *Les Trois femmes, nouvelle, par
l'auteur des 'Lettres de Lausanne,'
publiée pour le soulagement d'une de
ses amies dans le malheur.* London:
Imprimerie de Baulis, et se trouve
chez J. Deboff, Dulau & Co, &
chez tous les marchands de nouveautés, 1796.
2t. in-18; t.I:156p, t.II:137p; First
published in German as *Drei
Weiber . . .* , Leipzig, 1795; other
editions: (1) Paris: Libraires de
nouveautés, 1797, 2t. in-12; (2)

Charrière (*continued*)
Paris: Mourer et Pinpar, 1797,
2t. in-18; (3) Paris, Mourer et Pinpar, an VI, 2t. in-18; (4) Lausanne:
Mourer, 1798, 2t. in-12; (5) *L'abbé
de la Tour ou recueil de nouvelles et
autres, écrits divers*, t.I, Leipzig:
Pierre Philippe Wolf, 1798; (6) *Les
Trois femmes . . .* , Paris: A. Nepveu,
1808, 323p.; (7) Paris: A. Nepveu,
1809, in-8, 323p.
[BGR]; [Monglond].
novel.

Chastenay, comtesse Victorine de b.
circa 1770. *Les Mystères d'Udolphe,
par Anne Radcliffe, traduit de
l'anglais sur la troisième édition.*
Paris: Maradan, 1797.
in-12; other editions: (1) Paris: n.p.
1797, 6t. in-18; (2) Paris: Maradan,
1808; (3) Paris: Maradan, 1819, 4t.
in-12.
[BGR]; JT 22.ix.97; Mag. enc. III
1797 ii 526; Monglond.
novel / translation.

Chéret, madame. *Evénement de Paris
et de Versailles, par une des dames
qui a eu l'honneur d'être de la députation à l'Assemblée Générale.* Paris:
Garnery et Volland, n.d. [1789].
in-8, 7p.
[Monglond]; [MW]; [CHF], x, 582;
BN: 8 Lb(39). 7941.
politics.

Choiseul-Meuse, comtesse Félicité
de. *Alberti ou l'erreur de la nature,
par Madame de C**, auteur de
'Coralie ou le danger de se fier à soi-
même,' Suivi de Mélusine.* Paris:
Marchand, 1799.
in-12.
[BGR]; JT 20 germ., 5 mess., 5
therm. vII, 25 brum. VIII; Monglond.
novel.
———. *Coralie ou le danger de se fier à
soi-même, par Madame de CH . . .*

Paris: imprimerie de Chaigneau
aîné, 1797.
2t. in-24; other editions, (1) Paris:
Devaux, an VI, 2t. in-18; (2) Paris:
n.p. an VII, 2t. in-12; (3) Paris: an
VIII, in-12; (4) N.l.: n.p., 1816, 2t.
in-8.
[BGR]; JT 16 germ. VI; Monglond.
novel.

Clabaux, veuve Dauchez. *Prévarica-
tion des juges du tribunal révolutionnaire d'Arras, qui ont mal et iniquement appliqué la peine de mort. A la
Convention Nationale.* Paris: imp.
de Guffroy, n.d. [1794].
in-4.
[CHF], ix, 91; BN: 4 Lb(41). 4157.
politics.

Clairon, Claire Josephe Hippolyte
Leris de La Tude (called mademoiselle) 1723–1803. *Mémoires et
réflexions sur l'Art dramatique, publiées par elle-même.* Paris: F. Buisson, 1798.
in-8; II-360p; other edition:—2me
édition. revue, corr. et augm.,
Paris, F. Buisson, an VII, in-8, VIII-
379p; listed in BLC under Legris
de la Tude, 1799, in-8, with a portrait.
[Monglond]; [CHF], ix, 422; BN:
Ln(27) 4360; BLC.
memoir / theater.

Clément, Albertine née Hémery
madame fl. 1799. *Le Démocrite
français, Journal politique, de littérature et des spectacles. Rédigé par la
citoyenne Reyneri* (1799).
Cnne Hémery (à partir du 18 flor.
an VII); Réd: Cnne Reyneri.—
Cnnes Hémery et Reyneri (no. du
17 flor. an VII).—Cnne Hémery
(no. du 18 flor. an VII.—Cnnes
Hémery et Reyneri (à partir du 19
flor. an VII).—Cnne Hémery (à
partir du 26 flor. an VII).—Cnnes
Hémery et Reyneri (à partir du 2

Clément (*continued*)
prair. an VII);Imp: Imp. du Journal
le Démocrite français (Lachave),
rue Poupée des Arcs, no. 16.—J.-B.
Lesourd, rue Nicaise, no. 513 (à
partir du 27 vent. an VII).—Imp.
du Démocrite française (à partir
du 17 flor. an VII).
[Monglond]; [MW];BN: Lc2 2729.
journal.
————. *Journal des dames et des modes*
41 volumes (1797–1839).
Paris, rue Montmartre; in-8; Mme
C. Wuiet is listed [by Tourneux] as
one of the first editors, along with
C. J. B. Lucas de Rochemone, J. J.
Lucet, Louis Dubois, etc.; this text
is listed under Hémery's name in
MW, with the note 'Réd., sous
le Consultat'; BLC lists name
Clément-Hemery; ABF: 231, 343.
[Monglond]; [MW]; BN: Rés. 8
Lc(24).4.
journal.
————. *Le Juif errant, Journal politique
et littéraire, ou relation véridique de
tous les événements relatifs à La
République française. Rédigé par la
citoyenne Clément Hémery* (1799).
[Monglond]; [MW]; [CHF]; BN: 8
Lc(2).2727.
journal.
————. *Prospectus du Journal le Juif er-
rant.* N.l.: n.d.
in-8; 2p.
[MW]; BN: 8ø Lc(2).2727.
prospectus / journal.
Clermont-Tonnerre, comtesse de.
Mon Portefeuille, dédié à ma femme.
Paris: Valade, 1791.
in-8; la comtesse de Clermont-
Tonnerre et Bouchard (Le cheva-
lier A. de).
[Monglond].
poetry.
Coicy, madame de. *Demandes des
femmes aux états généraux, par l'au-*

*teur des 'Femmes comme il convient
de les voir.'* N.l.: 1789.
in-8, 16p.
[Monglond]; BLC.
politics.
Coisy de Montigny, madame H. J. M.
de. *Mémoire . . . présenté à l'Assemblée Nationale.* Paris: imp. de Laurens jeune, n.d.
in-4; 4p.
[MW]; [CHF] ix, 428; BN: 4ø
Ln(27). 4502.
politics.
Colleville, Anne Hyacinthe de Saint-
Léger dame de 1761–1824. *Les
Dangers d'un tête-à-tête ou histoire
de Miss Mildmay, traduite de
l'anglais de Sir Higues Kelly, par A.
Colleville, de Cherbourg.* Paris: Le
Prieur, 1800.
in-12, 2v.
[BGR]; JT 10 fruct. VIII; Mag. enc.
vI 1800 iv 141; Monglond.
novel / translation.
Colon, Elisabeth Lardi veuve Joseph.
*Elisabeth Lardi . . . à la Convention
Nationale.* Paris: imp. de Dupont,
n.d.
in-8; 18p.
[MW]; [CHF] ix, 433; BN: 8 Ln(27).
4624.
politics.
Condorcet, Marie Louise Sophie de
Grochy marquise de 1764–1822.
Lettres sur la sympathie. [1798].
[Monglond].
philosophy / translation.
————. *Théorie des sentimens moraux,
ou essai analytique sur les principes
des jugemens moraux que portent naturellement les hommes, d'abord sur
les actions des autres et ensuite sur
leurs propres actions. Suivi d'une
Dissertation sur l'origine des
langues. Traduit de l'anglais sur la
7me et dernière édition, par Sophie
Grouchy, Vve Condorcet, qui y a joint*

Condorcet (*continued*)
huit lettres sur la sympathie. Paris:
F. Buisson, 1798.
2 vol. in-8; other edition:—2me
éd., revue et corr. Paris, Barrois
l'aîné, 1810, 2 vol. in-8,
BN: R.51408–51409.
[Monglond]; BN.
philosophy / translation.
Corbin, Marie Thérèse Lucidor dame.
*Discours . . . prononcé . . . au temple
de la raison, l'an 2e de la liberté.*
Paris: Coulubrier, n.d.
in-8; 2p.
[MW]; BN: 8 Lb(41). 5315.
politics.
———. *Pétition sur la réclamation de la
citoyenne Corbin à la Convention
Nationale.* N.l.: n.d. [1791].
in-4; 8p.
[MW]; BN: 8ø Lb(41). 530.
politics.
———. *Pétition sur la réclamation de la
citoyenne Corbin, à la Convention
Nationale (3 Fèvrier).* N.l.:
n.d.[1793].
in-4.
[CHF], iii, 30a.
politics.
Corday, Marie-Anne-Charlotte 1768–
1793. *Lettres de Marie Anne Charlotte Corday.* Paris: [1794].
in-4; 4p.
BLC.
politics.
———. *Véritable Lettre de Marie-Anne-
Charlotte Corday à Barbaroux . . .
l'autre à son père pour le consoler de
sa mort . . .* Paris: imp. de Guil-
homat, n.d. [1793].
in-8; 8p.
[MW]; [CHF] ix, 444; BN: 8ø
Ln(27). 4867.
politics.
Corémans, Marguerite Augustine
Kléber veuve. *A la nation française
et . . .à ses représentants.* Paris: imp.

de Dupont, n.d.[1796].
in-8; 39p.
[MW]; [CHF], iii, 146; BN: 8ø
Lb(42). 150; BLC.
politics.
Cottin, Sophie Ristaud dame 1770–
1807. *Claire d'Albe, par la C.****.
Paris: Maradan, 1799.
in-12, viii + 285p; other editions:
(1) Paris: Giguet et Michaud, an
XIII (1805), in-12, 283p.; (2) 3e édi-
tion, Paris: n.p., 1808, in-12; (3)
Paris: réimprimé à Londres, H.
Colburn, 1808, 2t. in-12; (4) Paris
& London: Colburn, 1811, 11t.; (5)
Paris: aux Cabinets littéraires,
1815–1816, 12t. in-12; (6) 4th ed.,
Paris: Michaud, 1817, 219p.; (7)
Paris: Foucault, 1817, 8t. in-12; (8)
Paris: Dabo, 1818, 12t. in-12.; (9)
Paris: Corbet, 1818, 12t.; (10) Paris:
Lebègue, 1820, in-12, 219p.; (11)
Paris: J. L. F. Foucault, 1820, 5t.
in-8.; (12) Paris: Roret et Roussel,
1820, 12t. in-12; (13) Paris: Dentu,
1820, 12t. in-18; (14) Paris: J. B.
Garnery, 1820, 12t. in-18; (15)
Paris: L. Tenré, 1820, 11t. in-12;
(16) Paris: Corbet, 1820, 12t. in-12;
ABF: 257, 301, 315–333.
[BGR]; JT 25 flor. VII; Monglond;
BLC.
novel.
———. *Malvina, par Madame ***, au-
teur de 'Claire D'Albe.'* Paris:
Maradan, 1800.
4t. in-12; p; other editions: (1)
Paris: Maradan, 1801, 4t. in-12;
(2) 2nd ed., Paris: Giguet et
Michaud, an xIII-1805, 3t. in-12;
(3) 3rd ed., Paris: L. G. Michaud,
1809, 3t. in-12; (4) London: Col-
burn, 1809, 3t.; (5) Paris: Michaud,
1811, 3t. in-12; (6) Paris: L. G.
Michaud, 1818, 2t.; (7) Paris:
Lebègue, 1820, 3t. in-12; (8) Paris:
J. B. Garnery, 1820, 3t.

Cottin (*continued*)
[BGR]; [Monglond]; BN: Y2
24709–24712.
novel.

Courtenai de la Fosse-Ronde, Sophie
Rémi madame de. *L'Argument des
pauvres aux États-Généraux*. N.l.:
n.d.[1789].
in-8; 15p.
[MW]; [CHF], x, 580 and ii, 522;
BN: 8ø Lb(39). 1589.
politics.

Couvert, citoyenne Millet femme.
*Pétition adressée à la Convention Na-
tionale . . .* Paris: imp. de L. Potier,
n.d.
in-4; 4p.
[MW]; [CHF] ix, 455; BN: 4ø
Ln(27).5116.
politics.

Daix, Sophie Joseph Eugénie. *Victimes
du système de sang longtemps à l'or-
dre du jour au tribunal révolution-
naire d'Arras. Marie-Joseph-
Antoinette, Louis-François-Joseph,
Cornil-Guislain-Joseph, Vaast-
François-Joseph, Marie-Louise-
Joseph, Louis-Benoist Lesergeant et
Sophie-Joseph-Eugénie Daix . . . à la
Convention Nationale*. Paris: imp.
de Guffroy, n.d.
in-4; 8p.
[MW]; BN: 8ø Lb(41). 4160.
politics.

Dalleaume, citoyenne. *Pétition au
corps législatif, par la citoyenne Dalleaume, épouse du citoyen de Frondeville, relative au remboursement
des rentes foncières (5 vendémiaire)*.
Lisieux: imp. de Mistral, n.d.
[1796].
in-8, 7p.
[CHF], iii, 1481 BLC; BN: 8 Lb(42).
92.
politics.

Daubenton, Marguerite 1720–1818.
Histoire de Zélie. 1789.

ABF: 281, 330–332.
[Monglond].
novel.
————. *Zélie dans le désert, par Mme
D****. Cinquième édition avec sup-
plément. Tome premier [quatrième]*.
Geneva & Paris: chez Dufart, 1796.
4 vol. in-18; first edition: 1786;
other edition, Paris: n.p. 4 vols.
in-18, 1804.
[Monglond].
novel.

Dauzay, Gabrielle. *Une Mère de famille
. . . au représantant du peuple Lan-
juinais*. N.l.[Paris]: n.d.[1794].
in-8; 4p.
[MW]; BN: Fp. 2783 and 8 Lb 41.
4416; BLC.
politics.

Defrance, Claude Jeanne née Chom-
pré madame 1747–1818. *Idylles sur
l'enfance et l'amour maternel, mises
en vers français, par Mme Defrance,
née Chompre . . .* Paris: imp. de
Crapelet, 1791.
in-8; other edition: Paris, Crapelet,
1800.
[Monglond].
pedagogy / poetry.

Dejassaud d'Erlach, Anne Charlotte
Marie. *Pétition au conseil des cinq-
cents, pour les héritiers légitimes de
René-Ange-Augustin Maupeou, en
réponse au rapport fait, le 19 frimaire
dernier, sur celle d'un prétendu enfant naturel Maupeou*. Paris: imp.
de Dupont, n.d.[1796].
in-8; 31p.
[MW]; BN: Fp. 2403; BLC.
politics.

Delaforest-Richard, madame. *Procé-
dures et pièces relatives à l'Assassinat
Juridique commis à Dijon le 21 germ.
an II en la personne de Frédéric-
Henri Richard, ci-devant président à
mortier au ci-dev. Parlement de Dijon
sous prétexte d'émigration*. Dijon:

Delaforest-Richard (*continued*)
    imp. de Vve Defay, 1795.
    in-4; 84p.
    [MW]; [CHF], xi, 95; BN: 4 Lb(41).
    4245.
    politics.
Deseine, madame Louis. *A la Conven-
    tion Nationale*. N.l.: 1794.
    in-4; 4p.
    [MW]; BN: 4 Ln(27). 27666.
    law.
Deshoulières, Antoinette Thérèse
    mademoiselle 1656–1718 and An-
    toinette du Ligier de la Garde,
    madame Deshoulières 1638–1694.
    Oeuvres. Paris: chez les libraires
    associés, 1790.
    2 vol. in-12; other edition, Paris:
    Desray, an VII, 2 vols. in-8.
    [Monglond].
    literature.
Desmarest, citoyenne de Corbeil. *Éle-
    ments d'instruction républicaine, par
    la citoyenne Desmarêts* (sic), *de Cor-
    beil, chef-lieu de district . . . imprimés
    aux frais et par ordre de la Société
    Populaire de la Commune de Corbeil*.
    N.l.: imprimé à l'institution na-
    tionale des Enfants-Aveugles, sec-
    tion et près l'Arsenal, 1794.
    in-8.
    [CHF], ii, 762; BN: 8ø Lb(40). 954.
    pedagogy / politics.
    ———. *Premiers Éleméns de l'instruc-
    tion républicaine*. Paris: Cailleau,
    1794 [an II].
    in-18; 44p.
    [BN]; [CHF], iii, 53; BN: 8
    Lb(41) 916.
    pedagogy.
Desmoulins, citoyenne. *Souscription
    de bienfaisance présentée par une in-
    fortunée à la Convention Nationale*.
    Paris: l'auteur, n.d. [1793?].
    in-8; 6p.
    [MW]; BN: Ye.Pièce.4902; BLC.
    politics.

Despalle, Victoire. *Observations
    adressées à messieurs du Comité Ec-
    clésiastique par les mandataires des
    imprimeurs-libraires des différentes
    liturgies de France . . .* Paris: imp.
    de N.-H. Nyon, 1792.
    in-4; 4p.
    [MW]; BN: Fp.7178.
    commercial.
Dhont, mademoiselles. *Ode présentée à
    M. Jean Dhont leur frère et à Mlle
    Rose de Pau, à l'occasion de leur
    mariage célébré à Bruges le 29 juin
    1798 (vieux style)*. [Bruges]: imp. de
    J. de Busscher et fils, n.d., [1798].
    in-8; 3p.
    [Mongond]; BN: Ye. 42033.
    poetry.
Dromgold, citoyenne. *Pétition . . . à la
    Convention Nationale*. Paris: imp.
    de Migneret, n.d.[1794].
    in-8; 6p.
    [MW]; [CHF]; BN: 8 Ln(27).6259.
    politics.
Du Châtelet, Gabrielle Emilie le Ton-
    nelier de Breteuil marquise 1706–
    1749. *Doutes sur les religions
    révélées, adressés à Voltaire. Ouvrage
    posthume*. Paris: 1792.
    in-8; 72p.
    [Monglond].
    philosophy.
    ———. *Lettres du roi de Prusse et de la
    marquise du Châtelet*. N.l.: n.p.,
    1790.
    in-8.
    BLC.
    letters.
Du Noyer, Anne Marguerite Petit
    madame 1663–1719. *Lettres his-
    toriques et galantes, ouvrage curieux.
    Nouv. éd. corr. et augm. de plusieurs
    lettres très intéressantes*. Paris &
    Avignon: François Seguin, 1790.
    12 vol. in-12; first edition: 1713.
    [Monglond]; BLC; BN: Z. 15172.
    literature.

Du Petit-Thouars, Félicité. *Mémoire
adressé . . . aux actionnaires et à
l'équipage du diligent, expédié au
mois d'août 1792 pour aller à la
recherche de M. de la Peyrouse . . .*
Paris: imp. de Gueffier, n.d.
in-4; 23p.
[MW]; BN: 4 Ln(27).32144.
politics / commercial.
Dubarry, Anne Marie Thérèse
Rabaudy-Montoussin veuve. *La
Citoyenne Anne-Marie-Thérèse
Rabaudy-Montoussin, Veuve de Jean-
Baptiste Dubarry . . . au corps législatif.* Paris: imp. de le Normand,
n.d. [1795].
in-4; 4p.
[MW]; BN: 4 Ln(27).6303; BLC.
politics.
Dubois, veuve Alexis. *Adresse aux
représentants de la Commune de
Paris . . . contre M. l'Archevêque de
Toulouse, abbé de Saint-Victor.* Paris:
imp. de Rose, 1790.
in-8; 24p.
[MW]; BN: 8 Ln(27).6334.
politics.
Dubois, veuve Jean Baptiste Brazier.
*Accusateur public, juges et jurés du
tribunal révolutionnaire d'Arras,
imposteurs et prévaricateurs.
La citoyenne Dubois, veuve, avec
enfants, de Jean-Baptiste Brazier, . . .
la citoyenne Rosalie-Delphine-
Joseph Bossu, . . . et Victoire Hidou,
Veuve de Jean-Baptiste Bossu, . . .
à la Convention Nationale.*
Paris: imp. de Guffroy, n.d.
[1794].
in-4; 7p; Pièce.
[CHF], ix, 91; [MW]; BN 4 Lb(41).
4158.
politics.
———. *Chantes patriotiques de nos
républicains sur la prise de Charleroi.*
Coulubrier, 1794.
in-8.

[BN].
song.
———. *Chants patriotiques sur le
tombeau de Marat . . .* Paris: Coulubrier, n.d.
in-8; 2p; d: Veuve de Jean-Baptiste
Brazien (condamné à mort par le
tribunal révolutionnaire d'Arras,
poétesse républicaine).
[MW]; BN: Ye.54818.
song.
———. *Chants patriotiques sur le
tombeau de Marat le 20 germinal.*
Paris: Coulubrier, 1794.
in-8; 2p.
[BN]; BN: Ye. 54818.
song.
———. *Hymne à l'éternel chanté à la
section du muséum, le 30 germinal
. . .* Paris: Coulubrier, 1794.
in-8; 2p.
[BN]; BN: Ye. 20576.
song.
———. *Hymne pour les français en
l'honneur de l'être suprême.* N.l.: n.d.
in-8; 2p.
[MW]; BN: Ye.20577 and 55971
(796).
song.
———. *Hymnes et prières républicaines:
Adressés à la liberté.* Paris: Coulubrier, 1794.
in-8.
[BN].
song.
———. *Ombre de Marat aux républicains, air.* Coulubrier, 1793.
in-8.
[BN].
song.
———. *Le Réveil républicain par une
démocrate.* N.l.: n.d.
in-8; 4p.
[MW]; BN: 8 Ye.Pièce.4894.
song.
Dubreuil, Sophie et Dubreuil
François Darzier. *Hommage à la*

Dubreuil (*continued*)
*véritié contre l'oppression, l'injustice,
l'inhumanité et les rapines du Directoire et de ses représentants au Corps
Législatif, ou appel à leur cruauté
pour en obtenir la mort, par une
famille de rentiers et créanciers de
l'état réduits à l'agonie du désespoir
par l'extrême besoin.* N.l.: 1798.
in-8, 47p; other edition, Paris: n.p.,
1799.
[Monglond]; [MW]; BLC.
politics.

Duclozel, mademoiselle. *Mémoire
présenté par Mlle Duclozel, novice
prébendée du monastère de Montmartre, contenant sa pétition présentée à l'Assemblée Nationale, et ren-
voyée par décret du 27 août 1790,
pour lui en être rendu compte incessa-
ment.* Clermont-Ferrand: imp. de
A. Delcros, 1791.
in-4; 8p.
[CHF]; BN: Lk(7).5080.
politics.

Ducos, Angélique marquise de
Blanville née Caze de la Bove
madame d. 1821. *Clémence de Ville-
fort, par l'auteur de 'Marie de Sain-
clair.'* Paris: Dentu et Carteret, 1799.
in-12, ABF: 341, 268–269.
[BGR]; JT 5 prair. VII; Monglond.
novel.
———. *Henry, traduction de l'anglais.*
Paris: Maradan, 1797.
in-12; translation of *Henry, A Novel*
(1795) by Richard Cumberland;
other editions: (1) Paris: Maradan,
an VI, 6 part. in-18; (2) Paris:
Maradan, an VII, 2t. in-12.
[BGR]; Monglond.
novel / translation.
———. *Marie de Sinclair.* Paris:
Maradan, 1798.
in-12; 266p.
[BGR]; JT 16 flor. VI; Monglond.
novel.

Dufrénoy, Adélaïde Gillette Billet
madame 1765–1825. *Le Courrier
lyrique et amusant, ou passe-temps
des toilettes* 5 vols. (1785–1789).
in-8.
[Monglond]; BN: Z. 21686–21690.
journal.
———. *Le petit Armand, ou le bienfait
des perruques, fait historique en un
acte, mêlé de vaudevilles.* 1799.
performed at the *Théâtre des Trou-
badours,* 4 fructidor an VII.
[Monglond].
theater.
———. *Le Restaurateur, ou la gageure,
comédie-parade en un acte et en prose,
mêlée de Vaudevilles.* 1799.
performed at the *Théâtre du Vaudeville,* 13 prairial an VII.
[Monglond].
theater.
———. *Santa Maria ou la grossesse mys-
térieuse, traduit de l'anglais de Fox
par Madame Dufrenoy.* Paris: Cabinet littéraire, chez Vignon, 1800.
2t. in-12; translation of *Santa-
Maria or the Mysterious Pregnancy*
(1797) by John Fox.
[BGR]; JT 10 vend. IX; Monglond.
novel / translation.

Duligondiz, Marie Louise Charlotte
de Méru dame. *Pétition . . .* N.l.:
n.d.
in-8; 19p.
[MW]; BN: Fp.2384 et 8
Ln(27).6613bis.
politics.
———. *Pétition à la Convention Nationale.* Paris: Imp. nationale
[1793].
in-8; 14p; BLC suggests date
[1792].
[MW]; [CHF]; BN: 8ø Ln(27).6613;
BLC.
politics.

Dumesnil, Marie Françoise also
known as Marchand 1713–1803.

Dumesnil (*continued*)
  Mémoires de Marie-Françoise Dumesnil, en réponse aux mémoires d'Hippolyte Clairon; suivis d'une lettre du célèbre Le Kain et plusieurs anecdotes curieuses, relatives au théâtre français. Paris: Dentu, 1799.
  in-8.
  [CHF]; BLC.
  memoirs.
Duplessy, baronne fl. 1785. *Alexandrine de Châteaufort ou la fatale alliance, histoire française mise au jour par la cne Duplessy, orné* (sic) *de quatre figures.* Paris: Jouanaux, 1799.
  2 part. in-12; Gay lists 2 part. in-18; Monglond gives information: 4 part. 2 tomes – tome I: iv-161p, tome II: 167p; BLC lists an VII [1798/1799], with plates; ABF: 356, 289.
  [BGR]; [Monglond]; BN: Ye 31528–31529; JT 30 vent. Ve; BLC.
  novel.
———. *Le Mariage de la soeur du diable, roman mystérieux.* Paris: Marchand, 1799.
  in-18; 175p.
  [BGR]; Monglond.
  novel.
Dupray, madame. *Chanson des dames des marchés S. Paul, des Quinze-Vingts, la Halle et d'Aguesseau . . .* N.l.: n.d. [1789].
  in-16; 3p.
  [MW]; BN: Ye.54832.
  song.
Duval, madame Françoise veuve. *Discours fait et prononcé par Mme Vve Duval.* Caen: Chalopin, 1791.
  in-8; 10p.
  [CHF]; BN: 8ø Lb(40).2607.
  politics.
Elisabeth, Philippine Marie Hélène de France dite madame Elisabeth 1764–1794. *Lettre de Madame Élisa-*

beth, adressée à la Convention Nationale; avec les discours des deux enfants du ci-devant roi de France. Paris: Moreau, jeune, n.d. [1793].
  in-8; 8p.
  [CHF]; BN: 8 Lb(41).2720.
  politics.
———. *Le Rendez-Vous de Madame Élisabeth . . . avec l'abbé de S. Martin . . . dans le jardin des Tuileries. Reimprimé . . . sur l'édition originale . . . de 1790.* London: Imprimerie particulière de Lord C***, 1875[1st pub. 1790].
  in-12; 20p.
  BLC.
  politics.
Fare-Goujon, Louise. *Réclamation de deux mères . . . contre un jugement du tribunal révolutionnaire, sur un crime qui n'était pas contre-révolutionnaire, aux citoyens-représentans du peuple française.* Paris: Dupont, n.d.[1793].
  in-4; 6p.
  [MW]; [CHF], iii, 86; BN: 8 Lb(41).1124; BLC.
  politics.
Fars-Fausselandry (née Paysac) vicomtesse de (1751–1830). *Quelques-uns des fruits amers de la Révolution et une faible partie des journées des 2 et 3 septembre 1793 [sic pour 1792].* N.l.[Paris?]: n.d.[1792].
  in-8; 16p.
  [Monglond]; [MW]; [CHF]; BLC; BN: 8 Lb(39).10886.
  politics.
Favras, Victoire Edwige Caroline princesse d'Anhalt-Chambourg Marquise de b. circa 1759 et Thomas de Mahy marquis de Favras. *Correspondance pendant leur détention [publiée par de Mahy Savonnière].* N.l.: n.d.[1790].
  in-8; 107p; other ed: N.l.: n.d., in-8,

Favras (*continued*)
58p, BN: 8 Lb(39).3010; ABF: 391,
400–401.
[Monglond]; [MW]; [CHF];
BLC.
correspondence.

Femmes françaises. *Les Femmes
françaises à la Convention Nationale.*
N.l.: n.d.
in-8; 16p.
BLC.
politics.

————. *Les Femmes françaises à la nation.* N.l.: 1795.
in-8; 16p.
BLC.
politics.

————. *Les Femmes françaises, pour la
seconde fois à la nation.* N.l.: [1795].
in-8; 24p.
BLC.
politics.

Ferrand, veuve. *Le Triomphe de la
liberté et de l'égalité. Almanach
républicain. Chansons nouvelles et
analogues aux années 1789, 90, 91,
92.* Paris: Laurens jeune, 1793.
in-32; 115p.
[Monglond]; [MW]; BN: Ye 22159
(from Monglond)—MW lists in
addition Ye 12259, 22535, 34121.
almanac / poetry.

Ferrant, citoyenne Leclair femme.
*Mémoire sur la conduite du cit. Fer-
rant, avant et depuis la Révolution
avec copies de pièces citées . . .*
N.l.[Paris]: 1794.
in-4; 11p.
[MW]; BN: 4 Ln(27).7517.
politics.

Fléchet, mademoiselle Jenny. *Mes
Loisirs.* Paris: imp. de Lottin l'âiné,
1792.
in-8; 9–13p.
[Monglond]; BN: 8
Ye.Pièce.5575.
poetry.

Fleury, madame Moylin fl. 1800. *Les
Malheurs d'Élisabeth, ou les victimes
de la perfidie.* Paris: n.p., 1799.
in-18; ABF: 404.
[Monglond].
novel.

Flinville, Éléonore de. *Le Curé anglais
ou la famille Primrose, traduit de
l'anglais de Goldsmith par Eléonore
de Fl . . .* Paris: Imprimerie à Prix-
Fixe et chez les marchands de
nouveautés, 1799.
2t. in-18; pp variously 163, 156;
translation of *The Vicar of Wakefield*
(1766) by Oliver Goldsmith.
[BGR]; Monglond.
novel / translation.

Fontanier, Joséphine. *Discours
prononcé à l'Assemblée Générale de la
section de l'unité, le 30 prair. an II
. . . en offrant de la charpie et du
plomb.* N.l.: n.d.[1793].
in-8; 4p.
[MW]; [CHF], x, 732; BN: 8
Lb(40).2190.
politics.

Fontette de Sommery, mademoiselle
fl. 1780–1785. *L'Oreille, conte Asia-
tique.* Paris: Barrois l'aîné, 1789.
3t. in-12; other edition: 1789, 2t.
in-12, pp variously 167, 146; ABF:
409, 30; 1060, 160.
[BGR]; Monglond; BLC.
novel.

————. *Le Rosier et le brouillard, conte
par le même auteur de (sic) l'Oreille.*
Paris: Cailleau, 1791.
in-8.
[BGR]; Monglond.
novel.

Formentin, madame Madeleine-
Victoire. *Dénonciation à l'Assemblée
Nationale et aux 48 sections, des
juges et du greffier du tribunal de
Sainte-Geneviève; par Denis-Louis
Formentin, . . . et Magdeleine-
Victoire Lourdet, son épouse . . .*

Formentin (*continued*)
  N.l.[Paris]: n.d.[1792].
  in-8; 8p.
  [CHF]; BLC; BN: Fp. 1781.
  politics.
Fouquet, madame. *Recueil des
  remèdies faciles et domestiques*. Paris:
  Villier, 1798.
  2 vol. in-12.
  [NL].
  medicine / health.
Fourquevaux, Marie Angélique
  Hélène Félicité. *Aperçu pour la
  citoyenne Fourqueaux*. Paris: imp.
  du Cercle social, n.d.
  in-8; 7p.
  BN: 8 Ln(27).7921.
  politics.
  ———. *Marie-Angélique-Hélène-Félic-
  ité Fourquevaux, au comité de la Convention Nationale*. N.l.: n.d.
  in-8; 16p.
  [CHF]; BN: Fp.2168.
  politics.
  ———. *Marie-Angélique-Hélène-
  Félicité Fourquevaux, au Corps
  Législatif*. N.l.: n.d.
  in-4; 15p.
  [CHF]; BN: 4 Ln(27).7920.
  politics.
  ———. *Observations de la citoyenne
  Fourquevaux au Conseil des Anciens,
  sur la résolution prise par celui des
  Cinq-Cents relativement à ses biens
  vendus au nom de la nation*. Paris:
  imp. de Brasseur, n.d.
  in-8; 8p.
  [CHF]; BN: 8 Ln(27).7923.
  politics.
Fray, Mademoiselle. *Recueil d'airs,
  avec accompagnement de fort–piano,
  par Mlle Fray, dédiée à M. Son Père.
  Oeuvre 1re. Gravé par Mlle Chaunec*.
  Paris: n.p., 1791.
  [FC].
  music.

Froidure de Rezelle, mademoiselle.
  *Histoire de Pierre le Cruel, roi de
  Castille et de Léon . . . traduit par
  Mlle Froidure de Rezelle*. Paris:
  Briand, 1790.
  2 parties en I vol., in-8; translation
  from Spanish of text by J.-T. Dil-
  lon.
  [Monglond]; BLC.
  history / translation.
Fumelh, madame de fl. 1785. *Discours
  à la nation française*. N.l.[Paris]:
  n.d.[1789].
  in-8; 21p.
  [Monglond]; [MW]; BN: 8
  Lb(39).1314 and Lb(39).1314; BLC.
  politics.
  ———. *Oeuvres diverses*. Geneva: n.p.,
  1790.
  in-12; ABF: 426,167–168.
  [Monglond].
  novel.
  ———. *Second Discours à la nation
  française*. Paris: Lacloye, 1789.
  in-8; 35p.
  [Monglond]; [MW]; [CHF], ii, 511;
  BN: 8 Lb(39).1315; BLC.
  politics.
Gacon-Dufour, Marie Armande
  Jeanne d'Humières madame
  1753–c. 1835. *Georgeanna ou la
  vertu persécutée et triomphante, traduction de l'anglais, par l'auteur des
  'Dangers de la coquetterie,' ornée de
  figures d'après les dessins de Chail-
  loux*. Paris: Lepetit, 1798.
  2t. in-18; t.I:180p, t.II:196p; ABF:
  427, 308–313.
  [BGR]; JT 24 flor., 8 prair. VI; Monglond.
  novel / translation.
Gas, Jeanne Louise Bertrand veuve.
  *Adresse à l'Assemblée Nationale . . .
  contenant la relation exacte du pillage
  de la maison du Sieur Gas, de son af-
  freux asassinat et des excès commis*

Gas (*continued*)
envers sa famille. Paris: Gattey, 1790.
in-8; 23p; 2nd, 3rd, and 4th eds., 1790; ABF: 436, 285–288.
[MW]; [CHF], ii, 617; BN: 8 Lb(39).3894; BLC.
politics.

———. *Nouvelle Adresse de la veuve Gas et de ses enfans, à l'Assemblée Nationale en réponse à la lettre que M. Voulland . . . adressée à MM. les Députés* . . . Paris: les marchands de nouveautés, 1790.
in-8; 23p.
[MW]; [CHF], ii, 637a; BN: 8 Lb(39).4377; BLC.
politics.

Gauche, citoyenne Driot femme du citoyen. *Aux Citoyens composant le Comité Révolutionnaire et l'Assemblée Générale des Sans-Culottes.* Paris: imp. de l'Union, n.d.
in-4; 3p.
[MW]; [CHF]; BN: 4 Ln(27).8326.
politics.

Gaudichon, mère. *La Nourrice de Barras au président du Conseil des Cinq-Cents.* Paris: imp. de Coesnon-Pellerin, n.d. [1797].
in-fol.plano.
[CHF], iii, 158; BN: Fol.Lb(42).391.
politics.

Gauthier, madame de. *Voyage d'une française en Suisse et en franche-comté depuis la Révolution.* London Neuchâtel: n.p. 1790.
2 vol. in-8; other edition, Paris: Debray, an X - 1802, in-8.
[Monglond]; BLC.
travel.

Gautier-Lacépède, madame fl. 1785. *Sophie ou mémoires d'une jeune religieuse, écrits par elle-même, adressés à la princesse de L***, & publiés par Madame G.* . . Paris: Belin, De-

senne, 1790.
in-8; 295p; other edition: (2nd) Paris: *au bureau de la correspondance des artistes et des amateurs des sciences et des arts*, 1792, in-8, 295p.
[BGR]; [Monglond]; BN: Y2.69008.
novel.

Gelieu, madame de. *La Nature et l'art par Mistress Inchbald, auteur de 'Simple Histoire,' nouvelle traduction par Mlle de G. et Mme de C.* Paris: imp. chez Fauche-Borel, 1797.
in-8, 240p; collaborative translation, with dame Isabelle-Agnès-Elizabeth van Tuyll van Scrooskerken van Zuylen de Charrière, of *Nature and Art* (1796), by Mrs. Elizabeth Simpson Inchbald; other editions: (1) Geneva: J. J. Paschould, & Paris: Buisson, Tavernier, Petit, Huet, 1797, 2t. in-18, (2) Paris: Tavernier, an VI, 2t. in-18.
[BGR].
novel / translation.

Genlis, Stéphanie-Félicité Ducrest de Saint-Aubin marquise de Sillery comtesse de 1746–1830. *Nouveau Théâtre sentimental, à l'usage de la jeunesse.* Paris: n.p., 1791.
in-8, 104p.
[FC].
pedagogy.

———. *Épître à l'asile que j'aurai, suivi de deux fables, du chant d'un jeune savage, de l'épître à Henriette Sercey, et des réflexions d'un ami des talents et des arts.* Hamburg: P.-F. Fauche, 1796.
in-8; 61p.
[Monglond]; [MW]; BN: Ye 23222.
poetry.

———. *Catéchisme de morale.* Dresden: Walther, 1800.
in-8.

Genlis (*continued*)
[Monglond].
pedagogy.
———. *Les Chevaliers du cygne ou la cour de Charlemagne, conte historique et moral, pour servir de suite aux 'Veillées du château' et dont tous les traits qui peuvent faire allusion à la Révolution française, sont tirés de l'histoire, par Madame de Genlis, auteur du 'Théâtre d'éducation,' d'Adèle et Thèodore,' Etc.* Paris, Lemierre, & Hamburg: P.-F. Fauche, 1795.
3t. in-8; t.I:xxiv + 381p, t.II:406p, t.III:434p; BN lists Lemierre, 1795, in-8; other editions: (1) Hambourg: P.-F. Fauche, 1795, 3t. in-12; (2) Hamburg: P.-F. Fauche, 1797; (3) Paris: Maradan, an XIII - 1805; (4) Paris: Maradan, 1811; (5) Paris: Maradan, 1818, 3t. in-12; (6) Paris: Maradan, 1819.
[BGR]; [Monglond]; [MW]; BLC.
novel.
———. *Correspondance de Louis-Philippe-Joseph, duc d'Orléans.* 1800.
in-8.
BLC.
letters.
———. *Discours sur l'éducation de M. le Dauphin et sur l'adoption, par Mme de Brulart, ci-devant Mme de Sillery, gouvernante des enfants de la maison d'Orléans.* Paris: Onfroy, 1790.
in-8; 72p.
[Monglond]; [MW]; BN: 8 Lb(39).4391 et 8 R.7042; BLC.
pedagogy.
———. *Discours sur l'éducation et sur différents sujets. Nouv. éd.* Berlin: Laurens, 1797.
in-8.
[Monglond].
pedagogy.
———. *Discours sur l'éducation publique du peuple.* Paris: Onfroy, 1791.

in-8; 36p.
[Monglond]; [MW]; BN: Rp.4672.
pedagogy.
———. *Discours sur la suppression des couvents de religieuses et sur l'éducation publique des femmes.* Paris: Onfroy, 1790.
in-8; xxiv-84p.
[Monglond]; [MW]; BN: 8 Lb(39).8436 et 8 R.7219; BLC.
politics / pedagogy.
———. *Discours sur le luxe et sur l'hospitalité, considérés sous leurs rapports avec les moeurs et l'éducation nationale.* Paris: Onfroy, 1791.
in-8; 46p.
[Monglond]; [MW]; BN: Rz.2987.
pedagogy.
———. *Herbier moral, ou recueil des fables nouvelles et autres poésies fugitives.* Hamburg & London: Pierre Chateauneuf et l'Homme, 1799.
in-8; other editions: (1) Paris: Moutardier, n.d., [1799], in-12; (2) Paris: Maradan, an IX - 1801.
[Monglond]; BLC.
pedagogy / poetry.
———. *Leçons d'une gouvernante à ses élèves, ou fragments d'un journal, qui a été fait pour l'éducation des enfants de Monsieur d'Orléans.* Paris: Onfroy, 1792.
2 vols. in-12; MW lists 1791, 371–582p; BLC lists 1791, in-8.
[Monglond]; [MW]; BN: R.23261–23262; BLC.
pedagogy.
———. *Leçons d'une gouvernante et journal d'éducation.* Bern: Société typographique, 1797.
2 vols.
[Monglond].
pedagogy.
———. *Lettre adressée à Monseigneur le duc d'Orléans sur l'enseignement de ses enfans proposé . . . par Madame de Sillery.* n.d.: [1789?].

Genlis (*continued*)
in-8.
BLC.
letter.
————. *Le Libraire, comédie en 1 acte.*
N.l.: 1798.
in-12.
[MW]; BN: 8 Yth. 21187.
theater.
————. *Les Mères rivales ou la calom-*
nie, par Madame de Genlis. Berlin:
F. T. de la Garde, 1800.
3t. in-8; other editions: (1) Berlin:
F. T. de la Garde & Paris: Barba,
1800; (2) Paris: Maradan, Hein-
richs, 1800; (3) Paris: chez l'éditeur,
à l'ancienne librairie de Dupont,
an IX, 4t. in-8; (4) Paris: chez l'éditeur, à l'ancienne librairie de
Dupont, an IX, 4t. in-8; (5) Berlin:
J. F. de la Garde, an X, in-12; (6)
5th ed., Paris: Maradan, 1808; (7)
6th ed., Paris: Maradan, 1813, 3t.
in-12; (8) 7th ed., Paris: Maradan,
1819, 3t. in-12.
[BGR]; [Monglond]; JT 20 brum.
IX; Mag. enc. VI 1800 iv 144, VI
1801 v 285.
novel.
————. *Manuel du voyageur, ou recueil*
de dialogues, de lettres, etc., suivi
d'un itinéraire raisonné à l'usage des
français en allemagne et des alle-
mands en France, par Mme de Genlis,
avec la traduction allemande par
S.-H. Catel. Pour servir de suite . . .
aux 'exercices de prononciation, de
grammaire et de construction.'
Berlin: F.-T. de Lagarde, 1799.
in-8; 200p; other editions: (1)
Berlin: J. F. de la Garde, 1800,
in-16; (2) Breslau: G. T. Korn, 1807,
in-8, 343p; (3) Paris: Charles Barrois, 1810, in-8 oblong, 207p.
[Monglond]; [MW]; BN: X. 11658,
G. 23897, X. 11659, and X. 16300.
pedagogy / travel.

————. *Modèles de conversation et de*
lettres avec traduction allemande par
Catel. Berlin: Köchly, 1799.
gr. in-8.
[Monglond].
pedagogy.
————. *Nouvelle Bibliothèque uni-*
verselle des romans, dans laquelle on
donne l'analyse raisonnée des romans
anciens et modernes, française ou
traduits dans notre langue, avec des
anecdotes et des notices historiques et
critiques, concernant les auteurs et
leurs ouvrages; ainsi que les moeurs,
les usages de temps, les circonstances
particulières et relatives, et les per-
sonnages connus, déguisés ou emblé-
matiques. Paris: rue André-des-
Arts, (puis) Demonville, 1798–
1805.
112 vols. in-12; edited by Mme de
Genlis, Mme de Staël, P. Blan-
chard, H. Coiffier, J. M. Des-
champs, G. F. Desfontaines de la
Vallée, J. J. M. Duperche, Fabre
D'Olivet, J. Fiévée, A. H. Kératry,
Labaume, J. L. Laya, J.M.J.B.
Legouvé, Lemoine, J. Monbron,
Mabille, Millin, F. J. Noël, Petitot,
L.J.B.E. Vigée.
[Monglond]; BN: Y2 56742–56853.
novels.
————. *Oeuvres.* Bern: Société ty-
pographique, 1793.
21 vols. in-12.
[Monglond].
literature.
————. *Le Petit La Bruyère.* Vienna:
Mayer, 1799.
in-8; other editions: (1)Paris:
Maradan, 1801, in-8; (2) Leipzig:
Greshammer, 1802; (3)—3rd ed.,
Leipzig: Greshammer, 1810, in-12.
[Monglond].
pedagogy.
————. *Les Petits émigrés ou correspon-*
dance de quelques enfans, ouvrage fait

Genlis (*continued*)
*pour servir à l'éducation de la jeu-
nesse, par Madame de Genlis*. Paris
& Berlin: Onfroy & J. F. de La
Garde, 1798.
2t. in-8; other editions: (1) Paris:
1798, 2t. in-12; (2) London: n.p.
1799, 2t. in-8; (3) Paris: Maradan,
an XI; (4) 4th ed., Paris: Maradan,
1808, 2t. in-12; (5) 5th ed., Paris:
Maradan, 1812, 2t. in-12; (6) 6th
ed., Paris: Maradan, 1819, 2t.
in-12; (7) 7th ed., Paris: Lecointe et
Durey, 1825, 2t. in-12; (8) 8th ed.,
Paris: Lecointe et Durey, 1828, 2t.
in-12; (9) Hamburg: n.p., 1798, 3t.
[BGR]; [Monglond]; [MW]; BLC.
novel/pedagogy.
———. *Précis de la conduite de Mme de
Genlis, depuis la Révolution. Suivi
d'une lettre à M. de Chartres et de
réflexions sur la critique*. Hamburg:
B.-G. Hoffman, 1796.
in-8; IV-296p; other edition, Hamburg & Paris: Cérioux, n.d., in-12.
[Monglond]; [MW]; BN: 8ø Ln(27)
8491 A; BLC.
memoir.
———. *Réflexions d'un ami des talents et des arts*. Paris: n.p., 1798.
in-8.
[Monglond].
art.
———. *Théâtre à l'usage des jeunes personnes, ou théâtre d'éducation*.
Berlin: n.p. 1795.
4 vols. in-8; first edition: 1779–
1780; other edition, Paris: n.d.
Maradan, 5 vols. in-12.
[Monglond].
theater/pedagogy.
———. *Les voeux Téméraires ou l'en-
thousiasme, par Mme de Genlis, auteur du 'Théâtre d'éducation,' d'Adèle
et Théodore,' &c &c &c*. Hamburg,
Paris & London: P. Chateauneuf &
Bernard & l'Homme, 1798.

2t. in-8; other editions: (1) Leipzig:
n.p. 1798, 2t. in-8; (2) Altona: n.p.
aux dépens de l'auteur, 1799, 2t.
in-8; (3) Hamburg: n.p. 1799, 3t.
in-12; (4) Vienna: n.p. J. W. Degen,
1799, in-12, 3t; (5) Paris: Maradan,
an X, 3t. in-12; (6) 4th ed., Paris:
Maradan, 1807, 3t.; (7) 5th ed.,
Paris: Maradan, 1813, 3t. in-12.
[BGR]; [Monglond]; [MW]; JT 20
vent., 10 flor. VII.
novel.
Geoffroy, madame. *Aux Citoyens
membres du Directoire du Département de Paris*. N.l. [Paris]: n.d.
[1794].
in-8; 3p.
[MW]; [CHF]; BN: 8 Ln(27).8520,
47065 (2 ex.); BLC.
politics.
Getnonville, comtesse de fl. 1785.
*L'Épouse rare ou modèle de douceur,
de patience et de constance, anecdote
aussi intéressante qu'amusante &
écrite dans le simple* (sic), *par
Madame la comtesse de Getnon-Ville*.
Malta & Paris: Froullé, 1789.
in-12; 192p; ABF: 451, 347–348.
[BGR]; [Monglond]; BN: Y2 z.80.
novel.
Gilles, Lauchard femme Jean-
Baptiste. *Mémoire à la Convention
Nationale . . . contenant des éclair-
cissemens importans sur des chefs
d'accusation contre Louis Capet*.
Paris: imp. de Noiroeil, n.d.[1793].
in-4; 8p.
[MW]; [CHF], xi, 23; BN: 4
Lb(41).2511; BLC.
politics.
Giovane, Julie baronne de Muders-
bach duchesse de. *Idées sur la
manière de rendre les voyages des
jeunes gens utiles à leur propre culture, au bonheur de la société, accompagnées de tablettes et précédées d'un
précis historique sur l'usage des voy-*

Giovane (*continued*)
ages. Vienna: n.p., 1798.
in-8.
[Monglond].
travel/pedagogy.

―――. *Lettres sur l'éducation des princesses*. Vienna: J. Stahel, 1791.
in-8; 63p.
[Monglond]; BN: R.54805.
pedagogy.

―――. *Plan pour faire servir les voyages à la culture des jeunes gens qui se vouent au service de l'état dans la carrière politique, accompagné d'un précis historique de l'usage de voyager et d'une table pour faciliter les observations statistiques et politiques; le tout suivi de l'esquisse d'un portefeuille à l'usage des voyageurs et de celle d'une carte statistique*. Vienna: imp. de Vve Alberti, 1797.
in-4.
[Monglond]; BN: G. 3537.
travel/pedagogy.

Girardin, Sophie Victoire Alexandrine comtesse de Bohm de 1762–1845. *Observations pour les créanciers bailleurs de fonds d'avance des ci-devant fermiers généraux*. N.l.: n.d. [1798].
in-8; 16p.
[CHF], iii, 164; BLC; BN: 8 Lb(42).510.
politics/commercial.

Girieux, Anne Marie Dubreuil de Sainte-Croix comtesse de 1752–1825. *Lettre à Mme la comtesse de Beauharnais (5 août 1789)*. N.l.: n.d. [1789].
in-8; ABF: 458, 224–225.
[Monglond]; [CHF].
letter.

Giroux, Suzanne, also known as Suzanne Gireux madame Bertand Quinquet and madame de Morency b. circa 1772. *Euphémie, ou les suites du siège de Lyon; roman*

historique, orné de gravures, par l'auteur d' 'Illyrine.' Paris: chez Bertrandet, 1801.
4 vol. in-12; t.I:x-208p, t.II:210p, t.III:187p, t.IV:211p.
[Monglond]; BN: Y2 55213–55215.
novel.

―――. *Illyrine ou l'écueil de l'inexpérience, par G . . . De Morency*. Paris : Rainville & Favre, l'auteur & Mlle Durand & tous les marchands de nouveautés, 1799.
3t. in-8; t.I:viii + 339p, t.II:360p, t.III:397p; volumes I & II published, 1799, volume III published 1800; other edition, 2nd ed., Paris: n.p., an VII–an VIII, 3t. in-8.
[BGR]; BN: Y2 55213–55215; JT 20 pluv. VIII; Monglond.
novel.

Glezen, Geneviève Rose Marie Lemétayer dame. *Pétition Au Corps Législatif . . .* Paris: imp. de Baudouin, n.d.
in-8; 18p.
[MW]; BN: 8 Ln(27).8826.
politics.

Gobelet, veuve. *Adresse à l'Assemblée Nationale 30 août 1791*. Troyes: imp. de Vve Gobelet et fils, n.d. [1791].
in-8; 20p.
[MW]; BN: Vp.8285; BLC.
politics/commercial.

Gonzague, Anne de princesse palatine 1616–1684. *Mémoires*. London & Paris: Valade, 1789.
in-8; xlvii-338p; first edition, 1786.
[Monglond]; BLC; BN: 8 Lb(37).161.
memoir.

Gonzagues, E. Rangoni princesse de. *Lettres de Madame la Princesse de G***, écrites à ses amies pendant le cours de ses voyages d'Italie en 1779 et années suivantes*. Gênes: Y. Gravier, 1789.

Gonzagues (*continued*)
2 vol. in-12.
[Monglond].
travel / correspondence.
———. *Lettres sur l'Italie, la France, l'Allemagne et les Beaux-arts.* Hambourg: P.-F. Fauche, 1797.
2 vols. in-8.
[Monglond]; BN: G.10833–10834.
travel.

Goubet, veuve Anne-Françoise Dauvin. *Amis et patriotes sacrifiés par jugement rendu par le tribunal révolutionnaire de Cambray. Marie-Marguerite Payen, Vve Payen . . . et Anne-Françoise Dauvin, Vve Goubet . . . à la Convention Nationale.* Paris: imp. de Guffroy, n.d.[1794].
in-4; 8p.
[MW]; [CHF]; BN: 4 Lb(41).1706.
politics.

Gouges, Marie Gouze called Olympe de 1755–1793. *Action héroïque d'une Française, ou la France sauvée par les femmes.* Paris: Guillaume junior, n.d. [1790].
in-8; 7p.
[Monglond]; [MW]; [OF]; BN: 8 Lb(39).8602.
politics.
———. *Adresse au Don Quichotte de nord. [suivi de: La Fierté de l'innocence, ou le silence de véritable patriotisme].* Paris: Imp. nationale, 1792.
in-8; 16p.
[Monglond]; [MW]; [OF]; BN: 8 Lb(41).87; BLC.
politics.
———. *Adresse aux représentants de la nation. Mémoire pour Mme de Gouges contre la Comédie Française.* N.l. [Paris]: n.d. [1790].
in-4; 46p.
[Monglond]; [MW]; [OF]; BN: 4 Ln(27).8954; BLC.
theater.

———. *Ambassade au roi. Adresse à la reine. Adresse au Prince de Condé. Observation à M. Duveyrier sur sa fameuse ambassade . . .* N.l. [Paris]: n.d. [1791].
in-8; 24p.
[MW]; [OF]; BN: 8 Lb(39).5174; BLC.
politics.
———. *Arrêt de mort . . . contre Louis Capet.* N.l. [Paris]: n.d. [1793].
in-8; 4p.
[MW]; [OF]; BN: 8 Lb(41).2589; BLC.
politics.
———. *Avis pressant à la Convention par une vraie républicaine.* N.l.: n.d. [1793].
in-8; 16p.
[Monglond]; [MW]; [OF]; BN: Lb(41).2969.
politics.
———. *Avis pressant, ou réponse à mes calomniateurs.* N.l.: n.d. [1789].
in-8; 16p.
[Monglond]; [MW]; [OF]; BN: 8 Lb(39).1848.
politics.
———. *Bienfaisante, ou la bonne mère, conte mêlé d'anecdotes. La Bienfaisante récompensée, ou la vertu couronnée, comédie en un acte et en prose mêlée d'ariettes.* N.l.: n.d.[1793?].
in-8; 57p.
[OF]; BLC; BN: 8 Yth.2024.
theater.
———. *Le bon Sens français, ou l'apologie des vrais nobles, dédiées aux Jacobins.* N.l.: n.d. [1792].
in-8; 56p.
[Monglond]; [MW]; [OF]; BN: 8 Lb(39).1848.
politics.
———. *Le Bonheur primitif de l'homme, ou les rêveries patriotiques.* Amsterdam & Paris: Royez, 1789.

Gouges (*continued*)
in-8; 126p.
[Monglond]; [MW]; [OF]; BN:
R.37509 et 8 R. 5870 (2 ex.); BLC.
politics.
———. *Les Comédiens démasqués, ou
Mme de Gouges ruinée par la
Comédie-Française, pour se fair jouer.*
Paris: imp. de la Comédie-
française, 1790.
in-8; IV-53p.
[Monglond]; [MW]; [OF]; BN: 8
Ln(27).8953; BLC.
theater.
———. *Complots dévoilés des sociétaires
du prétendu Théâtre de la
République.* Paris: Imp. F.-M.
Boileau, 1793.
[Monglond].
theater.
———. *Correspondance de la cour.
Compte mal rendu et dernier mot à
mes chers amis, à la Convention Na-
tionale et au peuple, sur une dénonci-
ation faite contre son civisme, aux Ja-
cobins.* N.l.: n.d. [1792].
in-8; 24p.
[Monglond]; [MW]; [OF]; BN: 8
Lb(41).207; BLC.
politics.
———. *Le Couvent ou les voeux forcés,
drame en 3 actes, représenté en 2
actes et remis en trois au Théâtre-
Française Comique et Lyrique au
mois d'octobre 1790.* Paris: Vve
Duchesne, 1792.
in-8; xii-83p.
[Monglond]; [MW]; [OF]; BN: 8
Yth. 4193 et 23243 (2 ex.); BLC.
theater.
———. *Le Cri du sage, par une femme.*
N.l.: n.d. [1789].
in-8; 8p.
[MW]; [OF]; BN: 8 Lb(39).1803;
BLC.
politics.
———. *Départ de Necker et de Mme de*

*Gouges ou les adieux de Mme de
Gouges aux français et à M. Necker.*
Paris: 1790.
in-8; 41p.
[Monglond]; [MW]; BN: 8
Lb(39).4038; BLC.
politics.
———. *Dialogue allégorique entre la
France et la vérité. Dédié aux États
Généraux.* N.l.: n.d. [1789].
in-8; 32p.
[Monglond]; [MW]; [OF]; BN: 8
Lb(39).1741; BLC.
politics/philosophy.
———. *Discours de l'aveugle aux
français.* N.l. [Paris]: n.d. [1789].
in-8; 19p.
[Monglond]; [MW]; [OF]; BN: 8
Lb(39).1846; BLC.
politics/philosophy.
———. *Les Droits de la femme. A la
reine.* N.l. [Paris]: n.d. [1791].
in-8; 24p.
[MW]; [OF]; BN: *E.5568 et 8
Lb(39).9989 (2 ex.); BLC.
politics.
———. *L'Entrée de Dumouriez à Bruxelles, ou les vivandières, pièce en cinq
actes et en prose.* Paris: Regnaud,
1793.
in-8; 148p; performed at the
Théâtre de la République, January
23, 1793.
[Monglond]; [MW]; [OF]; BN:
Yf.12247; BLC.
theater.
———. *L'Esclavage des noirs, ou
l'heureux naufrage, drame en 3 actes
en prose.* Paris: Vve Duchesne, 1792.
in-8; 50p; performed at the
Comédie Française in December
1792.
[Monglond]; [MW]; [OF]; BN: 8
Yth. 6166 et 22643 (2 ex.); BLC.
theater.
———. *L'Esprit français, ou problème à
résoudre sur le labyrinthe des divers*

Gouges (*continued*)
    complots. Paris: Vve Duchesne,
    1792.
    in-8; viii-32p.
    [Monglond]; [MW]; [OF]; BN:
    Lb(39).5845; BLC.
    politics.
    ———. *Les Fantômes de l'opinion
    publique*. N.l.: n.d.
    in-8; 8p.
    [MW]; BN: 8 Lb(41).2360.
    politics.
    ———. *Grande Éclipse du soleil Ja-
    cobiniste et de la lune feuillantine . . .*
    N.l.: n.d. [1793].
    in-8.
    BLC.
    politics.
    ———. *Lettre à mgr le duc d'Orléans,
    premier prince du sang*. N.l.: n.d.
    [1789].
    in-8; 8p.
    [Monglond]; [MW]; BN: 8
    Lb(39).1911; BLC.
    letter / politics.
    ———. *Lettre aux représentants de la
    Nation*. Paris: imp. de L. Jorry, n.d.
    [1789].
    in-8; 8p.
    [Monglond]; [MW]; BN: 8
    Lb(39).1847; Q; BLC.
    letter / politics.
    ———. *Lettres à la reine, aux généraux
    de l'armée, aux amis de la constitu-
    tion et aux françaises citoyennes. De-
    scription de la fête de 3 juin*. Paris:
    imp. de la Société typographique,
    n.d. [1792].
    in-8; 16p.
    [Monglond]; [MW]; [OF]; BN: 8
    Lb(39).10603; BLC.
    letter / politics.
    ———. *Mes Voeux sont remplis, ou le
    don patriotique*. N.l. [Paris]: n.d.
    [1789].
    in-8; 4p.
    [Monglond]; [MW]; [OF]; BN: 8

    Lb(39). 7327; BLC.
    politics.
    ———. *Mirabeau aux Champs-Élysées,
    comédie en un acte et en prose*. Paris:
    Garnery, n.d. [1791].
    in-8; XXI-46p; performed at the
    Comédie italien, April 15, 1791.
    [Monglond]; [MW]; [OF]; BN: 8
    Yth. 11834, 11835 et 22666 (3 ex.);
    BLC.
    theater.
    ———. *Oeuvres de la citoyenne de
    Gouges en deux volumes formant le
    recueil de ses oeuvres dramatiques et
    politiques. Se Trouvent chez le Jay
    Père . . .* N.l.: n.d. [1791].
    in-8; 16p.
    [Monglond].
    politics.
    ———. *Olympe de Gouges, défenseur
    officieux de Louis Capet, au président
    de la Convention Nationale*. 1791.
    in-8; other ed. 1792, n.l.
    [Monglond].
    politics.
    ———. *L'Ordre national, ou le comte
    d'Artois inspiré par Mentor, dédié
    aux États Généraux*. N.l.: n.d.
    [1789].
    in-8; 24p.
    [Monglond]; [MW]; [OF]; BN: 8
    Lb(39).2055; BLC.
    politics.
    ———. *Pacte national . . . adressé à
    l'Assemblée Nationale*. Paris: imp.
    de la Société typographique, 1792.
    In-fol. piano.
    [MW]; [OF]; BN: Fol.Lb(39).5690.
    politics.
    ———. *Pour Sauver la patrie, il faut re-
    specter les trois ordres, c'est le seul
    moyen de conciliation qui nous reste*.
    N.l.: n.d. [1789].
    in-8; 8p.
    [Monglond]; [MW]; [OF]; BN: 8
    Lb(39).1696; BLC.
    politics.

Gouges (*continued*)

————. *Le Prélat d'Autrefois, ou So-phie et Saint-Elme, fait historique mis en action, comédie en trois actes et en prose.* Paris: Cailleau, 1795. in-8; 103p; performed at the *Théâtre de la Cité-Variétés*, March 18, 1794. [Monglond]; [OF]; BN: 8 Yth. 14596.
theater.

————. *Le Prince philosophe, conte oriental par l'auteur de la pièce intitulée 'L'Esclavage des nègres.'* Paris: Briand, 1792.
2 part. in-12; Ier part:261p, 2e part:261p.
[BGR]; [Monglond]; [MW]; [OF]; BN: Y2 60745–60746; FC 92 VIII 2768; MF 21.iv.92; Q.
novel.

————. *Projet sur la formation d'un tribunal populaire et suprême en matière criminelle présenté le 26 mai 1790 à l'Assemblée Nationale.* Paris: imp. du Patriote français, n.d. [1790].
in-8; 8p.
[Monglond]; [MW]; [OF]; BN: 8 Lf(113).82; BLC.
politics / law.

————. *Réponse à la justification de maximilien ROBESPIERRE, adressée à Jérôme PÉTION. Pronostic sur Maximilien Robespierre, par un animal amphibie* [Signé : Polyme]. N.l. [Paris]: n.d. [1791].
in-8; 16p.
[Monglond]; [MW]; [OF]; BN: Lb(41).2359; BLC.
politics.

————. *Réponse au champion américain, ou colon très aisé à connaître (18 janvier 1790).* N.l.: n.d. [1790].
in-8; 8p.
[Monglond]; [MW]; [OF]; BN: 8 Lk(9).84.
politics.

————. *Remarques patriotiques, par la citoyenne auteur de la 'lettre au peuple.'* N.l.: n.d. [1789].
in-8; 48p et pl.
[Monglond]; [MW]; BN: 8ø Lb(39).749; BLC.
politics.

————. *Repentir de Mme de Gouges.* N.l. [Paris]: n.d. [1797].
in-8; 4p.
[MW]; [OF]; BN: 8 Ln(27).8956; BLC.
politics.

————. *Séance royale. Motion de mgr le duc d'Orléans, ou les songes patriotiques . . .* N.l.: 1789.
in-8; 32p.
[Monglond]; [MW]; [OF]; BN: 8 Lb(39).7829.
politics.

————. *Sera-t-il roi, ne le sera-t-il Pas?* . . . N.l. [Paris]: n.d. [1791].
in-8; 16p.
[MW]; [OF]; BN: 8 Lb(39).5136; BLC.
politics.

————. *Testament politique, [4 juin 1793].* N.l.[Paris]: n.d.[1793].
in-8; 12p.
[Monglond]; [MW]; [OF]; BN: 8 Lb(41).3049; BLC.
politics.

————. *Le Tombeau de Mirabeau.* N.l.: n.d. [1791].
in-8; 2p.
[Monglond]; [MW]; BN: 8 Lb(39)4784; BLC.
politics.

————. *Les trois Urnes, ou le salut de la patrie.* 1793.
in-8.
[Monglond]; [OF].
politics.

Goujon, veuve née Ricard. *Réflexions adressées à la Convention Nationale sur la question de savoir si elle doit laisser juger par la commission mili-*

Goujon (*continued*)
taire les représentans du peuple ar-
rêtés le premier prairial. N.l. [Paris]:
1795.
in-8; 7p.
[MW]; BN: 8 Lb(41).1829; BLC.
politics.
———. *La citoyenne Ricard, veuve*
Goujon, aux représentans du peuple.
N.l.: n.p. 1795.
in-8; 8p.
[MW]; BN: 8 Lb(41).1869; BLC.
politics.
Graffigny, Françoise d'Issembourg
d'Happoncourt madame de
1695–1758. *Lettres d'une péruvi-*
enne, par Mme de Grafigny. nouv.
éd., augmentée d'une suite qui n'a
point encore été imprimée [Par Mme
Morel de Vindé]. Paris: P. Didot
l'aîné, 1797.
2 vol. in-12; t.I:255p, t.II:239p.
[Monglond]; BN: Z.15589–15590.
novel.
Grandval, madame. *Pétition à*
l'Assemblée Nationale, pour lui de-
mander une loi qui accorde aux en-
fants naturels le droit d'hériter de
leurs pères et mères libres . . . Paris:
imp. de Demonville, n.d.
in-8; 15p.
[MW]; BN: 8 F.Pièce.2892.
politics.
Gravier, Citoyenne. *Aux Citoyens*
représentans du peuple, membres des
comités de salut public et de sûreté
générale. N.l.: n.d.[1794].
in-8; 7p.
[MW]; [CHF]; BN: 8 Lb(41).3945;
BLC.
politics.
Grégoire, veuve. *Prospectus d'une ex-*
pédition pour la côte du Mozambique,
pour y traiter trois cens noirs. N.l.:
n.d. [1791].
in-4; 2p; [Dated: Havre, 2 août
1791].

[MW]; BN: 4 Or(3).2.
commercial.
Grisard, madame. *Pétition au sujet de*
la révision d'un jugement du tribunal
criminel du département de l'Yonne
qui a condamné à 8 années de fers
Pierre-Joseph Grisard. N.l.: n.d.
in-4; 4p.
[MW]; BN: 4 Ln(27).29098.
politics.
Guérin-Albert, madame. *Avis aux*
mères républicaines, ou mes réflexions
sur l'éducation des jeunes citoyennes
. . . N.l.: imp. de la citoyenne Fon-
rouge, n.d.
in-8; 49p.
[MW]; BN: 8 R.13625 et 14220 (2
ex.).
pedagogy.
Guibert, Louise Alexandrine
comtesse de 1758–1826. *Agatha ou*
la religieuse anglaise, traduit de
l'anglais. Paris: Maradan, 1797.
3t. in-12; translation of *Agatha or a*
Narrative of Recent Events (1796),
author unknown; other edition,
Paris: Maradan, an VII, 4t.
[BGR];[Monglond]; BN: 8 4(2)
62042.
novel/translation.
———. *Margaretta, comtesse de Rains-*
ford, traduit de l'anglais par A. L. de
G . . . Paris: Pougens et Buisson,
1797.
2t. in-12; translation of *Margaretta,*
Countess of Rainsford, a Sentimental
Novel (1769), author unknown.
[BGR]; [Monglond]; Mag. enc. III
1797 ii 566.
novel/translation.
Guizot, madame Pauline de née
Meulan 1773–1827. *La Chapelle*
d'Ayton ou Emma Courtney. Paris:
Maradan, 1799.
5t. in-12; translation of *Memoirs of*
Emma Courtney (1798), by Mary
Hays; other edition, Paris:

Guizot (*continued*)
  Maradan, 1810, 4t. in-12.
  [BGR]; [Monglond]; JT 20 mess.
  VII; Monglond.
  novel / translation.
  ———. *Les Contradictions ou ce qui peut en arriver*. Paris: Maradan, 1799.
  in-12; 275p.
  [BGR]; [Monglond]; Mag. enc IV 1799 v 142.
  novel.
Guyon, Jeanne Marie Bouviers de la Motte madame 1648–1717. *L'Ame amante de son dieu, representée dans les emblèmes de H. Hugo, et dans oeux d'O. Vaenius sur l'amour divin. Avec des Figures nouvelles, accompagnées de vers*. Paris: n.p. 1790.
  in-8; nouvelle édition augumentée.
  BLC.
  religion.
  ———. *Discours chrétiens et spirituels sur divers sujets qui regardent la vie intérieure*. Paris: n.p., 1790.
  2 vol. in-8; first edition: 1716.
  [Monglond]; BLC.
  religion.
  ———. *Les Justifications de Mme J.-M.-B. de la Mothe-Guion, écrites par elle-même . . . avec un examen de la IXe et Xe conférence de Cassien, touchant l'état fixe d'oraison continuelle, par feu M. de Fénelon . . .* Paris: libraires associés, 1790.
  in-8; first edition: 1720.
  [Monglond]; BN: T.I.D. 90281.
  religion.
  ———. *Oeuvres. [Publiées par Dutoit Mambrini.]* Paris: libraires associés, 1790.
  40 vol. in-8.
  [Monglond].
  literature.
  ———. *Opuscules spirituels*. Paris: n.p. 1790.

2 vols. in-18; first edition: 1712.
  [Monglond]; BLC.
  religion.
  ———. *La Vie de Mme Jeanne-Marie Bouvières de la Mothe-Guion, écrite par elle-même*. Paris: n.p., 1790.
  3 vols. in-8 (Sup.); first edition: 1720.
  [Monglond]; BLC.
  memoir.
Guyton de Morveau, Claudine Poullet Picardet fl. 1785. *Traité de caractères extérieures des fossiles*. Dijon: n.p., 1790.
  in-12; translation of Gottlob Werner's text; ABF: 224–225.
  [WS]; BLC; BN: S. 20551.
  science / translation.
Haudry, mademoiselle. *Emma ou l'Enfant du malheur, traduit d'anglais sur la seconde édition*. Paris: Buisson, 1792.
  2t. in-12; translation of *Emma or the Child of Sorrow* (1776), author unknown; other editions: (1) Paris: n.p., 1788, 2t. in-12; (2) Paris: Dufart, 1795, an 4e, 2t. in-12.
  [BGR]; [Monglond]; BN: Y(2) 32401.
  novel / translation.
  ———. *Le Fils naturel ou mémoires de Gréville, traduit de l'anglais*. Paris: Duchesne, 1798.
  in-12, 220p.; Original ed. P. de Lormel, 1786, in-12; 216p; translation of *The Bastard or the History of Mr. Greville* (1784), author unknown.
  [BGR].
  novel / translation.
  ———. *Tout s'arrange à la fin ou l'histoire de M. Melfort. Écrite dans le courant de 1790*. Pithiviers: Cocatrix l'aîné, 1796.
  3 part. in-12; other edition, Pithiviers, Cocatrix l'aîné & Paris: le Marchand, [an IX].

Haudry (*continued*)
[BGR]; [Monglond]; BN:Y(2) 62832
& Y(2) 62839.
novel.

Hidou, Victoire veuve de Jean Baptiste Bossu. *Accusateur public, juges
et jurés du tribunal révolutionnaire
d'Arras, imposteurs et prévaricateurs.
La citoyenne Dubois, veuve, avec enfants, de Jean-Baptiste Brazier, . . . La
citoyenne Rosalie-Delphine-Joseph
Bossu, . . . et Victoire Hidou, veuve de
Jean-Baptiste Bossu, . . . à la Convention Nationale.* Paris: imp. de Guffroy, n.d. [1794].
in-4; 7p.
[CHF]; BN: Lb (41) 4158.
politics.

Hue de la Colombe, Elisabeth Victoire. *Lettres à son neveu.* N.l.: n.d.
in-8; 3p.
[MW]; BN Ln(27).65190 et
65109.A.
letters.

Huguenin, Marie Catherine. *Mémoire
. . . au Directoire Exécutif pour la justification de son parent Jean-Louis
Jaquin, ministre du culte catholique à
Beine (Yonne) . . . condamné à la dé-
portation . . . en vertu d'un arrêté du
6 niv. an VI.* Auxerre: imp. de L.
Fournier, 1798.
in-4; 11p.
[MW]; [CHF]; BN: 4 Ld(4).4075;
BLC.
politics.

Huot, Jeanne. *Pétition de Jeanne Huot,
ex-religieuse . . . au Conseil des Cinq-
Cents (3 brumaire an VII).* N.l.: n.d.
[1799].
in-fol.
[CHF].
politics.

Hurville, madame. *Lettre.* N.l. [Paris]:
n.d.[1794].
in-8; 24p.
[MW]; [CHF]; BN: 8 Lb(41).1290;

BLC.
letter / politics.

Huzard, Mme M. R. *Epreuves de caractères qui sont le plus en usages.*
Paris: Imp. de la citoyenne M. R.
Huzard, 179–.
broadside: 41.5 x 22.5 cm.
Houghton Library, Harvard University.
commercial.

Hyver, citoyenne Penon femme.
*Adresse . . . à la Convention Na-
tionale . . .* Paris: Imp. de la Vve
d'A. J. Gorsas, 1793.
in-8; 20p.
[MW]; [CHF]; BN: 8 Lb(41).1396.
politics.

————. *Pétition présentée à la Convention Nationale . . . le 29 niv. an II . . .*
N.l. n.d.[1794].
in-8; 4p.
[MW]; BN: 8 Ln(27).10044.
politics.

Jodin, mademoiselle. *Vues législatives
pour les femmes, adressées à l'Assemblée Nationale.* Angers: Mame,
1790.
in-8; IV-86p.
[Monglond]; [MW]; BN: 80 R.
3944.
politics.

Jullien, Rosalie Ducrollay madame.
*Copie de la lettre écrite . . . au citoyen
. . . à Valence . . .* N.l. [1793]: n.d.
in-4; 4p.
[MW]; BN: 4 Lb(41).3171.
letter.

Kennens, madame et Radet J. B.
*Le Dîner au Pré-Saint-Gervais,
comédie en un acte et en prose, mêlée
de vaudevilles.* Paris: Migneret,
1797.
in-8; 64p; performed at the *Théâtre
du Vaudeville,* November 19, 1796.
[Monglond]; BN: 2 ex. 8 Yth. 5206
et 5207; BLC.
theater.

Kéralio, Marie Françoise née Abeille
madame de fl. 1755–1790. *Les Vi-
sites par Mademoiselle D** K****.
Paris: Gattey, 1792.
in-8; 154p; ABF: 558: 69, 74, 77.
[BGR]; BN: Y(2). 73510; FC 92 II
2151; Monglond.
novel.
Kéralio-Robert, Louise Félicité
Guynement de 1758–1821. *Adresse
aux femmes de Montauban . . .* N.l.:
n.p., 1790.
in-8; 8p; ABF: 558, 78–99.
[MW]; [CHF]; BN: 8 Lb(39).3410.
politics.
————. *Les Crimes de Marie-
Antoinette*. Paris: Prudhomme,
1793.
in-8.
[BN].
politics.
————. *Les Crimes des reines de France,
depuis le commencement de la monarchie jusqu'à Marie-Antoinette, publiés par L. Prudhomme; avec cinq
gravures*. Paris: bureau des Révolutions de Paris, 1791.
in-8; other editions: (1) Neuchâtel:
Société typographique, 1792, in-12;
(2) Paris: Prudhomme, an II
(1794), in-8.
[Monglond]; BLC.
politics.
————. *Discours sur l'administration
des hôpitaux*. N.p., n.d. [1792].
[MW] BN: 8ø Lb(40).2418.
politics.
————. *Histoire d'Élisabeth, reine d'Angleterre, tirée des écrits originaux
anglais . . .* 1786–1789.
5 vols. in-8.
[Monglond].
history.
————. *Journal d'état et du citoyen, par
Mlle de Kéralio, de l'Académie d'Arras et de la Société Patriotique Bre-
tonne* (1789).

Edited by Mlle de Kéralio, Imp.:
N. H. Nyon, Paris, appeared from
October 1, 1789, in-8; continued by
*Mercure national, ou Journal d'État
et du Citoyen* [by Mlle de Kéralio
(later Mme Robert) et MM. Carra,
Masclet et Hugou de Bassville],
December 31, 1789–August 30,
1790, edited by L. Guynement
(formerly de Kéralio), Hugou de
Bassville, Fr. Robert et Mme
Guynement-Robert (formerly de
Kéralio) Imp: L. Potier de Lille,
Paris, in-8; BN: 8 Lc2 215; contin-
ued by *Révolutions de l'Europe et
Mercure National Réunis*; changes
title: *Mercure National et Révolutions de l'Europe* (as of September
14, 1790); edited by, Mme Robert,
L.-F. Guynement de Kéralio, A.
Tournon, Hugou de Bassville,
Robert, Imp. des Révolutions de
l'Europe, Lefort (as of October 1,
1790), J. Bigot (December 14,
1790), Roland (as of December 31,
1790), Cordier et Meymac (January 19, 1791), L. Potier de Lille (as
of February 11, 1791), Paris; BN: 8
Lc2.178–179.
[Monglond]; [MW]; BN: Lc2 214.
journal.
————. *Louise Robert à M. Louvet, . . .*
Paris: imp. de Baudouin, n.d.
[1792].
in-8; 4p; Pièce.
[CHF]; BN: 2 ex. 8 Lb(41) 2302 et 8
Lb(27) 1762.
politics.
————. *Mercure National et étranger,
ou Journal Politique de l'europe
pour faire suite aux deux journaux
connus, l'un sous le title de Mercure National et Révolutions
de l'Europe, l'autre sous celui de
Journal Général de l'Europe. Par
Louise Robert, Fr. Robert . . .
et P.-M.-H. Lebrun*

Kéralio-Robert (*continued*)

2 vols. in-8; the *Journal général de l'Europe,* by Lebrun and Smits, united temporarily with the *Mercure* by Mme de Kéralio: edited by Louise Robert (Mlle de Kéralio), Fr. Robert, P. M. H. le Brun Imp: Lefort, Paris, in-8.
[Monglond]; [MW]; BN: Lc2 96. journal.

———. *Observations sur quelques articles du project de constituton de M. Mounier.* Paris: imp. de Nyon, n.d. [1789].
in-8; 18p.
[Monglond]; [MW]; BN: 8 Lb(39).7802 et 11760 (2 ex.). politics.

Labrousse, Clothilde Suzanne Courcelles de 1747–1821. *Discours de Mlle S. de la Brousse, sur les objections qu'on lui a faites sur la constitution et qu'elle a prononcé, d'une manière tres-intelligible . . . par-tout où l'on a voulu . . .* N.l.[Grenoble]: n.d. [1792].
in-8; ABF: 567, 342–347.
[Monglond]; BLC.
prophecy / politics.

———. *Lettre de Mlle de la Brouse du 20 février 1790.* 1790.
in-8; 16p.
[Monglond]; BLC; CHF.
prophecy / politics.

———. *Prophéties . . . concernant la révolution française, suivies d'une prédiction qui annonce la fin du monde.* N.l.[Paris]: n.p., 1790.
in-8; 16p.
[MW]; [Monglond]; BN: 8 Lb(39).8907; BLC.
prophecy / politics.

———. *Prophéties de Mlle Suzette de La Brousse, concernant la Révolution française suivies d'une prédiction que annonce la fin du monde. No. 1.* N.l.: n.p., 1790.

in-8.
[CHF]; BN: 8ø Lb(39) 8907; BLC.
politics.

———. *Recueil des ouvrages de la célèbre Mlle La Brousse . . . actuellement prisonnière au Château Saint-Ange à Rome . . . [publié par Pontard].* Bordeaux: Brossier, 1797.
in-8; 296p.
[Monglond]; [MW]; BN: 8 Ld(4).6687; BLC.
politics.

Lacombe, Claire called Rose. *Discours prononcé à la barre de l'Assemblée Nationale . . . le 25 juillet 1792 . . .* N.l.[Paris]: n.d.[1792].
in-8; 3p.
[MW]; BN: 8 Le(33).3.X (63; BLC.
politics.

———. *Rapport fait . . . à la Société des Républicaines Révolutionnaires, de ce qui s'est passé le 16 septembre à la Société des Jacobins . . .* N.l.: n.d.
in-4; 15p.
[MW]; BN: 4 Fm.35160.
politics.

Lacombe, veuve de. *Précis des observations remises au comité des finances de l'Assemblée Nationale, concernant l'affaire des messageries . . . par les sieurs Le Prieur, Doyen, Barbereux, de Nanteuil l'aîné, de Nanteuil le jeune, Le Clerc et la dame veuve de La Combe, tous anciens fermiers des messageries.* Paris: imp. de Demonville, 1790.
in-4.
[CHF].
politics / commercial.

———. *Résumé présentée à l'Assemblée Nationale par les sieurs Le Prieur, Doyen, Barbereux, de Nanteuil l'aîné, de Nanteuil le jeune, Leclerc et la dame veuve de La Combe . . . tous anciens fermiers généraux des messageries. En Réponse au dernier mémoire publié par les sieurs Caulet*

Lacombe (*continued*)
*d'Hauteville et consorts, chargés du
service actuel des messageries.* Paris:
imp. de Demonville, 1790.
in-4.
CHF.
politics.
Lacour, citoyenne. *Affaires de l'Orient.
Faits.* Paris: imp de Guérin,
n.d.[1793].
in-8; 8p.
[MW]; [CHF]; BN: 8 Lb(41).876;
BLC.
politics.
――――. *Lettre . . . aux députés extraordinaires du Conseil Général de la
Commune de l'Orient pour servir de
réponse à trois feuilles imprimées
ayant pour titre: 'Mémoire, dernières
paroles de M. Gérard, et copie de l'at-
taché du département.'* Paris: imp de
Guérin, n.d. [1792].
in-8; 16p.
[MW]; BN: 8 Ln(27).10849; BLC.
politics.
――――. *Lettre de la citoyenne Lacour
aux députés extraordinaires du Conseil Général de la commune de l'Orient . . .* Paris: 1792.
in-8.
BLC.
politics.
――――. *Réponse . . . à l'écrit imprimé
qui a pour titre: 'Correspondance de
M. Gérard fils aîné, négociant de
l'Orient.'* Paris: imp de Guérin,
n.d.
in-8; 8p.
[MW]; BN: 8 Ln(27).10850; BLC.
politics.
Laférandière, Marie Amable Petiteau
marquise de 1736–1817. *Romance
de Paul et Virginie [avec la musique,
par Madame la Comtesse de Cau-
mont, sa fille].* Paris: imp. de Didot
jeune, 1789.
in-32; 26p; words and music; ABF:

575, 243–245.
[Monglond]; BN: Ye. 25021.
poetry / music.
LaFayette, Marie Adrienne de
Noailles marquise de 1759–1807.
*Notice sur la vie de A. L. H.
d'Aguesseau, duchesse d'Ayen . . .
imprimée par G. E. J. Montmorency
Albert-Luynes.* Dampierre: n.p.,
1800.
in-4; 135p.
[Monglond]; BN: 4 Ln(27) 23010;
BLC.
literature.
Lafite, Marie Elisabeth née Bouée
madame de 1737–1794. *Miss Lony,
traduit de l'allemand de Mme de la
Roche, par Mme **.* Lausanne: L.
Luquiens, Durand l'aîné et Comp.,
1792.
in-8; 201p; translation of *Geschichte
von Miss Lony und der schöne Bund*
(1789), by Frau von Maria Sophie
Gutermann la Roche.
[BGR]; [Monglond]; BN: Y(2)
47325; FC 92 III 2257.
novel / translation.
――――. *Entretiens, drames et contes
moraux à l'usage des enfans, par
Madame de la Fite.* N.l.: 1791.
Original ed, LaHaye; Detune,
1778, in-12; xii +453p; other editions: (1) La Haye: Detune, 1781;
(2) 2nd ed., La Haye: Detune,
1783, 2t. in-12; (3) La Haye: Detune, 1788, in-12; (4) 4th ed, n.1.,
1791, 2t., pp variously xii + 309,
322; (5) 5th ed., Paris: J.-C. Pon-
celin, 1801, 2t. in-12; (6) Paris: n.p.
1809, 4t. in-12; (7) Paris: 1820, 4t.
in-18; ABF: 576, 291–292, 296–298.
[BGR]; [Monglond].
novel / pedagogy.
――――. *Eugénie et ses élèves ou lettres
et dialogues à l'usage des jeunes personnes, par Madame de La Fite, auteur des 'Entretiens, drames & contes*

Lafite (*continued*)
  moraux à l'usage des enfans.' Paris:
  Onfroy et Née de la Rochelle,
  1792.
  Original ed., 1787, part. in-12;
  t.I:xxiv + 212, t.II:218–416; other
  editions: (1) Amsterdam: n.p.
  1787, 2t, xx + 195p; (2) Dresden:
  Walther, 1792.
  [BGR]; [Monglond]; JL xvi 1787.
  novel / pedagogy.
———. *Pensées sur les moeurs des*
  grands . . . N.l.: n.p., 1790.
  in-8; translation of Hannah More.
  BLC.
  translation / philosophy.
———. *Réponses à démêler ou essai*
  d'une manière d'exercer l'attention.
  On y a joint divers morceau qui ont
  pour but d'instruire ou d'amuser les
  jeunes personnes, par Madame de la
  Fite. London: J. Murray, 1790.
  in-8; iv + 271p; other editions: (1)
  Lausanne: n.p., 1791, in-12; (2)
  Hamburg & Leipzig: n.p., 1792,
  in-12; (3) Lausanne: n.p., 1807,
  in-12.
  [BGR]; [Monglond]; BLC.
  novel / pedagogy.
LaGrave, comtesse de fl. 1795–1805.
  Le Château d'Alvarino ou les effets de
  la vengeance, par L. C. Lagrave, au-
  teur de 'Sophie de Beauregard,' 'Za-
  beth,' 'Minuit,' Etc. Paris: Leprieur,
  1800.
  2t. in-12; pp variously xvi + 223,
  250; other edition: Paris: Delarue
  & Lille Castiaux, [n.d.], 3t. in-18,
  t.I:100p, t.II:99p.
  [BGR]; [Monglond]; JT 30 frim.
  VIII; Mag. enc. V 1799 v 426.
  novel.
———. *Minuit ou les aventures de Paul*
  de Mirebon, par l'auteur de 'Sophie
  de Beauregard' et de 'Zabeth.' Paris:
  Leprieur, 1799.
  in-12; 223p.

[BGR]; [Monglond]; BN: Y2 53715;
  JT 30 pluv. VII; Mag. enc. V 1799
  iii 568.
  novel.
———. *Sophie de Beauregard ou le véri-*
  table amour, par L.C.L.G. Paris: de
  l'imprimerie de Legras et Cordier,
  chez Leprieur, 1799.
  in-12; t.I:216, t.II:211.
  [BGR]; [Monglond]; JT 8 vend.
  VII.
  novel.
———. *Zabeth ou la victime de l'ambi-*
  tion, par l'auteur de 'Sophie de Beau-
  regard.' Paris: Leprieur, 1799.
  2t. in-12; t.I:263p, t.II:224p.
  [BGR]; [Monglond]; BN* Y2
  74735–74736; JT 5 pluv. VII.
  novel.
LaHaye, Angélique Charlotte Pignon
  veuve de. *Dénonciation présentée au*
  comité de législation de la Convention
  Nationale contre le représentant du
  peuple Dupin, par les veuves et en-
  fans des ci-devant fermiers généraux.
  Paris: Dupont, 1795.
  in-8; 55p; another edition, signed
  by M. Paulze, veuve Lavoisier,
  Pignon, veuve de la Haye, Papil-
  lon-Sannois, fils de Papillon-
  d'Autroche, 7 thermidor an III.
  [MW]; [CHF]; BN: 8 Lb(41).1924 et
  4485; BLC.
  politics.
———. *Lettre adressée au cit. Royé*
  défenseur des créanciers et intéressés
  à la liquidation des fortunes des ci-
  devant fermiers genéraux. N.l.: n.d.
  [1795].
  in-8; 4p.
  [MW]; BN: 8 Lb(41).5516.
  commercial / politics.
———. *Rentes foncières constituées*
  avant 1791. Pétition. Omission à ré-
  parer dans la loi du 18 Fruct. an IV et
  dans le projet de loi sur les transac-
  tions. Paris: imp. de Gueffier,

LaHaye (*continued*)
n.d.[1797].
in-8; 4p.
[MW]; [CHF]; BN: 8 Lb(42).1282.
politics / commercial.
Lamarck, Marie Anne Françoise de
Noailles Comtesse de 1720. *Obser-*
vations . . . sur une assertion de M.
Camus. N.l. [Paris]: n.d. [1790?].
in-8; 6p; ABF: (family): 786, 388–
430.
[MW]; BN: 8 Ln(27).11158.
commercial.
Lambert, Anne Thérèse de Margue-
nat de Courcelles marquise de
1647–1733. *Avis d'une mère à son*
fils. London: A. Dulau &. Co.,
1799.
in-12; ii-77p; two other eds.: both
Paris: n.p., 1800.
BLC.
novel.
LaMotte, citoyenne. *Anniversaire du*
14 juillet . . . Paris: Daniel, n.d.
in-12; 4p.
[MW]; BN: Ye.56375 (533[3]).
song.
LaMotte-Geffrard, Marie Anne Antoinette de. *Affaire de 1773, du régi-*
ment royal-comtois, rappelée à
l'Assemblée dite Nationale par M.
Chabroud, en 1790 et 1791, écrit des-
tiné à la seconde législature . . . N.l.:
n.p. 1791.
in-8; 2 parts in 1 vol.; ABF: (family) 591, 76.
[MW]; [CHF]; BN: 8 Lb(39).10182.
politics.
———. *Dénonciations publiées par un*
aristocrate; des différens individus qui
ont contribu, à l'arrestation du Rio, à
Varennes . . . et contre M. Chabroud,
dit le blanchisseur des criminels dits
de lèse-nation . . . [lettre de M.-A.-A.
de la Motte-G, Ffrard (sic) . . . à
Monsieur Chabroud.]. Worms: n.p.,
1792.

in-8.
BLC.
politics.
LaMotte, Jeanne de Luz de Saint-
Rémy de Valois comtesse de
1756–1791. *Adresse à l'Assemblée*
Nationale, pour être déclarée
citoyenne active. London: n.p.,
1790.
in-8; 14p.
[Monglond]; [MW]; [CHF]; BN: 8
Lb(39).3640; BLC.
politics.
———. *Lettre . . . à la reine de France.*
Oxford: n.p., n.d. [1789].
in-8; 16p.
[Monglond]; [MW]; BN: 8
Ln(27).11291; BLC.
politics.
———. *Lettre . . . aux françois.* Paris:
Lacloye, n.d.[1789].
in-8; 8p.
[Monglond]; [MW]; [CHF]; BN: 8
Ln(39).7572.
politics.
———. *Mémoires justificatifs écrits par*
elle-même. Paris: n.p., 1789.
in-8; 260p; first edition: 1788; other
editions: n.l., 1789, 2 vols. in-12;
five different 1789 London editions: (1) 257p, in-8 (fictitious imprint; printed in France); (2) 2
vols., in-8; (3) in-8, 204p; (4) in-8,
258p; (5) in-8, 260p.
[Monglond]; [MW]; BN: Rés.
Ln(27).1128 (4 ex.); BLC.
memoir.
———. *Second Mémoire justificatif.*
London: n.p., 1789.
in-8; 78p; other editions: (1) London: n.p., 1790, in-8; (2) Paris
(Leipzig, Fr. Fleischer): n.d., 2
parties in-8; (3) Bern: Haller, n.d.
[Monglond]; [MW]; Rés. Ln(27)
11289, 11289 alpha, 11289 beta (3
ex.); BLC.
memoir.

———. *Supplique à la nation, et requête à l'Assemblée Nationale, en révision de son procès.* N.l.: imp. patriotique, n.d. [1790].
in-8; 8p.
[Monglond]; [MW]; [CHF]; BN: 8 Lb(39).3639.
politics.

———. *Vie de Jeanne de Saint-Rémy de Valois, ci-devant comtesse de la Motte, écrite par elle-même.* Paris: Garnery, 1792.
2 vols. in-8.
[Monglond]; [MW]; BN: 8 Ln(27).11294.A.
memoir.

———. *Vie et aventures de la comtesse de Valois de la Motte, écrites par elle-même. Avec figures.* London: n.p., 1793.
in-12; VIII-425p.
[Monglond]; [MW]; [OF]; BN: Rés. Ln(27).11295.
memoir.

LaQueuille, marquise J.C.M. de. *Lettre en réponse à Mme la comtesse de *** [21 mars 1792].* Bruxelles: n.p., n.d. [1792].
in-8; Pièce; 16p; ABF: 599, 373–378.
[Monglond]; BN: 8 Lb (39) 5828.
politics.

LaQueuille, marquise J.C.M. de et Condé L. J. duc de Bourbon prince de. *Réponse des princes et français émigrés aux décrets de l'Assemblée Nationale du 8 novembre 1791 et à la proclamation du roi.* Tournay: imp. de J. Serre, 1791.
in-8; 16p.
[Monglond]; BN: 8 Lb(39) 5542.
politics.

Laugier, Marie. *Les Épreuves du républicain, ou l'amour de la patrie, essai patriotique en 3 actes, mêlés de chants . . . musique du cit. Champein . . .* Paris: Maradan, 1794.

in-8; IV-59p; performed at the *Opéra-comique national,* 17 therm. an II.
[MW]; BN: 8 Yth.6123.
theater.

———. *Circulaire sur la police de la récolte de la farine.* N.l.: n.d. [1794].
in-8; 4p.
[MW]; BN: Sp.602.
agriculture / commercial.

———. *La Commission d'agriculture et des arts aux autorités constituées. récolte de la farine. Police de cette récolte.* N.l.: n.d.
in-4; 4p.
BN: Sp. 602.
agriculture.

———. *Moyens propres à rendre plus économique l'emploi des farines provenant des grains nouvellement récoltés, et à augmenter la qualité du pain qu'elles doivent donner . . .* Paris: imp. de la 'Feuille du cultivateur,' n.d.
in-8; 4p.
[MW]; BN: S.21969.
agriculture / commercial.

Laveaux, madame Étienne Mayneaud Bizefranc de née Guillermin. *Réponse aux calomnies coloniales de Saint-Domingue. L'Épouse du républicaine Laveaux . . . à ses concitoyens . . .* Paris: imp. de Pain, n.d. [1794?].
in-4; 1–3.
[MW]; [CHF]; BN: 4 Lk(12).447; ABF: 724, 341–342.
politics.

Leblanc, mademoiselle. *Journal Politique d'Avignon* (1790).
[Sullerot].
journal.

Leboindre, Françoise. *Département de la Sarthe. Premier mémoire pour Clément Négrier. Les citoyennes Françoise Leboindre, épouse de Clément Négrier, et Anne-Louise-*

Leboindre (*continued*)
Françoise Morre de Posset, sa mère,
au Directoire Exécutif. Le Mans:
imp. de Monnoyer, n.d. [1796].
in-4; 6p.
[CHF]; BN: 4 Ln(27) 15112.
politics.

Lebrun, Louise Elisabeth Vigée called
Vigée-Lebrun 1755–1842. *Lettre à*
M. de Calonne. N.l.[Paris?]: 1789.
in-8.
[Monglond]; [CHF]; BLC; BN: 2
ex. 8 Lb(39). 1427 et 8 Ln(27). 3408.
politics.

Léger, Marie Jeanne Guerrier veuve
Claude. *La Veuve et les neuf enfants*
de Claude Léger, cultivateur et meu-
nier, à la Convention Nationale.
N.l.[Paris?]: n.d.[1794].
in-8.
[CHF]; [BLC]; [MW]; BN: 8
Lb(41).1247.
politics.

Legroing-La-Maisonneuve, mademoiselle Françoise Thérèse Antoinette comtesse de 1764–1837.
Essai sur le genre d'instruction qui
paraît le plus analogue à la destina-
tion des femmes. Paris: imp. de Dufart, 1799.
in-18; 69p; other edition: 2nd ed.,
Paris: l'auteur, an X—1801, in-18,
154p.
[Monglond]; BN: R. 23193 et Rz.
3788.
pedagogy.
———. *Zénobie, reine d'Arménie.* London: n.p., 1795.
in-8; 294p; 2nd ed., Paris: Delance,
an VII, 300p.
[BGR]; [Monglond].
novel.

LeNormand, Marie Anne Adélaïde
mademoiselle 1772–1843. *Le Mot à*
l'oreille, ou le Don Quichotte des
dames, nouveau journal républicain,
par Mlle Le-Normand, propriétaire -

rédactrice [c'est l'illustre Sybille]
(1797).
Imp: Augustin, 8 p. in-8; ABF: 645,
367–381.
[Monglond]; [MW]; [CHF]; BN:
Lc2 2702.
prophecy / journal.

Léonard, veuve Bourdeaux. *A M. le*
Maire de Paris. N.l.: n.d. [1789].
in-8.
[CHF].
politics.

Leprince de Beaumont, Jeanne Marie
1711–1780. *Éducation complète, ou*
abrégé d'histoire universelle. Berlin:
Sander, 1791.
3 vols. in-8, fig.; other editions,
1745, 1762 & 1763.
[Monglond].
pedagogy.

LeRebours, Marie Angélique née
Anel madame 1731–1821. *Avis aux*
mères qui veulent nourrir leurs en-
fants, par la Citoyenne L. R. 1799.
in-12; first edition in 1767; ABF:
650, 140, 145–151.
[Monglond].
pedagogy / health.

LeRoi, baronne de Messey madame.
Proposition d'une femme citoyenne
pour établir les moyens de remédier à
toutes les calamités qui environnent
la France, rétablir l'ordre dans les tri-
bunaux et dans toute espèce d'admin-
istration, regagner la confiance et
faire renaître l'harmonie dans tous les
coeurs française. Paris: imp. de Momoro, 1789.
in-18; 4p.
[Monglond]; [MW]; [CHF]; BN: 8
Lb(39).2266.
politics.

Lesieur, citoyenne. *Exposé sommaire de*
l'abus des pouvoirs de métier, curé de
Melun, et délégué de Dubouchet,
représentant du peuple et commis-
saire dans le département de Seine-

Lesieur (*continued*)
  *et-Marne depuis le 11 septembre
  jusqu'au 16 novembre* . . . Paris:
  imp. de Cellot, n.d. [1793].
  in-8; 16p.
  [MW]; [CHF]; BN: 8ø
  Ln(27).12448; BLC.
  politics.
————. *Pétition faite à la Convention
  Nationale* . . . *le 26 brumaire de l'an
  IIe* . . . Paris: imp. de L.-M. Cellot,
  n.d.[1793].
  in-8; 6p.
  [MW]; [CHF]; BN: 8 Lb (41) 905;
  BLC.
  politics.
Lesurques, veuve Joseph. *Pétition. La
  Vve Lesurque au Directoire Exécutif*.
  Paris: Dépôt des lois, 1797.
  in-4; 23p; ABF: 657, 275–300.
  [MW]; [CHF]; BN: 4 Ln(27).12498;
  BLC.
  politics.
LeTellier, madame. *Mémoire à
  messieurs de l'Assemblée Nationale
  . . .* Paris: imp. du 'Journal gra-
  tuit,' (1789).
  In-fol; 3pp.
  [MW]; BN: Vp.22519.
  politics.
LeVacher de la Feutrie, madame S.
  M. fl. 1800. *Nella ou la carinthienne,
  par Madame S. M. L.* Paris: chez
  l'auteur, 1800.
  3 parts. in-12; t.I:xiii + 162p,
  t.II:219p, t.III:241p; other edition:
  Paris, 1801.
  [BGR]; [Monglond]; BN: Y2
  56143–56145); JT 10 vend. IX.
  novel.
Levasseur, Marie Thérèse 1721–1801.
  Lettre à Corancez. 1798.
  [Monglond].
  politics / society.
Lévis-Mirepoix, Marie Gabrielle Elisabeth de abbesse. *Discours . . . en
  réponse aux officiers du district [de*

*Montargis] entrant par force dans sa
  maison*. N.l.: n.d. [1790].
  in-8; 4p.
  [MW]; [Monglond]; [CHF]; BLC;
  BN: 8 Lb(39). 8586.
  politics / religion.
Lézardière, mademoiselle Marie
  Charlotte Pauline Robert de 1754–
  1835. *Esprit des lois canoniques et
  politiques qui ont régi l'église galli-
  cane dans les quatre premiers siècles
  de la monarchie*. Paris: Nyon l'aîné
  et fils, 1791.
  2 vols. in-8; parts of this text are
  included in volumes IV and V of
  *Théorie des lois politiques de la
  monarchie française*; ABF: 662, 212–
  218.
  [Monglond]; [CHF]; BN: 8 Ld(4)
  3312.
  philosophy / law.
————. *Théorie des lois positives de la
  monarchie française*. Paris: Nyon
  l'aîné et fils, 1792.
  8 vols. in-8.
  [Monglond]; BN: 8 Lc(4) 68.
  philosophy / law.
Loquet, mademoiselle Marie
  Françoise b. 1750. *Voyage de Sophie
  et d'Eulalie au palais du vrai bonheur,
  ouvrage pour servir de guide dans les
  voies du salut, par une jeune demoi-
  selle*. Paris: Onfroy, 1789.
  in-12; xiii-455p; ABF: 672, 213–
  214.
  [Monglond]; BN: D. 42340.
  pedagogy.
Lory de Narp, madame d. circa 1825.
  *Les Victimes de l'amour et de l'incon-
  stance ou lettres de Madame de
  Blainville*. Paris: Laurent jeune,
  1792.
  2t. in-18; other editions: (1) 1794,
  2t. in-18; (2) Paris: Laurent jeune,
  [1800], 2t. in-12.
  [BGR]; [Monglond].
  novel.

Los Rios, Charlotte Marie de 1726–
1802. *Abrégé historique de toutes les
sciences et des beaux-arts, pour faire
suite . . . L'Encyclopédie enfantine.*
Lausanne: n.p., 1789.
in-12; original edition, Dresden:
n.p., 1785; other edition, Bern: Société typographique, 1789, in-12;
ABF: 674, 73–74, 76–77; 895, 370.
[Monglond].
pedagogy.
———. *Encyclopédie enfantine, ou magasin pour les petits enfants.* Dresden: Walther, 1780–1791.
3 vols. in-8; first edition 1770.
[Monglond].
pedagogy.
Louise Marie, Princesse de France
1737–1787. *Méditations eucharis-
tiques.* Paris: Planche, 1789.
in-8; other edition, Lyon: Pitrat,
1810, in-12; ABF, 678, 392–394.
[Monglond].
religion.
Lowendahl, Charlotte de. *Adresse aux
représentans des françois, en réclamation du bien patrimonial de la branche
directe et du nom de Lowendal . . .*
N.l.: n.d.
in-4; 10p; ABF: 669, 204–211; 680,
123–125 (for father).
[MW]; [CHF]; BN: 4 Lm(3).608.
politics / petition.
———. *Aux Représentants de la nation
françoise.* N.l.: n.d.[1790?].
in-4; 8–4-2p.
[MW]; [CHF]; BN: 4 Lm(3).610.
politics.
———. *A M. Camus président du
comité des pensions.* Paris: n.p.,
1790.
in-4.
BLC.
politics.
———. *Notice sur la famille de Lowendal, pour les militaires qu'elle pouvra
intéresser.* N.l.: n.d.

in-4.
[CHF].
politics.
———. *Résumé court et nécessaire de
plusieurs mémoires qui auroient dus
être inutiles.* N.l.: n.p., 1791.
in-8; 16p.
[MW]; [CHF]; BN: 4 Lm(3).609.
politics.
Lubert, mademoiselle de c. 1710–
1779. *Histoire sécrete du Prince Cro-
qu'étron et de la Princesse Foirette.*
N.l.: n.p., 1790.
original edition 1743; ABF: 680,
419–420.
[BGR].
novel.
Luxce-Dumas, Marguerite de. *Mémoire présenté à l'Assemblée Nationale . . . contre M. Leberthon fils,
président au parlement de Bordeaux.*
Paris: imp. des frères Chaigneau,
n.d.
in-8; 8p.
[MW]; [CHF]; BN: 8 Ln(27).13071.
politics.
Luynes, Guyonne Elisabeth Josèphe
de Laval Montmorency duchesse
de 1755–1830. *Épître au lac de
Genève.* Dampierre: n.p., 1795.
in-8; 15p.
[Monglond]; BN: Rés. Ye 4345.
poetry.
———. *A ma Belle-Mère. Traduction en
vers de l'élégie de Gray sur un
cimetière de village.* Dampierre:
n.p., 1797.
in-12; 8p; manuscript note: 'Imprimé au château de Dampierre par
Mme de Luynes, née Montmorency.'
[Monglond]; BN: Rés. Ye 4344.
poetry / translation.
———. *La Vie et très surprenantes adventures de Robinson Crusoe d'York,
marin, qui vécut huit et vingt ans
dans une inhabitée isle sur la côte
d'Amérique, près de l'embouchure de*

Luynes (*continued*)
la Grande Rivière Orénoque avec une relation de sa délivrance de cet endroit et (de) ses ensuite surprenantes aventures. Dampierre: G.E.J.M.A.L., 1797.
2t. in-4; t.I:vi + 495p, t.II:361p; translation of *The Life and Surprising Adventures of Robinson Crusoe* (1719), by Daniel Defoe; interlinear translation for teaching English.
[BGR]; Monglond.
novel / translation / pedagogy.
———. *Le vrai Bonheur, ou la foi de Tobie récompensée, poème tiré de l'écriture sainte, destiné par l'auteur à sa fille.* Dampierre: 1798.
in-8; 7p; printed at the château de Dampierre by Mme de Luynes.
[Monglond]; BN: Rés. Ye 4346; Barb.
poetry.
Machet-Vélye, veuve. *La Famille de l'un des cent soixante conspirateurs du Luxembourg, mis à mort les 19, 21, et 22 messidor . . .* N.l.: n.d.
in-12; 23p.
[MW]; BN: 8 Ln(27).13128.
politics.
Magniez, veuve Floride Lemaire. *Le Tribunal révolutionnaire de Cambray, exécuteur des vengeances personnelles de Joseph Lebon, représentant du peuple. Floride Lemaire, veuve de Joachim Magniez, . . . à la Convention Nationale.* Paris: imp. du Guffroy, n.d. [1795].
in-4; ABF: 688, 271–273.
[CHF].
politics.
Maintenon, Françoise d'Aubigne marquise de 1635–1719. *Mémoires et lettres de Madame de Maintenon.* Maestricht: J. E. Dufour et P. Roux, 1789.
6 vols.; in-12; first edition: 1778.

[Monglond]; BN: 80 Lb(37) 181F.
memoir / letters.
Malarme, Charlotte de Bournon comtesse de 1753—c. 1830.
Clarence Weldone, ou le pouvoir de la vertu. Paris: Lepetit, 1799.
2 vols. in-12; first edition: 1780.
[Monglond]; [NL].
novel.
———. *Miladi Lindsey ou l'épouse pacifique.* Paris: Cailleau, an VI.
other edition, Paris: Lepetit, an VII, 2t. in-12.
[BGR]; [Monglond]; [NL].
novel.
———. *Miralba, chef de Brigands, par Charlotte Bournon-Malarme, académicienne.* Paris: Maradan, 1800.
in-12; t.I:323p, t.II:322p; other edition, Paris: Lecointe et Durey, 1821, 2t. in-12, t.I:281p, t.II:284p.
[BGR]; [Monglond]; [NL]; JT 25 pluv. VIII.
novel.
———. *Théobald Leymour ou la maison murée, par Charlotte Bournon-Malarme, académicienne.* Paris: Maradan, 1799.
in-12; t.I:263p, t.II:278p, t.III:254p.
[BGR]; [Monglond]; [NL]; JT 10 vent. VII.
novel.
———. *Les Trois frères ou Lydia Churchill, par Charlotte Bournon-Malarme.* Paris: Maradan, 1798.
2t. in-12; t.I:287p, t.II:241p.
[BGR]; [Monglond]; JT 1.i.09.
novel.
———. *Les Trois soeurs et la folie guérie par l'amour ou les heureux effets de l'amour filial, par Mme Bournon-Malarme.* Paris: Laurent jeune, 1796.
4t. in-18; t.I:213p, t.II:192p, t.III:159p, t.IV:152.
[BGR]; [Monglond]; [BLC].
novel.

Mallard, Marie Barbe Guillot dame.
Mémoire justificatif . . . N.l.: n.d.
[1791].
in-4; 8p.
[MW]; BN: 4 Ln(27).13309.
politics.
———. *Observations pour la dame Mallard, nourrice du roi.* N.l.: n.d.
[1790].
in-8; 4p.
[MW]; BN: 4 Ln(27).13308.
politics.
Marat, Albertine. *Réponse aux dé-
tracteurs de l' 'ami du peuple' . . .*
Paris: imp. de Marat, n.d.[1793].
in-8; 8p.
[MW]; BN: 8 Ln(27).13395; BLC.
politics.
Marat, S. Evrad madame. *Lettre à
M.L.B.D.B., En faveur de son mari,
au sujet de la défense qu'il a prise de
M. Necker . . . contre M. Marat . . . et
réponse en conséquence par le
B. D. B. (16–17 février).* N.l.: 1790.
in-8.
[Monglond]; [CHF].
politics.
Marbeuf, Henriette Françoise Michel
Marquise de. *Précis pour la
citoyenne Marbeuf—Mémoire.* N.l.:
n.d.
in-4; 4–17p.
[MW]; BN: 4 Ln(27).13407.
politics.
———. *Réponse de la citoyenne Marbeuf, à une calomnie aussi atroce
qu'absurde, insérée dans différents
journaux.* Paris: imp. de la rue
Mélé, n.d.
in-4; 2p.
[MW]; BN: 4 Ln(27).13408.
politics.
Marchand, madame. *Journal du Pas-
de-Calais.*
editor.
[MW]; BN: 8 Lc(9).18 (4).
journal.

———. *La Rédactrice du 'Journal du
Pas-de-Calais,' aux citoyens de la
ville d'Arras, le dimanche 22 mai
1791.* N.l.: 1791.
in-8; 4p.
[MW]; [CHF], ii, 660; BN: 8
Lb(39).4937.
politics / journal.
Marguerite d'Angouleme, reine de
Navarre 1492–1549. *Heptaméron
français, ou nouvelles de Marguerite,
reine de Navarre.* Bern: Société typographique, 1791.
3 vols. gr. in-8, fig.
[Monglond].
literature.
Marie Antoinette, Queen consort of
Louis XVI King of France 1755–
1793. *Déclaration de la reine.* N.l.:
1791.
in-8.
BLC.
politics.
———. *Demandes de Marie-Antoinette,
à la commune de Paris.* [Paris]: n.p.
[1793].
in-8.
BLC.
politics.
———. *Lettre . . . pour être présentée
. . . à la Convention Nationale . . . sur
la mort de Louis XVI . . .* Paris: imp.
de Carron, 1793.
in-8; pièce; other edition, Paris:
rue Percée, No. I, n.d., in-8, 8p.
[Monglond]; [BLC].
letter.
———. *Marie-Antoinette d'Autriche,
reine de France, à la nation.* Paris:
rue du Sépulcre, No. 15, n.d.
[1789].
in-8; other edition, Paris: rue du
Sépulcre, No. 15, n.d., in-8.
[Monglond]; [BLC].
politics.
———. *Réponse de la reine [to the Address of J. S. Bailly, February 5,*

Marie Antoinette (*continued*)
1790]. Paris: n.p., 1789[1790].
in-8.
BLC; BN: 8 Lb(40). 68.
letter.

————. *Testament de Marie-Antoinette d'Autriche*, . . . Paris: imp. de le Gros, n.d. [1790].
in-8.
[Monglond]; [CHF].
politics.

Marie Christine de Lorraine, et Albert-Casimir archiduc d'Autriche. *Recueil de lettres de leurs altesses royales Albert et Marie-Christine au comte de Trauttmannsdorff*. Brussels: E. Flon, 1790.
in-8; 24p; other editions, (1) Brussels: J. J. Jorez, 1790, in-8, viii-15p; (2) Brussels: de Trez, in-8, viii-13p; (3) Malines: Van der Elst, in-8, vii-12p.
[Monglond]; BN: M. 22745.
correspondence.

Mariette, madame. *Les Contes de fées de Perrault mis en vers par la cit. M****. Paris: Blanchon, 1798.
2 vols. in-12.
[Monglond].
poetry.

Marion, mademoiselle. *Mlle Marion à ses concitoyens*. Paris: imp. de Nouzou, n.d.
in-8.
[CHF].
politics.

Martin, Marie. *Le Patriotisme des dames citoyennes, discours prononcé à la tribune de l'Assemblée Patriotique . . . le 7e novembre de l'an second de la liberté*. Marseille: imp. de P.-A. Favet, n.d.
in-8; 8p.
[MW]; BN: 8 Lb(39).11061.
politics.

Maurville, comtesse de. *Motion en faveur des officiers du roi destitués par les ministres, proposée à l'Assemblée Nationale . . .* N.l.: 1789.
in-8; 21p.; ABF 723, 230–231 (for husband: conte de Maurville).
[MW]; [CHF]; BN: 8 Ln(27).13855.
politics.

Mayeur, citoyenne. *Monsieur Pamphletin, ou la liberté de la presse, opéra en un acte, mêlé de vaudevilles*. 1794.
performed at the *Théâtre des Variétés amusantes*, 6 frimaire an III.
[Monglond]; J.T., 13 frimaire an III, 59–60.
theater.

Ménard, madame. *Les Malheurs de la jalousie ou lettres de Murville et d'Elénore Melcour, par Mme Ménard*. Paris: Lepetit, 1796.
4t. in-18; t.I:12 + 13–167, t.II:152, t.III:139, t.IV:144; other editions, (1) Paris: Lepetit, 1798, 4t. in-18; (2) Paris: Lepetit, 1799, 4t. in-18.
[BGR]; [Monglond]; [NL]; JT 16.xii.97.
novel.

————. *Les Veillées d'une femme sensible, par Mme Ménard*. Paris: Lepetit, 1796.
2t. in-18; t.I:16 + 17–158p, t.II:160p.
[BGR]; [Monglond]; JT 16.xii.97; Q.
novel / pedagogy.

Ménouvrier, Marie Anne Campion femme. *Pétition présentée et lue au Conseil des Cinq-Cents, le 29 messidor, l'an IV . . . pour réclamer contre les abus du divorce sur la simple allégation d'incompatibilité d'humeur et de caractère*. N.l.: n.d. [1796].
in-8; Pièce.
[CHF].
politics.

Mérard de Saint-Just, Anne Jeanne Félicité d'Ormoy madame 1765. *Le Château noir ou les souffrances de la*

Mérard de Saint-Just (*continued*)
jeune ophelle, par Anna d'Or. Mér.
St. J., auteur de la 'Mère Coupable.'
Paris: Leprieur, 1799.
in-12; 273p; other edition, Paris:
Delarue, n.d. [1821], 2t. in-18.
[BGR]; [Monglond]; [NL]; JT 20
mess. VII; Mag. enc. V 1799 iii 276.
novel.

————. *Démence de Madame de*
Panoren son nom Rozadelle Saint-
Ophèle, suivi d'un conte de fées, d'un
fragment d'antiques, d'une anecdote
villageoise et de quelques couplets,
par l'auteur de 'l'Histoire de la
Baronne d'Alvigny ou la joueuse.'
Paris: rue Helvétius, Nø 605, 1796.
in-18; 250p.
[BGR]; [Monglond]; BN: Y(2).
52877, Rés. Y(2). 3224 et 3225.
novel.

————. *Dangers de la passion du jeu.*
Paris: Maradan, 1793.
in-12; 192p; other edition: London
& Paris, Maradan, 1788, in-12,
192p.
[BGR]; JL xvi 1788.
novel.

————. *Opuscules ou bergeries.* Paris:
n.p., 1798.
in-8; first edition:1784.
[Monglond].
novel.

————. *Le petit Lawater* (sic), *ou*
tablettes mystérieuses, dans lesquelles
se trouvent la lunette de l'astrologue,
la fortune favorable, le jeu de cartes
intéressant, le thot moderne, le petit
livret d'or des anciens, nostradamus
rajeuni, les hiéroglyphes parlants, les
couleurs disent tout, ou l'arc-en-ciel
du destin; les femmes comme il y en a,
morphée qui ne dort plus, vous aurez
le quine, la sybile de l'autre siècle, la
sorcière du tems présent, le physicien
divertissant, le petit-cousin du grand
et petit Albert, Tissot ressuscité, ou le
médecin des bonnes gens; le docteur
ami des belles, etc., etc. par l'auteur
de l'histoire de la baronne d'Alvigny.
Paris: chez Demoraine, 1800.
3 vols. in-12.
[Monglond]; BN: V. 21196.
almanac.

Méré, Elisabeth Guénard baronne de
called Guénard de Faverolles,
called de Boissy, and called J. H. F.
de Gelly 1751–1829. *La Comtesse de*
Suède, ouvrage traduit de l'Allemand
de Geller[t] (sic), *dédi é à S. M. le roi*
suède. Paris: Valade, Laporte, 1797.
2 parts. in-12; pp variously 4 +
156, 197; translation of *Leben der*
*schwedischen Gröfin von G****
(1747–1748), by Christian
Furchegott Gellert; other edition,
Paris: Mérigot père, Mérigot
jeune, Volland, 2 parts. in-12.
[BGR].
novel / translation.

————. *Irma ou les malheurs d'une jeune*
orpheline, histoire indienne, avec des
romances, publiée par la ce gd. Delhy
& Paris: chez l'auteur et les
marchands de nouveautés, 1800.
in-12; t.I:218p, t.II:226 + 8p; other
editions: (1) Delhy & Paris: Le-
rouge, l'auteur, an VIII, 4t. in-18,
t.I:216p, t.II:22p6, t.III:196p,
t.IV:195p; (2) Delhy & Paris: chez
l'auteur et les marchands de nouveautés, an VIII, in-12, t.I:216p,
t.II:226p, t.III:192p, t.IV:190p; (3)
Paris: n.p., 1801, 2t. in-12 ou 4t.
in-18; (4) Delhy & Paris: Barba, an
XI—1803, 4t. in-18, t.I:227p,
t.II:240p, t.III:213p, t.IV:210p; (5)
6th ed., Paris: veuve Lepetit, 1815,
4t. in-18; (6) 10th ed., Paris: veuve
Lepetit, 1816, 5t. in-12; ABF: 731,
310–322.
[BGR]; [NL]; JT 5 niv., 15 germ., 30
mess. VIII; Monglond.
novel.

———. *Lise et Valcour ou le bénédictin,
par la cne. G***d*. Paris: Pigoreau,
1799.
2t. in-18; t.I:iv + 176p, t.II:178p.
[BGR]; [Monglond].
novel.
———. *Zulmée ou la veuve ingénue,
nouvelle traduction de l'italien*.
Paris: Mlle Durand, 1800.
in-18; 147p; purported translation.
[BGR]; [Monglond].
novel.

Mérigot, mme. *La Cuisinère républicaine* . . . Paris: Mérigot jeune,
1795.
in-24; 42p; other edition: an III,
in-18, 42p.
[Monglond]; BN: 2 ex. v. 35834 et
Rés. V. 2622.
technical / cookbook.

Merlin, Henriette Payen veuve. *Mau-
vaise Application de la peine de mort
prononcée par les juges du tribunal
révolutionnaire d'Arras*. N.l.: n.d.
in-4.
[CHF].
politics.

Miaczynski, M. F. Chaboteau veuve J.
*Adresse aux Consuls sur les enfants
abandonnées*. N.l.: n.d. [1800].
in-8; 12p; ABF: 738, 30–33.
[Monglond]; BN: 80 R. Pièce 7045.
politics.

Mique, mademoiselle Catherine.
*Dénonciation faite de Richard Mique,
architecte de la reine, ses cruautés, sa
barbarie envers son frère, qu'il a fait
mourir à Bicêtre, et présentée à
l'Assemblée Nationale; par Catherine
Mique, fille de l'infortuné Mique*.
Paris: imp. de Pougin, n.d. [1789?].
in-8; 16p; other edition: N.1.: n.d.,
in-8, 19p, BN: 8 Ln(27). 14220a.
[CHF]; BLC; B: 8 Ln(27) 14220.
politics.

Miremont, Anne d'Aubourg de la
Bove comtesse de. *Traité de l'éducation des femmes, ou cours complet
d'instruction*. Paris: Pierres, 1779–
1789. .
7 vols. in-8.
[Monglond]; BN: R.23186–23192.
pedagogy.

Moitte, A. M. A. Castellas Mme.
*L'Ame des romaines dans les femmes
françaises*. Paris: Gueffier jeune,
1789.
in-8; 7p.
[Monglond].
history / politics.
———. *Suite de l'ame des romaines
dans les femmes françaises*. Paris:
Knapen, n.d. [1789].
in-8; 4p.
[Monglond]; [MW]; BN: 8
Lb(39).7711.
history / politics.

Monneron, Marie Uranie Rose
madame. *Le Temple de la mode, par
M. ****. Lausanne: Jean Mourer,
1789.
in-12; 316p.
[BGR]; [Monglond].
novel.

Monnet, Marie Moreau madame.
*L'Intrigue secrète, ou la veuve,
comédie en un acte et en prose*. Paris:
imp. Cailleau, 1793.
in-8; performed at the *Théâtre du
Palais*, March 27, 1793.
[Monglond].
theater.
———. *Lisia, opéra en un acte, musique
de Scio*. Paris: imp. Cailleau, 1794.
in-8; performed at the *Théâtre de la
rue Feydeau*, July 8, 1793.
[Monglond].
theater.
———. *Les Montagnards, comédie en
trois actes et en prose*. Paris:
citoyenne Toubon, 1793.
in-8; 64p; performed at the *Théâtre
National maintenant réuni à celui de
l'Égalité, ci-devant Français*, 24

Monnet (*continued*)
vendémaire an II, October 15,
1793.
[Monglond]; [MW]; BN: 8
Yth.12225 et 21048 (2 ex.); J.T., 29
brumaire an III, 749–752.
theater.
Montalembert, Marie Joséphine de
Comarrieu marquise de m. 1775 d.
1832. *Elise Duménil, par Marie de
Comarrieu, Marquise de Montalembert.* London: A. Dulau, 1800.
5t. in-12; t.I:210p, t.II:225p,
t.III:249p, t.IV:257p, t.V:314p; original edition: 1798; other edition,
Paris: Giguet et Cie, 1801.-9., 6t.
in-12, t.I:12 + 13–236p, t.II:236p,
t.III:232p, t.IV:236p, t.V:234p,
t.VI:238p; ABF: 753, 57, 72–73.
[BGR].
novel.
Montanclos, Marie Emilie née Mayon
de (and later de Princen) (1736–
1812). *Alison et Silvain, ou les habi-
tants de Vaucluse, opéra en un acte,
musique de Mengozzi.* Paris: Barba,
1803.
in-8; performed at the *Théâtre
Montansier,* 13 prairial, June 1,
1799.
[Monglond].
theater.
———. *Robert-Le-Bossu, ou les trois
soeurs, comédie en un acte et en
vaudeville.* Paris: Barba, 1799.
in-8; performed at the *Théâtre
Montansier-Variétés,* 22 pluviôse an
VII, February 10, 1799.
[Monglond]; BLC.
theater.
Montansier, Marguerite Brunet,
called mademoiselle de 1730–
1820. *Dernières Observations des
propriétaires du Théâtre National à la
Convention Nationale.* Paris: imp.
de A.C. Forget, n.d. [1793].
in-8; 4p; ABF: 753, 190–228.

[MW]; BN: Yf.1251 (3).
theater.
———. *Encore 7 Millions pour le Grand
Opéra? Ça ne prendra pas: Rendez la
salle à Montansier.* N.l.: n.d.[1794?].
in-4; 11p.
BLC.
theater.
———. *Mémoire justificatif.* Paris:
imp. de Potier, n.d. [1793].
in-4; 16p; performed on 10
frimaire an II.
[Monglond]; [MW]; BN: 4
Ln(27).14550.
theater.
———. *Note essentielle relative à l'affaire des propriétaires du Théâtre National, volés, incarcérés, vexés par
l'ancien comité de salut public qui,
pour la forme au moins, avait or-
donné de payer leurs créanciers et de
les indemniser.* Paris: imp. de A.C.
Forget, n.d.
in-8; 4p.
[MW]; BN: Yf.1251 (2).
theater.
———. *Les Propriétaires du Théâtre National à la Convention Nationale.*
[Paris]: De l'École typographique
des femmes, n.d. [1794].
in-4; 4p.
[Monglond].
theater.
———. *Réfutations des mensonges inti-
tulés: observations sur l'affaire du
théâtre des arts, rue de la loi, par les
créanciers de ce même théâtre.* Paris:
Imp. A.-C. Forget, n.d. [1795].
in-4; 8 p.
[Monglond]; [MW]; BN: Yf.1041 et
1519 (2 ex.).
theater.
———. *Réponse au message du Directoire Exécutif en date du 9 ventôse an
VI (27 février 1798), sur le Théâtre de
la République et des Arts.* Paris: imp.
Ch. Tutot, 1798.

Montansier (*continued*)
in-4.
[Monglond].
theater.

Montolieu, Jeanne Isabelle Pauline
née Polier de Bottens (and later de
Crousaz) (1751–1832). *La Sylphide
ou l'ange gardien, nouvelle traduite
de l'anglais.* Lausanne & Paris: n.p.,
1795.
in-18; translation of *The New Sylph
or the Guardian Angel* (1788), author unknown—this work was
often attributed to Georgiana
Cavendish, duchesse de Devon-
shire; other editions: (1) Leipzig:
Wolf (Schmidt), 1795, in-32; (2)
Lausanne: Pott, 1795, in-18; (3)
Paris: n.p., 1796, 126p; (4) Lausanne: n.p., 1796, pet. in-12; (5)
Paris: A. Bertrand, 1813, 2t.,
t.I:209p, t.II:334p.
[BGR]; Monglond.
novel / translation.

Montrond, Angelique Marie Darlus
du Taillis comtesse de d. 1827. *Le
long Parlement et ses crimes, rap-
prochements faciles à faire.* Paris:
imp. d'un royaliste, 1790.
in-8; 151p.
[Monglond]; [MW]; BN: 8
Lb(39).9495.
politics.

Morel de Vindé, madame Charles
Gilbert de Terray de née Choppin.
*Suite des lettres d'une péruvienne,
traduites en italien par le citoyen
Pio—Continuazione delle lettere
d'una peruviana . . .* Paris: Desenne,
1798.
in-8; vii–231p; ABF: 764, 86–99.
[Monglond].
novel.

Mouret, madame fl. 1790. *Annales de
l'éducation du sexe ou journal des
demoiselles, par Mme Mouret, de-
scendante de La Fontaine et auteur*

*du 'Plan d'éducation pour le sexe,'
Présenté à l'Assemblée Nationale,
Nos. 1–8* (1790).
ABF: 769, 338–339.
[MW]; [Monglond]; BN: R.44622–
44625.
journal.

Néret, madame et Néret J. M. *Extrait
de l'analyse botanique de la 'Flore
française' [de Lamarck].* Compiègne:
Bertrand, 1790.
in-8.
[Monglond].
botany.

Necker, Susanne Curchod madame
1739–1794. *Des Inhumations préci-
pitées.* Paris: imp. royale, 1790.
in-8; 22p.
[Monglond]; [MW]; BN: 8
Tc(54).14.
medicine / health.

———. *Mélanges extraits des manu-
scrits de Mme Necker.* Paris:
Pougens, 1798.
3 vols. in-8; other edition: Paris,
Pougens, 1801, 2 vols. in-8.
[Monglond]; [MW]; BN: Z.24360–
24362 et Rés. Z.3142–3144 (2 ex.).
literature.

———. *Réflexions sur le divorce.* Lausanne & Paris: P. S. Aubin, n.d.
[1794].
in-8; 100p.; other editions: (1)
Hamburg: Lunebourg, Hérold et
W., 1795, in-8; (2) Paris: Ch.
Pougens, an X (1802).
[Monglond]; [MW]; BN: R. 44809.
society.

Nesmond, comtesse de. *Contes en
l'air.* Paris: Royez, 1789.
in-16; 282p; other edition, Paris:
veuve Duchesne et fils, 1791, in-
18, ix + 11–271p.
[BGR]; [Monglond].
novel.

Oudin, Élisabeth Duval femme. *Compliment au roi . . .* N.l.: n.d.

Oudin (*continued*)
in-8; 4p.
[MW]; BN: 8 Ye.Pièce.4306 et 4667
(2 ex.).
poetry.

Palloy, femme. *L'Épouse de Palloi au
peuple toujours juste.—copie de la
lettre adressée à M. Rolland* . . .
Paris: imp. de L.-P. Couret, n.d.
[1793?].
in-8; 7p.
[MW]; [CHF]; BN: 8ø
Ln(27).15677.
politics.

————. *Adresse à la Convention Nationale, le 26 vent. l'an II . . . par la
famille Palloy, le lendemain de sa
mise en liberté par les huissiers de la
Convention* . . . Paris: imp. de Renaudière jeune, n.d. [1794].
in-4; 7p.
[MW]; BN: 4 Lb(41).1025.
politics.

————. *Lettre de la dame Palloy en
faveur de son mari incarcéré* . . . N.l.:
imp., n.d.[1793].
in-4; 1p.
[CHF]; [MW]; BN: 4ø ln(27).15673.
politics.

Pautigny, Jeanne. *Pétition à l'Assemblée Nationale.* N.l.: n.d.[1792].
Paris, January 26; in-4; 4p.
[MW]; [CHF]; BN: 4 Lb(39).10403.
politics.

Payen, Marie Marguerite veuve C. M.
*Amis et patriotes sacrifiés par juge-
ment rendu par le tribunal révolutionnaire de Cambray. Marie-
Marguerite Payen, Vve Payen . . . et
Anne-Françoise Dauvin, Vve Goubet
. . . à la Convention Nationale.* Paris:
imp. de Guffroy, n.d. [1794].
in-4; 8p.
[MW]; [CHF]; BN: 4ø Lb(41).1706.
politics.

Payen, veuve Thérèse. *Violation de
toutes les formes voulues par les lois*

*pour appliquer iniquement la peine de
mort. A la Convention Nationale.*
Paris: imp. de Guffroy, n.d. [1794].
in-4.
[CHF].
politics / law.

Perruchot, Perrine fl. 1795. *Clémentine
ou le legs fatal, par John Seally,
traduit de l'anglais par Perrine
Perruchot, orné de trois gravures.*
Paris: Raphel et Bertrandet,
1799.
2t. in-18; t.I:xii + 168p, t.II:164p;
translation of *The Loves of Calisto
and Elmira or the Fatal Legacy*
(1776), by John Seally; ABF: 823,
424.
[BGR]; Monglond.
novel / translation.

Persan, madame le Fournier Warge-
mont de. *Copie de la lettre écrite à
M. le Président de l'Assemblée Nationale* . . . N.l.: n.p., 1790.
in-8; 3p.
[MW]; [CHF]; BN: 8 Ln(27).16102.
politics.

Peutat, madame. *Discours des
citoyennes d'Avallon, armeés de
piques, aux amis de la constitution,
lors de l'installation du buste de
Mirabeau, prononcé par Mme Peutat.*
Avallon: imp. de A. Aubry, n.d.
in-8; 7p.
[MW]; [CHF]; BN: Lb(40).2511.
politics.

Philippeaux, veuve. *Réponse de Philippeaux.* N.l.: n.d.
ABF: 831, 63–87.
[CHF].
letter.

Picquenard, veuve. *Au Roi et aux
représentants de la nation, dénonciation contre M. le Baron de Breteuil
. . .* N.l.: n.d. [1790].
in-8.
[CHF].
politics.

Pinel, citoyenne. *Adresse à messieurs du comité de salubrité, à l'Assemblée Nationale* . . . N.l.: n.p., 1796. in-8; 16p; ABF: 838, 216–243. [MW]; BN: 8 Te(101). 8. medicine / health.

Pitel, madame also known as Madame Bouquet and Madame Bouquet-Quillau. *Étrennes comme il y en a peu, ou mélange agréable des plus jolies choses de tout genre pour l'année commune mil sept quatre-vingt-dix.* Falaise, Bouquet, & Paris: Moutard, 1790. in-32. [Monglond]. almanac.

Polier, Marie Élisabeth madame de 1742–c. 1820. *Bibliothèque germanique. Par Mme de Polier, le C. A. [Griffet de] Labaume et le C. De-maimieux, inventeur de la 'pasigra-phie,' membre de l'Académie des Sciences de Harlem.* Paris: chez les frères Levrault, 1800. 2 vols. in-8; Ier volume, an VIII, 728p, II volume, an IX-1800, 496p.; ABF: 845, 317, 331–333. [Monglond]; BN: Z.43239–43240. literature.

———. *Le Club des Jacobins, ou l'amour de la patrie, comédie en un acte, traduite de l'allemand et mise en 2 actes.* Paris: n.p., 1792. in-8; translation of Kotzebue's play. [Monglond]. theater / translation.

———. *Journal Littéraire de Lausanne, ouvrage périodique [par Mme la Chanoinesse M. E. de Polier]* (1794–1798). 10 vols. in-8. [Monglond]. journal.

———. *Recueil d'historiettes traduites de l'allemand par Madame la Chanoi-nesse de P.* Lausanne: L. Luquiens & Paris, Bossange et Comp., 1792. in-12; 237p; other editions: (1) Paris & Lausanne: Buisson & Mourer cadet, 1782; (2) Lausanne: Mourer cadet, & Paris: les marchands de nouveautés, 1787, in-12, 237p. [BGR]. novel / translation.

Polignac, comtesse Diane de. *Mémoire sur la vie et le caractère de Mme la duchesse de Polignac, avec les anecdotes intéressantes sur la révolution française et sur la personne de Marie-Antoinette de France.* Hamburg: P.-F. Fauche, 1796. in-8; x-52p; other editions: (1) Paris: au bureau général des nouveautés, an V, in-18, 108p.; (2) London, Debrett, n.d. [Monglond]; [MW]; [CHF]; [NL]; BN: 8 Ln(27).16455. memoir.

Pompigny, madame de. *Le Franc marin, ou la gageure indiscrette.* N.l.: Marchands de nouveautés, 1795. in-8; ABF: 846, 355. [BN]. theater.

Pons, mademoiselle de. *Relation d'un voyage fait à Madrid en 1789 et 1790, par Mademoiselle de* . . . Paris: imp. de Monsieur, 1791. in-16; 68p. [Monglond]. travel.

Pont-Wullyamoz, Marie Louise Françoise de née Burnand 1751–1814. *Anecdotes tirées de l'histoire et des chroniques suisses.* Lausanne: Henri Vincent, 1796. 2t. in-12; t.I:377p, t.II:283p; ABF: 848, 246–247. [BGR]; [Monglond]. novel.

————. *Léonore de Grailly et Gaston de Foix, suivie de Dom Ramire ou la conquête de Grenade, anecdotes extraites de l'histoire de France et d'Espagne, par Madame de Wllyamor* (sic), *auteur des 'Anecdotes suisses.'* Paris: Lepetit, 1797.
2t. in-12, t.I:x + 204, t.II:viii + 191; other edition: Paris, Lepetit, an V - 1797, 3t. in-18.
[BGR]; [Monglond]; JT 16.xi.97; Q.
novel.

————. *Mélanges, par l'auteur des 'Anecdotes suisses.'* Vienna: imp. de la veuve Albert, 1799.
in-8; t.I:343p, t.II:318p.
[BGR].
novel.

————. *La Recette du médecin Nicoclès, anecdote orientale du règne de Cyrus.* Bern: chez Emanuel Haller, 1795.
2t. in-8; 120p; other edition, Vienna: veuve Albert, 1799, 2t. in-8, pp. variously 343, 318.
[BGR]; [Monglond].
novel.

Posset, Anne Louise Françoise Morre de. *Département de la Sarthe. Premier Mémoire pour Clément Négrier. Les citoyennes Françoise Leboindre, épouse de Clément Négrier, et Anne-Louise-Françoise Morre de Posset, sa Mère, au Directoire Exécutif.* Le Mans: imp. de Monnoyer, n.d.
in-4.
[CHF].
politics.

Poterlot, madame G. *Égalité, liberté . . . mémoire justificatif de Guillaume Poterlot, ex-administrateur du département des Ardennes . . . détenu en la maison d'arrêt du Luxembourg, aux représentants du peuple composant les comités de salut public, de sûreté générale et de législation . . . Paris, le 27 thermidor 2e année . . . la citoyenne femme Poterlot, . . . aux*

représentants du Peuple composant les comités de salut public et de sûreté générale . . . Paris: imp. de Charpentier.
in-4; Pièce.
[CHF].
politics.

Poullin de Flins, madame née Philippe de Pretot. *Étrennes de mnémosyne, ou recueil d'épigrammes et de contes en vers pour l'année 1789.* Paris: Knapen et fils, 1788–1789.
2 vols. in-12.
[Monglond].
almanac.

————. *Almanach dauphin, contenant l'anniversaire de Monseigneur le Dauphin, cantatille; avec un plan d'un cours nouveau de littérature française à l'usage de ce prince.* Paris: Guillot, 1789.
published 1784–1789, in-16; ABF: 853, 121–126.
[Monglond].
almanac.

————. *Tablettes annuelles et chronologiques de l'historie ancienne et moderne pour l'année 1789.* N.l.: n.p., 1789.
in-12.
[Monglond].
history / almanac.

Poulmaire, Catherine Friren veuve. *Précis pour la vve Poulmaire . . .* N.l.: 1797.
in-8; 6p; ABF: 853, 135.
[MW]; BN: 8 Ln(27).16588 (1).
politics.

————. *Réclamation supplémentaire de la vve Poulmaire . . .* Paris: Hautbout l'aîné, 1797.
in-8; 15p.
[MW]; BN: 8 Ln(27).16588 (2).
politics.

————. *Suite aux mémoires de la citoyenne veuve Poulmaire . . .* Paris:

Poulmaire (*continued*)
Hautbout l'aîné, 1797.
in-8; 8p.
[MW]; BN: 8 Ln(27).16588 (3).
politics.
Quatremère-d'Isjonval, madame
S. H. *Miss Belhowe et le Lord Clarendon ou les épreuves de l'amour et de
la vertu, par la citoyenne ***.* Paris:
J. M. Leguay, 1796.
in-18; other edition, Paris: Pon-
thieu, an V, 2t. in-18; ABF: 863,
144–152.
[BGR]; [Monglond].
novel.
Rayer, Marie Anne. *Réclamation de
deux mères . . . contre un jugement
du tribunal révolutionnaire, sur
un crime qui n'était pas contre-
révolutionnaire, aux citoyens-
représentans du peuple française.*
Paris: Dupont, 1793.
in-4; 6p.
[MW]; [CHF]; BN: 8 Lb(41).1124.
politics.
Raymond de Saint-Sauveur, Marie
Madeleine Victoire. *Mémoire ad-
dressé aux administrateurs du département de Seine et Oise.* Paris:
n.p., 1793.
in-8; 24p.
BLC.
politics.
———. *Mémoire aux représentans du
peuple français.* Paris: n.p.,
n.d.[1794?].
in-8.
BLC.
politics.
Renelle, L. E. Bouillon madame. *A la
Mère patrie, prologue exécuté par des
jeunes demoiselles à la fête donnée en
famille.* Berlin: n.p., 1790.
in-8.
[Monglond].
theater.

———. *Nouvelle Géographie, à l'usage
des instituts et des gouvernantes
françaises . . .* Berlin: Decker, 1786–
1790.
3 vols. in-8.
[Monglond].
pedagogy / natural sciences.
Reynery, madame. *Le Démocrite
français, journal politique, de littérature et des spectacles. Rédigé par la
citoyenne Reyneri* (1799).
see also: Clément, Albertine, née
Hémery.
[Monglond]; [MW]; [CHF]; BN:
Lc2 2729.
journal.
Riccoboni, Marie Jeanne de Heurlas
Laboras de Mezieres madame
1713–1792. *Histoire d'Ernestine.
Nouv. éd.* Paris: Pigoreau, 1798.
in-18; reprint—first edition: 1777.
[Monglond].
novel.
———. *Oeuvres complètes de Madame
Riccoboni, nouvelle édition, sur pa-
pier fin véline, revue avec le plus
grand soin, et ornée de son portrait
d'après l'original. Tome premier
[Quatorzième].* Paris: Volland aîné,
1796.
FC lists an 8 vols., 1786 edition;
Monglond lists an 1809 edition—
14 vols. in-12; other edition, Versailles: imp. de Lebel & Paris: Foucault, 1818, 6 vols. in-8.
[NL]; [Monglond].
literature.
Rigal, madame. *Discours prononcé . . .
dans une assemblée de femmes
artistes et orfèvres, tenue le 20 sept.
[1789], pour délibérer sur une contribution volontaire.* N.l.: n.p., 1789.
in-8; 7p.
[MW]; [CHF]; [BLC]; BN: 8
Ln(39).2362.
politics.

Rivarol, Louise née Mather Flint comtesse de d. 1821. *Effets du gouvernement sur l'agriculture en Italie, avec une notice de divers gouvernemens, trad. de l'anglais par Mme de Rivarol, précédés d'un mot sur les femmes, la République française et les moeurs, suivis d'une lettre d'un orateur célèbre [le comte de Rivarol sous le pseud. de Lucius Apuleius] sur l'ouvrage: 'De l'Influence des Passions' par Mme de Staël, et d'une réponse adressée à cet auteur.* N.l.: n.p., 1797.
in-8; ABF: 897, 36–39.
[Monglond].
translation / agriculture / society.

Roche, Regina Maria. *Le Curé de Lansdowne ou les garnisons, imité de l'anglois de Miss Dalton.* Paris: rue des Poitevins, hôtel Bouthillier, 1789.
2t. in-12; t.I:315p, t.II:234p (for 244); translation of *The Vicar of Lansdowne or Country Quarters,* by Dalton; other editions: (1) Mayence: Kupterburg, 1789; (2) Paris: LePetit, n.d., 3t. in-12.
[BGR]; BLC.
novel / translation.

Roland de la Platiere, Marie Jeanne Philipon madame 1754–1793. *Appel à l'impartial postérité, par la citoyenne Roland, femme du ministre de l'intérieur, ou receuil des écrits qu'elle rédigés pendant sa détention aux prisons de l'abbaye et à Sainte-Pélagie . . . imprimé au profit de sa fille unique, privée de la fortune de ses père et mère et dont les biens sont toujours séquestrés.* Paris: Louvet, 1795.
4 vols. in-8.
[Monglond]; [MW]; BN: 8 Lb(41).2101.
memoir.

———. *Copie littérale prise sur la minute, du style et de la main de Marie-Jeanne Roland . . .* Paris: Vve Gorsas, 1795.
in-8; 15p.
[MW]; BN: Lb(41).896.
politics.

———. *Discours prononcé . . . aux juges du tribunal révolutionnaire . . .* N.l.: n.d. [1794].
in-8; 11p.
[MW]; BN: Lb(41).895.
politics.

———. *La Femme Roland à ses juges.* N.l.: n.d. [1793].
in-8.
[Monglond]; [CHF].
politics.

———. *Lettres à Buzot.* BN: 8 Ln(27).17781.
[MW].
correspondence.

———. *Oeuvres de J. M. Ph. Roland, femme de l'ex-ministre de l'intérieur; contenant les mémoires et notices historiques qu'elle a composées dans sa prison en 1793, sur sa vie privée, sur son arrestation, sur les deux ministères de son mari et sur la révolution; son procès et sa condamnation à mort par le tribunal révolutionnaire; ses ouvrages philosophiques et littéraires faits avant son mariage; sa correspondance et ses voyages; précédées d'un discours préliminaire par L. A. Champagneux, éditeur; et accompagnées de notes et de notices du même, sur sa détention.* Paris: chez Bidault, 1800.
3 vols. in-8; t.I:xc-348p, t.II:444p, t.III:435 + 2p.
[Monglond]; [MW]; BN: Z. 23293–23295.
memoirs.

Roland, Fanny. *Sonates (3) pour le piano.* N.l.: n.p., 1797.
[BN].
arts / music.

Rome, madame née Marné de Morville fl. 1770. *Célestine ou la victime des préjugés par Charlotte Smith, traduit de l'anglais sur la seconde édition, par la citoyenne R* . . . Paris: F. Buisson, 1795.
4t. in-12; t.I:321p, t.II:316p, t.III:368p, t.IV:427p; translation of *Celestine, a Novel* (1791), by Mrs. Charlotte Turner Smith; ABF: 767, 416; 908, 382.
[BGR]; Monglond.
novel / translation.
———. *Eulalie ou le repentir.* Paris: Lottin, 1799.
3t. in-18.
[BGR]; [Monglond]; JT 25 flor. VII.
novel.

Rosni, madame. *Protestation des filles du Palais-Royal et véritable tarif, rédigé par Mmes Rosni et Sainte-Foix, présidentes du district des Galeries.* N.l.: n.d.
in-8; 7p.
[MW]; BN: Rés. 8 Lb(39).3807 et 3807.A (2 ex.).
society.

Roujol, veuve. *Pétition à la Convention Nationale.* N.l.: n.d. [1795].
in-4; 1p.
[CHF]; BLC; BN: 4 Ln(27) 17924.
politics.
———. *La veuve Roujol à la Convention Nationale.* Paris: imp. de Valade, n.d.
in-4; 7p.
[CHF]; BN: 4 Ln(27) 17925.
politics.

Rousseau, Woldemar Michel madame. *Conseils d'une mère à ses filles, 1789. par W.M***, épouse de J.R*** [Jean Rousseau].* Paris: imp. de Roederer et Corancez, 1796.
in-12; 96p; other edition: Leipzig: n.p., 1810, in-8.
[Monglond].
pedagogy.

Rumford, Marie Anne Pierrette comtesse de née Paulze (and later Lavoisier) (1758–1836). *Addition à la dénonciation présentée au comité de législation contre le représentant du peuple Dupin, par les veuves et les enfants soussignés des ci-devant Fermiers-Généraux.* N.l.: n.d. [1795].
in-8; Pièce; ABF: 922, 6–7.
[CHF]; BN: 8 Lb(41) 4485.
politics.
———. *Dénonciation présentée au comité de législation de la Convention Nationale, contre le représentant du peuple Dupin, par les veuves et enfants des ci-devant Fermiers-Généraux (22 messidor).* Paris: Dupont, 1795.
in-8; Pièce; 55p.
[CHF]; BN: 8 Lb(41) 1924.
politics.

Ryamperre, Louise de. *Différentes anecdotes sur le martyre de Marie-Antoinette d'Autriche, infortunée reine de France et de Navarre.* Vienna: Alberti, 1794.
in-8; XII-40p.
[MW]; BN: 8 Lb(39).11895.
politics / history.

Saint-Aignan, madame de. *Plaidoyer de Lysias, contre les membres des anciens comités de salut public et de sûreté générale.* Paris: Dupont, 1794.
in-8; ABF: 925, 29–40.
[CHF].
politics.

Saint-Chamond, Claire Marie née Mazzarelli de la Vieuville marquise de b. 1731. *Jean-Jacques à M. S. [Serevan] sur des réflexions contre ses derniers écrits; lettre pseudonyme.* Genèva & Paris: Dufresne, 1789.
in-12; first edition: Geneva, 1784; ABF: 926, 53–55.
[Monglond]; BN: Ln(27) 17971 A.
philosophy.

Saint-Clément, madame Vincent en
religion Mère. *Plainte . . . contre le
sieur Boulets, chirurgien du dit
Hôtel-Dieu*. Paris: n.p., 1790.
in-8; 7p.
[MW]; BN: 8 Lk(7).6904.
politics / medicine.

Saint-Eloy, Soeur de. *Adresse à
messieurs de l'Assemblée Nationale
présentée par les religieuses hospital-
ières de l'Hôtel-Dieu de Paris*. Paris:
Le Becq, 1790.
in-8; 7p.
[MW]; [CHF]; BN: 4 Lk(7).6905.
politics / religion.

Saint-Herem, Marguerite Larocque-
Budos veuve. *Marguerite Larocque-
Budos, Vve St.-Herem, au Directoire
Exécutif*. Paris: imp. de Moreau,
n.d. [1797].
in-4.
[CHF].
politics.

Saint-Sauveur, madame fl. 1800.
*Recueil de pièces intéressantes et
morales, convenables aux théâtres de
société, par Mme de S.S.* N.l.: n.p.,
1800.
in-12; ABF: 930, 300.
[Monglond].
theater.

Salm-Reifferscheid-Dyck, Constance
Marie de Theis née Pipelet princesse de 1767–1845. *Éloge historique
de M. Sedaine, lu . . . à la 54me séance
publique de Lycée des Arts, le 30 messidor an V*. Paris: Desenne, 1797.
in-8; 24p.
[Monglond]; [MW]; [OF]; [CHF];
BN: Ln(27) 18744.
literature.

———. *Épître aux femmes*. Paris: Desenne, 1797.
[Monglond]; [MW]; [OF]; BN:
Ye.49562; M.F., March 20, 1797,
353–361.
poetry.

———. *Appel aux françaises sur la
régénération des moeurs et la nécessité de l'influence des femmes dans un
gouvernement libre*. Paris: n.p.,
1791.
in-8; 44p; ABF: 839, 198–201, 204;
934, 317–339.
[Monglond].
politics.

———. *Rapport sur les fleurs artifi-
cielles de la citoyenne Roux-
Montagnac . . .* Paris: imp. du
Lycée des arts, n.d.
in-8; 14p.
[MW]; [OF]; BN: V.55711.
arts.

———. *Rapport sur un ouvrage du
citoyen Théremin, intitulé: de la Condition des femmes dans une
république*. Paris: Gillé, 1800.
in-8; 16p.
[MW]; [OF]; BN: Rz.3504 et 8 R.
Pièce. 6754.
politics.

———. *Romances*. N.l.: n.p., 1797.
[Monglond].
poetry.

———. *Sapho, tragédie mêlée de chants,
en trois actes et en vers*. Paris: l'auteur, n.d. [1794].
in-8; performed at the *Théâtre des
Amis de la Patrie*, 22 frimaire an III.
[Monglond]; [MW]; [OF]; BN: 8
Yth. 16118 et 16119 (2 ex.); J.T., 26
frimaire an III, 122–125.
theater.

———. *Vers sur les dissentions des gens
de lettres*. Paris: Desenne, 1798.
in-12, 12p.
[Monglond]; [MW]; [OF]; BN: 8 Ye
Pièce. 5539.
poetry.

———. *Vers sur les vers de société et de
fête*. Paris: Ruphy, 1800.
in-12.
[Monglond].
poetry.

Salverte, Aglaé Deslacs d'Arcambal dame Claret de Fleurieu then dame Baconnière de d. 1826. *Pauline, comédie en deux actes et en vers, par Mme de F****. Paris: imp. No. 13 de la rue de la Monnaie, n.d. [1791].
4t. in-8; perfomed at the *Théâtre de la Nation*, July 1, 1791; ABF: 935, 375–388.
[Monglond]; [MW]; BN: Yf.11248 et 8 Yth.13616 (2 ex.).
theater.

———. *Stella, histoire anglaise, par Aglaé D . . . F*. Paris: Maradan, 1800. 2t. in-12; t.I:207,t.II:204, t.III:183, t.IV:166.
[BGR]; [Monglond]; JT 15 therm. VIII; Mag. enc. VI 1800 iv 7.
novel.

———. *Un Pot sans couvercle et rien dedans ou les mystères du souterrain de la rue de la lune, histoire merveilleuse et véritable, traduite du français ou langue vulgaire par Louis Randol*. Paris: B. Logerot, marchands de nouveautés, 1799.
Louis Randol was a pseudonym used by Salverte.
[BGR]; JT 25 flor. VII; Monglond.
novel.

Sancy, madame de fl. 1795. *Alphonse d'Armoncourt ou la belle-mère*. Lausanne: A. Fischer et Luc Vincent, 1797.
in-12; t.I:196p, t.II:216p: other editions: (1) Paris: Mourer et Pinpar, 1797, 2t in 12; (2) Paris: Maradan, 1798, 2t. in-18; ABF: 936, 228.
[BGR]; [NL]; Mag. enc. III 1797 ii 148; Monglond.
novel.

Saussure, mademoiselle de. *Éloge historique de M. de Périgord, adressé à Mme *** [Mme Turretin] par Mlle D.S*. N.l.: n.d. [1800].
in-8.

[Monglond]; BN: Ln(27) 19329.
literature.

Savary, Marie Luce Caroline. *Exécution par le tribunal révolutionnaire d'Arras du projet annoncé par Joseph Lebon . . . d'envoyer à l'échafaud les fermiers cultivateurs du département du Pas-de-Calais . . .* Paris: Guffroy, n.d. [1794].
in-4; 4p.
[MW]; BN: 4 Lb(41).1560.
politics.

Schaumburg, madame M. J. de. *Histoire ecclésiastique et politique des souverains contemporains*. Leyde: n.p., 1792.
8 tableaux in-fol.
[Monglond]; BN: G.1578.
history.

Schomberg, comtesse de. *Journal de ce qui s'est passé à la tour du temple pendant la captivité de Louis XVI*. London: l'auteur, 1798.
in-8.
[Monglond]; [CHF]; BN: Lb(39) 47.
memoir.

Scordel, veuve. *A Messieurs les présidents et membres de l'Assemblée Nationale*. Paris: Prault, n.d.
in-4; 3p.
[MW]; BN: 8 Ln(27).18727.
politics.

Sémonin, Hélène Madeleine Jouvencel citoyenne. *Acte par lequel la citoyenne Sémonin abandonne tous ses droits sur les rigoles et aqueducs compris dans sa ferme de Vélizy*. Paris: imp. du Dépôt des lois, n.d. [1798].
in-8; 3p.
[MW]; BN: Fp. 1510 et 8 Ln(27).18810 (2 ex.).
commercial.

———. *Observations sur le contrat d'échange passé entre la nation et la citoyenne Vve Sémonin . . .* Paris:

Sémonin (*continued*)
    imp. du Dépôt des lois, n.d.
    in-8; 8p.
    [MW]; BN: Fp.2326 et 8
    Ln(27).18809 (2 ex.).
    commercial.
Sergent-Marceau, Marie called Emira
    1753–1834. *Au citoyen Guillard . . .*
    en réponse à un passage de son opin-
    ion sur les testamens militaires.
    Paris: Patar-Jouannet, n.d. [1798?].
    in-8; ABF: 953, 195.
    [MW]; BN: 8 Ln(27).18839.
    politics.
    ———. *Présentation au Conseil des*
    Cinq-Cents du portrait du Général
    Marceau. Paris: Imp. nat., 1798.
    in-8; 2p.
    [MW]; BN: 8 Le(43).1902.
    politics.
    ———. *Réponse . . . au discours*
    prononcé au Conseil des Cinq-Cents,
    le 17 messidor, par le citoyen Guillard
    . . . Paris: Fauvelle et Sagnier, n.d.
    [1799].
    in-4; 4p.
    [MW]; BN: 8ø Ln(27).18840; BLC.
    politics.
Sévigné, madame de. *On en Reviendra*
    Là . . . car . . . la raison finit toujours
    par avoir raison. Paris: n.p., 1791.
    in-8; 18p.
    [FC].
    literature.
    ———. *Le Stationnaire aux frontières,*
    ou l'appel au bon sens ([1791]).
    [FC].
    journal.
Simonneau, madame Jacques Guil-
    laume veuve du maire d'Étampes.
    Lettre . . . au président de l'Assemblée
    Nationale, lue à la séance du 31 mars
    1792. Paris: Imp. nat., n.d. [1792].
    in-8; 2p.
    [MW]; [CHF]; BN: 8 Le(34).63;
    BLC.
    politics.

Simons, Julie. *Sonates (2 grandes) pour*
    clavecin. Paris: Naderman, n.d.
    in-4.
    [BN].
    arts / music.
Société des citoyennes. *Les Evéne-*
    ments du jour (1791). edited by
    "une société des citoyennes."
    [Sullerot].
    journal.
    ———. *La Feuille du soir* ([1791?]).
    edited by "une société des
    femmes."
    [Sullerot].
    journal.
Souza Botelho, Adélaïde Marie Émi-
    lie née Filleul comtesse de Flahaut
    then marquise de 1760–1836. *Emi-*
    lie et Alphonse ou danger de se livrer
    à ses premières impressions, par l'au-
    teur d' 'Adèle de Sénage.' Hamburg
    & Paris: P.-F. Fauche & Charles
    Pougens, 1799.
    3t. in-12; t.I:176p, t.II:221p,
    t.III:104p (for 204); other editions:
    (1) Paris: Gide, an XIII—1803
    [sic, pour 1805], 3t. in-12, 199p.;
    (2) Paris: A. Eymery, 1821–1822,
    6t. in-8.
    [BGR]; JT 25 niv., 5 therm. VII;
    Monglond.
    novel.
    ———. *Mademoiselle de Tournon.*
    Rouen: Jean Racine, 1792.
    3 tomes en 1 vol. in-18.
    [Monglond].
    novel.
    ———. *Adèle de Sénage ou lettres de*
    Lord Sydenham. London: 1794.
    in-8; other editions: (1) Neuville:
    Pange, 1794; (2) Hamburg: Hoff-
    man, 1796, in-8; (3) Hamburg:
    chez B. G. Hoffman, 1797, 2t. pet.
    in-8, t.I:xxiv + 144p, t.II:280p (for
    208); (4) Geneva: J.-J. Paschoud &
    Paris: Maradan, 1798, 2t. in-12,
    t.I:240p, t.II:232p.; (5) Hamburg:

Souza Botelho (*continued*)
P.-F. Fauche et compagnie, 1801, 2t.; (6) Paris: Gide, an XIII—1805, 2t. in-12, t.I:xix + 212p, t.II:220p.; (7) Paris: Dentu, 1808, 2t. in-12; (8) Paris: A. Eymery, 1821–22, 6t. in-8.; ABF: 966, 175–208.
[BGR]; Monglond.
novel.

Staël-Holstein, Anne Louise Germaine Necker baronne de 1766–1817. *Courte république à l'auteur d'une longue réponse; par Mme la Baronne de *** [Staël].* Geneva: n.p., 1789.
in-8; 14p.
[Monglond]; [MW]; BN: 8 Ln(27).17891.
philosophy / politics.

———. *De l'Influence des passions sur le bonheur des individus et des nations. par mad. la Baronne Staël de Holstein. Première partie. 'Inde Ista Tanta Coacervatio Aliorum Super Alios Ruentium. Séneque, de Vita Beata.'* Lausanne: Jean Mourer, 1796.
in-8; 376p; other editions: (1) Hamburg: P.-F. Fauche, 1796, in-8; (2) Paris: chez Dufart . . . , Dessenne, anV—1797, 2 vols. in-12.
[Monglond]; [MW]; BN: 8 R.46059.
literature / philosophy.

———. *De la Littérature considérée dans ses rapports avec les institutions sociales; par Madame de Staël-Holstein. Tome premier [Second].* Paris: Maradan, 1800.
2 vols. in-8: t.I;LVI-335p, t.II:284p; other editions: (1) Leipzig: Wolf (Schmidt), 1800, in-8; (2) Paris: Maradan, an 9, 2 vols. in-8, t.I:394p, t.II:307p.; (3) Paris & London: Chez Colburn, 1812, 2 vols. petit in-8; and a Spanish translation published in 1829.
[Monglond]; [MW]; BN: Rés. p. Z.

1080.
philosophy / literature.

———. *Du Caractère de M. Necker et de sa vie privée.* Geneva: chez J.-J. Paschoud, 1790.
in-8, 153 + 354p.
[Monglond]; BN: Z.24359.
memoir.

———. *Jane Gray, tragédie en cinq actes et en vers, composée en 1787.* Paris: Desenne, 1790.
in-8.
[Monglond].
theater.

———. *Lettres sur les ouvrages et le caractère de J.-J. Rousseau, par Mme la Baronne de Staël-Holstein, épouse de M. l'ambassadeur de Suède auprès du roi de France, fille unique de M. Necker.* N.l.: 1789.
other editions: (1) N.l.: n.p., 1788, in-8; (2) N.l., n.p., 1789, in-8;in-8.; (3) N.l.: Au Temple de la vertu, 1789, in-8; 118p, (4) Paris: Pougens, an VI (1798); (5) London: Colburn, 1814.
[Monglond]; [MW]; [CHF].
philosophy.

———. *Marthésie.* London: n.p., 1790. Found in Luchet, J.-P.-L. de, Rivarol, Mirabeau et Choderlos de Laclos, eds., *la Galerie des dames françaises, pour servir de suite à la 'Galerie des États généraux'.*
Troisième partie, in-8, 207p.
[Monglond].
literature.

———. *Nouvelle Bibliothèque universelle des romans, dans laquelle on donne l'Analyse raisonnée des romans anciens et modernes, française ou traduits dans notre langue, avec des anecdotes et des notices historiques et critiques, concernant les auteurs et leurs ouvrages; ainsi que les moeurs, les usages de temps, les circonstances particulières et rela-*

Staël-Holstein (*continued*)
tives, et les personnages connus,
déguisés ou emblématiques. Paris:
rue André-des-Arts (puis), Demonville, 1798–1805.
112 vols. in-12; edited by Mme de
Genlis, Mme de Staël, P. Blan-
chard, H. Coiffier, J. M. Des-
champs, G. F. Desfontaines de la
Vallée, J. J. M. Duperche, Fabre
d'Olivet, J. Fiévée, A. H. Kératry,
Labaume, J. L. Laya, J.M.J.B.
Legouvé, Lemoine, J. Monbron,
Mabille, Millin, F. J. Noël, Petitot,
L.J.B.E. Vigée.
[Monglond]; BN: Y2 56742–56853.
literature.
————. *Petit Prosne aux roturiers . . .*
Par M.V.***. N.l.: n.d. [1789?].
in-8.
[BLC].
literature.
————. *Réflexions sur la paix, adressées*
à M. Pitt et aux française. N.l.: n.p.,
1795.
in-8; VIII-64p.
[Monglond]; [MW]; [BLC]; BN: 8
Lb(41) 1326 et *E.5285 (2 ex.).
politics.
————. *Réflexions sur le procès de la*
reine par une femme. N.l.: n.p., 1793.
in-8; 38p; other edition: London:
1793, in-8.
[Monglond]; [MW]; [CHF]; BN:
Lb(41) 3272.
politics.
————. *Recueil de morceaux détachés*
par Mad. la Bne. Stael de Holstein.
Lausanne & Paris: Durand, Ra-
vanel et Compe & Fuchs, 1795.
in-8; 203p.; other editions: (1)
Leipzig: Dyck, 1796; (2) Leipzig:
Dyck, 1814.
[BGR]; [Monglond].
novel.
————. *Zulma, fragment d'un ouvrage*
par Mad. la Baronne St*** de

H*******. London: n.p. 1794.
in-8; viii + 24p.
[BGR]; [Monglond].
novel.
Suard, madame A. *Soirées d'hiver*
d'une femme retirée à la campagne;
extrait des feuilles du 'Journal de
Paris' des 4, 8, 11, 14, 17, 20 et 24
novembre 1786. Orléans (Paris):
n.p., 1789.
in-12; ABF: 970, 79–102.
[Monglond].
memoir.
Suremain, Louise Marie. *Melchior ar-*
dent ou les aventures plaisantes d'un
incroyable, par Mme S***. Paris:
Lefort, Moutardier, 1800.
in-12; 210p.
[BGR]; [Monglond]; JT 20 vend.
VIII; B.
novel.
Surville, Marguerite Elisabeth
Clotilde de Vallon madame de.
"Extrait du quatrième chant d'un
poème manuscrit de Clotilde,
troubadour de quinzième siècle."
Journal Littéraire de Lausanne VIII
(1797): 189–197.
J.L.L. was published from 1794–
1798.
[Monglond].
poetry.
————. "L'Hermite de Fribourg. Nouvelle accompagnée d'une notice
sur Clotilde, ancien poète français
du quinzième siècle. Article en-
voyé au rédacteur de '*Journal Lit-*
téraire de Lausanne,' par l'auteur de
'Marcomeris ou le beau troubadour." *Journal Littéraire de Lausanne*
VIII (1797): 54–64; 145–164.
J.L.L. was published from 1794–
1798.
[Monglond].
poetry.
Suzan, mademoiselle. *Les deux Mères,*
ou la fierté punie, proverbe, par une

Suzan (*continued*)
   jeune personne âgée de douze ans. Valenciennes: J.-H.-R. Prignet, 1791.
   in-18.
   [Monglond].
   theater.
Tallien, Jeanne Marie Thérèse née
   Cabarrus then marquise de
   Fontenay then de Caraman
   princesse de Chimay 1773 or
   1775–1830 or 1835. *Adresse à la
   Convention Nationale.* N.l: n.d.
   ABF: 223, 346–351; 976, 313–318.
   [MW].
   pedagogy.
———. *Discours sur l'éducation, par
   la citoyenne Thérèsia Cabarrus-
   Fontenay, lu dans la séance tenue au
   temple de la raison de Bordeaux, le
   1er décadi du mois de nivôse an II . . .*
   N.l.: n.d. [1793].
   in-12; Pièce.
   [CHF].
   pedagogy.
Tardieu-Denesle, madame Henri. *Encyclopédie de la jeunesse, ou nouvel
   essai élémentaire des sciences et des
   arts, extraits des meilleurs auteurs,
   par Mme H.* Paris: H. Tardieu, 1800.
   in-12.
   [Monglond].
   pedagogy.
Tencin, Claudine Alexandrine Guérin
   marquise de 1681–1749. *Les Amans
   malheureux, ou le comte de Com-
   minge [par Mme de Tencin], suivis
   des lettres et du drame [par F.-T.-M.
   de Baculard d'Arnaud] . . .* Hamburg: P.-F. Fauche, 1793.
   in-18, 186p.
   BN: Yf. 6902.
   literature.
———. *Correspondance du cardinal de
   Tencin et de la marquise de Tencin, sa
   soeur, avec le duc de Richelieu, sur les
   intrigues de la cour de France depuis
   1742 jusqu'en 1757 et surtout pen-*
   *dant la faveur des dames de Mailly,
   de Vintimille, de Lauraguais, de
   Châteauroux et de Pompadour.* N.l.:
   1790.
   in-8.
   [Monglond]; [CHF].
   correspondence.
———. *Louise de Valrose, ou mémoires
   d'une autrichienne, traduits de l'allemand sur la troisième édition.* Paris:
   n.p., 1789.
   in-12; new, disguised, edition of
   Les Malheurs de l'amour, 1747.
   [Monglond].
   literature / translation.
Tencin, Claudine Alexandrine Guérin
   marquise de 1681–1749, Mme
   Coulanges, Mme Villars, Mme de
   L'Enclos, Mme Ninon, Mme de La
   Fayette and Mlle Aïssé. *Lettres de
   Mmes de Villars, de la Fayette, de
   Tencin, de Coulanges, de Ninon, de
   l'Enclos et de Mademoiselle Aïssé; ac-
   compagnées de notices biographiques,
   de notes explicatives, et de la coquette
   vengée, par Ninon de l'Enclos. 3me
   Éd.* Paris: Léopold Collin, 1797.
   3 vols. in-12; t.I:359p, t.II:352p,
   t.III:xxvp + 319p.
   [Monglond]; BN: Z. 14658–14660.
   correspondence.
Topin, Marie Catherine Lacorne
   dame. *Déclaration de la citoyenne
   Topin, sous-gouvernante de Louise-
   Eugénie-Adélaïde d'Orléans.* Paris:
   R. Vatar, n.d. [1793].
   in-8; 7p.
   [Monglond]; [MW]; BN: 8
   Lb(41).631.
   politics.
Tott, Claire de. *Pauline de Vergies ou
   lettres de Madame de Staincis, publiées par Claire de Tott.* Paris: Belin,
   1799.
   3t. in-12; t.I:286, t.II:264, t.III:280.
   [BGR]; [Monglond]; JT 1 niv. VII.
   novel.

Travanec, madame de. *Premier recueil de romances et chansons. Paroles et musique.* 1796.
[Monglond].
poetry / music.

Trois Etoiles, citoyenne. *Miss Bellhowe et le Lord Clarendon, ou les épreuves de l'amour et de la vertu.* Paris: chez G. M. Leguay, 1797.
in-18p 293p.
[BLC].
novel.

Valant, citoyenne. *La citoyenne Valant à ses concitoyens de la Section des Sans-Culottes, aux 47 autres sections, aux Jacobins, aux Cordeliers et à toutes les sociétés populaires.* Paris: de l'imprimerie conforme à la prononciation . . . , n.d.
in-8; 4p; ABF: 1008, 80–82.
[MW]; BN: 8 Ln(27).19959.
politics.

Valincourt, madame de fl. 1785. *Les Élans du coeur et de la raison, ou justice rendue à la Reine. Dédié aux français.* Paris: Baudouin, 1789.
in-8; 22p.
[Monglond]; [CHF]; BLC; BN: 8 Lb(39) 1686.
politics.

———. *Adresse des chefs de famille à l'Assemblée Nationale, sur la liberté individuelle, suivie de quelques réflexions sur les droits de l'homme, et d'un projet d'émulation civique.* Paris: imp. de Valleyre aîné, 1790.
in-8; ABF: 1009, 257–258.
[Monglond]; [CHF]; BLC.
politics.

———. *La Légende de tous les illustres français dont le nom s'est signalé depuis le premier mai 1789, présentée dans un songe à une française, dont l'esprit a été transport, au temple de mémoire, le 14 juillet 1790; son extase à l'aspect du spectacle enchanteur des confédérés du champ de mars.* Paris:

imp.de vve Delaguette, 1790.
in-8.
[Monglond]; [CHF]; BLC.
politics.

Van den Yver, madame. *Mémoire pour Madame Vandenyer; elle réclame la propriété de l'Île de Sèvres, dont le citoyen Seguin s'est emparé sans droit . . .* [Paris]: n.d.[1795?].
in-4.
[BLC].
politics.

———. *Pétition à la Convention Nationale . . .* Paris: Dupont, n.d. [1793].
in-8; 14p; ABF: 1011, 259.
[MW]; [CHF]; BN: 8 Lb(41).4244 et 8 Ln(27).20022 (2 ex.).
politics / commercial.

Vanesbecq, madame Grandmaison. *Adolphe ou la famille malheureuse, par Mme. G . . . Van . . .* Paris: Lepetit, 1797.
3t. in-18; t.I:181p, t.II:154p, t.III:171p.; ABF: 1012, 25.
[BGR]; [Monglond]; BN: Y2 13044–13046.
novel.

———. *Synaïb et Zora ou l'héritie de Babylone, par Madame G . . . V . . . , auteur D' 'Adolphe ou la famille Heureuse.'* Paris: chez les marchands de nouveautés, 1800.
2t. in-12; t.I:iv + 184, t.II:120 + 44; other editions: (1) Paris: Ouvrier, 1800, 2t. in-12 or 2t. in-18; (2) Paris: Ouvrier, 1801, 2t.
[BGR]; [Monglond]; JT 15 prair. VIII.
novel.

Varlé, citoyenne. *Procès de Joseph Lebon, membre de la députation du département du Pas-de-Calais à la Convention Nationale, condamné à la peine de mort par le tribunal criminel du département de la Somme (17 vendémiaire an IV). Recueilli au dit*

Varlé, (*continued*)

tribunal. Amiens: imp. des associés, n.d. [1795].
2 tomes en 1 vol. in-8; 371–196p.
[Monglond]; [MW]; BN: Lb(41) 2068.
politics.

Vasse, Cornélie-Pétronille-Bénédicte née Wouters baronne de 1737–1802. *Les Aveux d'une femme galante ou lettres de Madame la marquise de *** . . . Myladi Fanny Stapelton*. London: veuve Ballard & fils, 1796.
in-12; 174p; other editions: (1) London & Paris: veuve Ballard et fils, & Brusselles: B. le Francq, 1783, in-8, 142p; (2) London & Paris: veuve Ballard et fils, 1783, 170p; (3) London: Jean Nourse, 1783, in-8, 168p.; (4) London: 1786; (5) London: n.p., 1791.
[BGR].
novel.

———. *La belle Indienne ou les aventures de la petite-fille du grand mogol*, traduit de l'anglais par Cornélie de Vasse. Paris: Lepetit, 1798.
2t. in-12.
[BGR]; [Monglond]; JT 1.iii.98, 16, 30 germ. VI.
novel / translation.

———. *Constitutions des empires, royaumes et républiques de l'Europe, avec un précis de leurs finances, dettes nationales, resources, commerce, etc., etc., auquel on a joint des anecdotes, des nouvelles authentiques de Londres, du Brabant et d'Autres pays; ouvrage publié par numéro et par souscription, au profit des pauvres, et présenté à l'Ass. nat. par l'auteur, Madame la Baronne de Vasse*. Paris: n.p., 1790.
in-8; subscription—24 issues; ABF: 1074, 76–82.
[BLC].
politics / journal.

———. *d'Harcourt ou l'héritier supposeé*, traduit de l'anglais de Mary Robinson, auteur de 'Vancenza, Angelina, Hubert de Sevrac,' orné de figures d'après les dessins de challiou. Paris: au magasin des nouveaux romans, chez Lepetit, 1798.
3t. in-12; t.I:247p, t.II:238p, t.III:286p; translation of *Walsingham or the Pupil of Nature* (1792), by Mary Darby Robinson.
[BGR]; JT 1.ii.98, 16 germ., 8 mess., 20 therm. VI; Monglond.
novel / translation.

———. *Mémoire à l'Assemblée Nationale, pour démontrer aux français les raisons qui doivent déterminer à admettre les juifs indistinctement aux droits de citoyens*. Paris: Baudouin, 1790.
in-8; 9p.
[Monglond]; [MW]; [CHF]; BN: 8 Ld(184).40.
politics.

———. *Le Mariage platonique, imité de l'anglais par Madame la Baronne de Vasse*. Amsterdam & Paris: Maradan, 1790.
2t. in-12, t.I:216p, t.II:174p; translation of *The Platonic Marriage* (1786), by Mrs. H. Cartwright; other editions: (1) Lausanne: Jean Mourer, 1789; (2) Nantes & Paris: n.p., 1790, 2t. in-8.
[BGR]; [Monglond].
novel / translation.

———. *Nelson, ou l'avare puni*. Paris: Lepetit, 1798.
3 vols. in-12.
[Monglond].
novel.

Vauthier, mademoiselle. *Vers aux marquis (Marie Paul Jean Roch Gilbert) de La Fayette*. 1789.
[BN].
poetry.

Vicogne, Amélie Françoise Joseph
  Lallart veuve. *Encore un Crime de
  Joseph Lebon* . . . Paris: Guffroy,
  n.d.
  in-4; 7p.
  [MW]; BN: 4 Lb(41).1557.
  politics.
———. *Imprimeur traduit au tribunal
  révolutionnaire d'Arras par l'envie de
  métier, et condamné à mort par l'un
  des auteurs du fait qu'on lui
  imputait.* Paris: Guffroy, n.d.
  [1794].
  in-4; 4p.
  [MW]; [CHF]; BN: 4 Lb(41).1561.
  politics.
———. *Persécution du tribunal révolutionnaire d'Arras, contre la famille
  des Lallart, habitant cette commune*
  . . . Paris: Guffroy, n.d.
  in-4; 7p.
  [MW]; BN: 4 Lb(41).1558.
  politics.
Vildé, madame L. *Betzi ou l'infortunée
  créole, histoire véritable par
  la citoyenne L.V* . . . Paris:
  imprimerie de Chaignieau aîné,
  1800.
  2t. in-12; t.I:251, t.II:211.
  [BGR]; [Monglond]; JT 10 brum.
  VIII.
  novel.
Villiers, citoyenne. *Journal des lois et
  des faits.* Paris: Villiers [1797].
  in-8; 5–26 frimaire an VI.
  [CHF].
  journal.
Villiers, madame N. M. *Barra, ou la
  mère républicaine, drame historique
  en trois actes et en prose.* Dijon: P.
  Causse, 1793.
  in-8.
  [Monglond].
  theater.
Warens, Louise Françoise Loys de la
  Tour du Pil baronne de 1699–1762.
  Mémoires de Mme de Warens, suivis

*de ceux de Claude Anet, publiés par
  un C.D.M.D.P., pour servir d'apologie aux 'Confessions' de J.-J.
  Rousseau.* Paris: Obré, 1798.
  in-8; first edition: 1786.
  [Monglond]; [FC].
  memoir.
Wiesenhuetten, Frederike Henriette
  baronne de. *Hélène, par Madame la
  Baronne de ****, auteur du 'journal
  de Lolotte.'* Frankfurt: Philippe
  Henri Guilhauman, 1797.
  2 part. in-8; t.I:172, t.II:163; other
  editions: (1) N.l.: Cassel, 1797, 2t.
  in-12; (2) Lausanne: Henri Jansen,
  l'an VIII, 2 part. pet. in-8, pp variously 172, 163.
  [BGR]; [Monglond]; BLC; BN: Y2
  37591.
  novel.
———. *Historiettes et conversations à
  l'usage des enfans qui commencent à
  lire un peu couramment, par Madame
  de V* . . . Paris: au bureau de l'Ami
  des enfans, 1789.
  2t. in-18; t.I:136p, t.II:148p.; other
  editions: (1) Maestricht: Roux et
  cie, 1790, 298p.; (2) Liège: Latour,
  1794, 2 vols. in-12; (3) N.l.: Cotta,
  1796, in-12; (4) Paris: A.-A. Renouard, 1805, 3t. in-18; (5) Paris:
  Leprieur, 1805, in-12.; (6) Paris:
  Brunet, n.d. [1806?], 2t.; (7) Paris:
  Leprieur, 1812, in-12; (8) Paris:
  Moronval, 1814, in-12; (9) Leipzig:
  Koechly, 1817, in-8; (10) Nancy:
  Thomas, n.d., 2t. in-18.
  [BGR]; [Monglond].
  pedagogy.
———. *Journal de Lolotte, par Mme. la
  Baronne de W* . . . Frankfurt: n.p.,
  1793.
  2 parts. pet. in-8; Ier part:158p, 2e
  part:150p; other edition, Paris:
  n.p., an VIII, 2t., t.I:158p, t.II:150p.
  [BGR]; BLC.
  novel.

———. *Lydie de Gersin ou histoire d'une jeune angloise de huit ans, pour servir à l'instruction & à la amusement des jeunes françoises du même âge, traduction de l'anglois par Madame de V . . .* Paris: au bureau de l'Ami des enfans, 1789.
in-18, 160p; other editions: (1) Paris: A.-A. Renouard, 1803, 114p.; (2) Paris: Billois, 1812, in-12.
[BGR]; [Monglond].
novel.

Wuiet, madame Caroline plus tard Auffdienes 1766–1835. *Le Cercle, journal des arts et des plaisirs. Dédié aux muses et aux grâces.* Paris, Perny; 72 nos in-8.
[Monglond]; BN: Lc2 2715.
journal.

———. *Essai sur l'opinion publique, framents de poésies fugitives, dédiées à Mme Bonaparte.* Paris: Desenne, 1800.
in-12; ABF: 1044, 206–208.
[Monglond].
poetry.

———. *Journal des dames et des modes.* 41 vols (1797–1839).
Paris, rue Montmartre; in-8; founded in 1797 by Sellèque.
[Monglond].
journal.

———. *Le Phénix.* 162 nos. (1798).
Paris: rue Poissonnière; 162 nos; in-4.
[Monglond]; BN: Lc2 2721.
journal.

Publishers and Publishing Locations of French Women: 1789–1800

Paris Publishers: **336 Imprints**

Ancelle: 1
Barba: 6 (theater)
*Barrois, aîné:
*Baudouin: 4
*Belin et Desenne: 7
Bertrandet: 2
Bidault: 1
*Blanchon: 1
Bossange: 1
*Boulard: 1
*Bourdet: 1
Brasseur: 11
*Briand: 2
*Buisson: 5
*Cailleau: 6 (novels)
Cercle Sociale: 3
Chaignieau, aîné: 5
Collin: 1
Coulubrier: 8 (songs)
Debrai: 1
*Vve Delaguette: 1
*Demonville: 5
Demoraine:
Dentu: 2
*Didot, jeune: 1
*Didot l'aîné: 3
Vve Duchesne: 4
Dufart: 3
Dufresne: 1
Dupont: 9

*Durand: 2
Ecole Typographique des femmes:
Fauche-Borel: 4
Fauvelle et Sagnier: 1
*Froullé: 1
Garnery et Volland: 3
*Gattey: 2
Gillé: 1
Grand: 2
*Grégoire: 1
*Gueffier: 3
Guffroy: 14 (political pamphlets)
*Guillaume, jeune: 1
*Guillot: 1
Hautbout, aîné: 2
*Vve Hérissant: 1
Hugelet: 1
*Mme M.R. Huzard: 1
Imp. des Arts et Sciences: 1
Imp. de Augustin: 1
Imp. de Boileau: 1
Imp. du Carron: 1
*Imp. de Cellot: 2
Imp. de Charpentier: 1
Imp. de Coesnon-Pellerin: 1
Imp. de Couret: 1
*Imp. de Crapelet: 2
Imp. de l'Egalité: 1
Imp. des Femmes: 1
Imp. de la 'Feuille du Cultivateur': 1

Imp. de la 'Feuille des Spectacles' : 1
Imp. de Forget: 3 (theater)
Imp. de la Vve Gorsas: 2
Imp. de Guerin: 3
Imp. Guihomat: 1
Imp. à l'Institution Nationale des
    Enfants-Aveugles: 1
*Imp. de Jorry: 1
Imp. du Journal `Le Democrite
    français' (Lachave): 1
Imp. de LeGros: 1
Imp. du Lycée des Arts:
Imp. de Marat: 1
*Imp. de Momoro:
*Imp. de Monsieur: 1
Imp. Nationale: 5
Imp. de Noireil: 1
Imp. de Nouzou: 1
Imp. du Patriote français: 1
Imp. de Potier: 2
Imp. à Prix Fixe: 1
Imp. de Renaudière jeune: 1
Imp. de Roederer et Corancz: 1
Imp. de Roland: 1
Imp. de Rose: 1
*Imp. Royale: 1
Imp. d'un royaliste: 1
Imp. de Rozé: 1
Imp. de Ch. Tutot: 1
Imp. de l'Union: 1
*Knapen et fils: 3
*LaCloye: 2
*LaPorte: 1
*Laurens jeune: 5
LeBecq: 1
Leguay: 2
*LeJay: 1
Lemierre: 11
Le Normand: 1
*LePetit: 13 (novels)
Leprieur: 6 (novels)

*Mme Lesclapart: 1
Levrault, frères: 1
Logerot: 1
*Lottin, aîné: 2
Louvet: 1
*Maradan: 21 (novels)
Marchand: 3
*Mérigot, jeune: 1
Migneret: 2
*Monory: 1
*Moreau, jeune: 2
*Moutard: 1
Moutardier: 2
*N-H. Nyon: 4
Obré: 1
*Onfroy: 8 (belle lettres)
Pain: 2
Parait: 1
*Pierres: 1
Pigoreau: 2
*Planche: 1
Poignée: 1
Pougens: 6 (novels)
Pougin: 2
*Prault: 1
Prudhomme: 2
Rainville et Favre: 1
*Regnault: 2
*Royer: 11
Ruphy: 1
Saint-Marcel: 1
Tardieu: 1
*Valade: 4
*Valleyre, aîné: 1
*Vatar-Jouannet: 2
Vignon: 1
Villier:1
*Volland, aîné: 1

Total Parisian Publishers: 137
(* Former Guild members: 52)

French Publishers (Non-Parisian)
(Note: The total number of imprints from each city appears after the name of the city. Names of identifiable publishers within each city and the number of imprints attributed to each of them appear below in parentheses.)

Amiens: 1
Angers: 1
  (Mame: 1)
Angoulême: 1
  (Texier Tremeau: 1)
Arras: 3
  (Vve de J. B. Vicogne: 1)
Auxerre: 1
  (Imp. de L. Fournier: 1)
Avallon: 1:
  (Imp de A. Aubry:1)
Avignon: 2
  (François Seguin: 1)
Bordeaux: 1
  (Brossier: 1)
Brignoles: 1
  (Guichard: 1)
Caen: 2
  (Chalopin: 2)
Clermont-Ferrand: 1
  (Imp. de A. de Delcros: 1)
Compiègne: 1
  (Bertrand: 1)
Dampierre: 5
  (Imp. de G.E.J. Montmorency: 1)
*Dijon:*5
  (Causse: 1)
  (Frantin: 2)
  (Imp. Vve Defay: 1)
Gênes: 1
  (Y. Gravier: 1)

Grenoble: 1
Le Mans: 2
  (Imp. de Monnoyer: 2)
Lisieux: 1
  (Imp. de Mistral: 1)
Lyon: 2
  (De la Roche: 1)
Marseilles: 1
  (Imp. de P.-A. Favet: 1)
Metz: 1
Nîmes: 1
  (Vve Belle:1)
Pithiviers: 1
  (Cocatrix: 1)
Orléans: 1
Rouen: 1
  (Jean Racine: 1)
Toulouse: 7
  (Benichet, freres: 2)
  (Desclassans: 1)
  (Vialanes: 1)
Tournay: 1
  (Imp. de J. Serre: 1)
Troyes: 1
  (Imp. de Vve; Gobelet: 1)
*Valenciennes:*1
  (Prignet: 1)

Total Provincial Imprints: 50
Total Provincial Cities: 29

III. Foreign Publishers:
(Note: The total number of imprints from each city appears after the name of the city. Names of identifiable publishers within each city and the number of imprints attributed to each of them appear below in parentheses.)

Amsterdam: 1
Berlin: 12
  (Decker: 2)
  (De la Garde: 3)
  (Kochly: 1)
  (Laurens: 1)
  (Sander: 1)
Berne: 4
  (Emmanuel Haller: 1)
  (Société Typographique: 3)

Bruges: 1
  (J. de Busscher et fils: 1)
Brussels: 2
  (E. Flon: 1)
Dresden: 2
  (Walther: 2)
Frankfurt: 2
  (Philippe Henri Guilhauman: 1)
Geneva: 4
  (J. J. Paschoud: 1)

Hamburg: 9
  (Chateauneuf: 2)
  (P.-F. Fauche: 6)
  (Hoffman: 1)
Lausanne: 15
  (Fischer and Vincent: 1)
  (Imp. de J.B. Heubach: 1)
  (Louis Luquiens: 3)
  (Jean Mourer: 3)
  (Henri Vincent: 1)
Leipzig: 2
  (Pierre Philippe Wolf: 2)
Leyden: 1
London: 18
  Vve Ballard et fils
  Bernard: 2
  Deboff: 1
  Dulau & Co.: 2
  Murray: 1
  J. Ridgeway: 1

Maestricht: 1
  (Roux: 1)
Neuchâtel: 1
Oxford: 1
Rome: 1
  (Imp. papale: 1)
Vienna: 6
  (Imp. de la Vve Albert: 3)
  (Mayer: 1)
  (J. Stahel: 1)
Worms: 1
Zuylen: 1
  (Fondation du Chateâu de Zuylen: 1)

Total Foreign Imprints: 85
Total Foreign Cities: 20
No Place: 185
TOTAL IMPRINTS: 657

INDEX